Readers, Reading and Librarians

Readers, Reading and Librarians has been co-published simultaneously as *The Acquisitions Librarian,* Number 25 2001.

The Acquisitions Librarian Monographic "Separates"

Below is a list of "separates," which in serials librarianship means a special issue simultaneously published as a special journal issue or double-issue *and* as a "separate" hardbound monograph. (This is a format which we also call a "DocuSerial.")

"Separates" are published because specialized libraries or professionals may wish to purchase a specific thematic issue by itself in a format which can be separately cataloged and shelved, as opposed to purchasing the journal on an on-going basis. Faculty members may also more easily consider a "separate" for classroom adoption.

"Separates" are carefully classified separately with the major book jobbers so that the journal tie-in can be noted on new book order slips to avoid duplicate purchasing.

You may wish to visit Haworth's website at . . .

http://www.haworthpressinc.com

. . . to search our online catalog for complete tables of contents of these separates and related publications.

You may also call 1-800-HAWORTH (outside US/Canada: 607-722-5857), or Fax: 1-800-895-0582 (outside US/Canada: 607-771-0012), or e-mail at:

getinfo@haworthpressinc.com

Readers, Reading and Librarians, edited by Bill Katz (No. 25, 2001). *Reaffirms the enthusiasm of books and readers as libraries evolve from reading centers to information centers where librarians are now also web masters, information scientists, and media experts.*

Acquiring Online Management Reports, edited by William E. Jarvis (No. 24, 2000). *This fact-filled guide explores a broad variety of issues involving acquisitions and online management reports to keep libraries and library managers current with changing technology and, ultimately, offer patrons more information. This book provides you with discussions and suggestions on several topics, including working with vendors, developing cost-effective collection development methods to suit your library, assessing collection growth, and choosing the best electronic resources to help meet your goals.* Acquiring Online Management Reports *offers you an array of proven ideas, options, and examples that will enable your library to keep up with client demands and simplify the process of collecting, maintaining, and interpreting online reports.*

The Internet and Acquisitions: Sources and Resources for Development, edited by Mary E. Timmons (No. 23, 2000). *"For those trying to determine how the Internet could be of use to their particular library in the area of acquisitions, or for those who have already decided they should be moving in that direction . . . this volume is a good place to begin." (James Mitchell, MLS, Library Director, Bainbridge-Guilford Central School, Bainbridge, NY)*

Gifts and Exchanges: Problems, Frustrations, . . . and Triumphs, edited by Catherine Denning (No. 22, 1999). *"A complete compendium embracing all aspects of the matter in articles that are uniformly well-written by people experienced in this field." (Jonathan S. Tryon, CAL, JD, Professor, Graduate School of Library and Information Studies, University of Rhode Island)*

Periodical Acquisitions and the Internet, edited by Nancy Slight-Gibney (No. 21, 1999). *Sheds light on the emerging trends in selection, acquisition, and access to electronic journals.*

Public Library Collection Development in the Information Age, edited by Annabel K. Stephens (No. 20, 1998). *"A first-rate collection of articles . . . This is an engaging and helpful work for anyone involved in developing public library collections." (Lyn Hopper, MLn, Director, Chestatee Regional Library, Dahlonega, GA)*

Fiction Acquisition/Fiction Management: Education and Training, edited by Georgine N. Olson (No. 19, 1998). *"It is about time that attention is given to the collection in public libraries . . . it is about time that public librarians be encouraged to treat recreational reading with the same respect* that is paid to informational reading . . . Thank you to Georgine Olson for putting this volume together." (Regan Robinson, MLS, Editor and Publisher, Librarian Collection Letter)

Acquisitions and Collection Development in the Humanities, edited by Irene Owens (No. 17/18, 1997). *"CAN EASILY BECOME A PERSONAL REFERENCE TOOL."* (William D. Cunningham, PhD, Retired faculty, College of Library and Information Service, University of Maryland, College Park)

Approval Plans: Issues and Innovations, edited by John H. Sandy (No. 16, 1996). *"This book is valuable for several reasons, the primary one being that librarians in one-person libraries need to know how approval plans work before they can try one for their particular library . . . An important addition to the professional literature."* (The One-Person Library)

Current Legal Issues in Publishing, edited by A. Bruce Strauch (No. 15, 1996). *"Provides valuable access to a great deal of information about the current state of copyright thinking."* (Library Association Record)

New Automation Technology for Acquisitions and Collection Development, edited by Rosann Bazirjian (No. 13/14, 1995). *"Rosann Bazirjian has gathered together 13 current practitioners who explore technology and automation in acquisitions and collection development . . . CONTAINS SOMETHING FOR EVERYONE."* (Library Acquisitions: Practice and Theory)

Management and Organization of the Acquisitions Department, edited by Twyla Racz and Rosina Tammany (No. 12, 1994). *"Brings together topics and librarians from across the country to discuss some basic challenges and changes facing our profession today."* (Library Acquisitions: Practice and Theory)

A. V. in Public and School Libraries: Selection and Policy Issues, edited by Margaret J. Hughes and Bill Katz (No. 11, 1994). *"Many points of view are brought forward for those who are creating new policy or procedural documents . . . Provide[s] firsthand experience as well as considerable background knowledge . . . ."* (Australian Library Review)

Multicultural Acquisitions, edited by Karen Parrish and Bill Katz (No. 9/10, 1993). *"A stimulating overview of the U.S. multicultural librarianship scene."* (The Library Assn. Reviews)

Popular Culture and Acquisitions, edited by Allen Ellis (No. 8, 1993). *"A provocative penetrating set of chapters on the tricky topic of popular culture acquisitions . . . A valuable guidebook."* (Journal of Popular Culture)

Collection Assessment: A Look at the RLG Conspectus©, edited by Richard J. Wood and Katina Strauch (No. 7, 1992). *"A well-organized, thorough book . . . Provides the most realistic representations of what the Conspectus is and what its limitations are . . . Will take an important place in Conspectus literature."* (Library Acquisitions: Practice & Theory)

Evaluating Acquisitions and Collections Management, edited by Pamela S. Cenzer and Cynthia I. Gozzi (No. 6, 1991). *"With the current emphasis on evaluation and return on funding, the material is timely indeed!"* (Library Acquisitions: Practice & Theory)

Vendors and Library Acquisitions, edited by Bill Katz (No. 5, 1991). *"Should be required reading for all new acquisitions librarians and all library science students who plan a career in technical services. As a whole it is a very valuable resource."* (Library Acquisitions: Practice & Theory)

Operational Costs in Acquisitions, edited by James R. Coffey (No. 4, 1991). *"For anyone interested in embarking on a cost study of the acquisitions process this book will be worthwhile reading."* (Library Acquisitions: Practice & Theory)

Legal and Ethical Issues in Acquisitions, edited by Katina Strauch and A. Bruce Strauch (No. 3, 1990). *"This excellent compilation is recommended to both collection development/acquisition librarians and library administrators in academic libraries."* (The Journal of Academic Librarianship)

The Acquisitions Budget, edited by Bill Katz (No. 2, 1989). *"Practical advice and tips are offered throughout . . . Those new to acquisitions work, especially in academic libraries, will find the book useful background reading."* (Library Association Record)

Automated Acquisitions: Issues for the Present and Future, edited by Amy Dykeman (No. 1, 1989).
"This book should help librarians to learn from the experience of colleagues in choosing the system that best suits their local requirements . . . [It] will appeal to library managers as well as to library school faculty and students." (*Library Association Record*)

Readers, Reading and Librarians

Bill Katz
Editor

Readers, Reading and Librarians has been co-published simultaneously as *The Acquisitions Librarian*, Number 25 2001.

The Haworth Information Press
An Imprint of
The Haworth Press, Inc.
New York • London • Oxford

Published by

The Haworth Information Press, 10 Alice Street, Binghamton, NY 13904-1580

The Haworth Information Press is an imprint of The Haworth Press, Inc., 10 Alice Street, Bing-hamton, NY 13904-1580 USA.

Readers, Reading and Librarians has been co-published simultaneously as *The Acquisitions Librarian* ™, Number 25 2001.

The development, preparation, and publication of this work has been undertaken with great care. However, the publisher, employees, editors, and agents of The Haworth Press and all imprints of The Haworth Press, Inc., including The Haworth Medical Press⑤ and Pharmaceutical Products Press⑥, are not responsible for any errors contained herein or for consequences that may ensue from use of materials or information contained in this work. Opinions expressed by the author(s) are not necessar-ily those of The Haworth Press, Inc.

Cover design by Thomas J. Mayshock Jr.

Library of Congress Cataloging-in-Publication Data

Readers, reading and librarians/Bill Katz, editor.
    p. cm.
    "Readers, reading and librarians has been co-published simultaneously as The acquisitions librarian, number 25, 2001."
    Includes bibliographical references and index.
    ISBN 0-7890-0699-5 (alk. paper)
    1. Books and reading. 2. Libraries and readers. 3. Book selection. I. Katz, William A., 1924-II. Acquisitions librarian.

Z1003.R28 2000
028'.9–dc21
                                       00-044873

INDEXING & ABSTRACTING

Contributions to this publication are selectively indexed or abstracted in print, electronic, online, or CD-ROM version(s) of the reference tools and information services listed below. This list is current as of the copyright date of this publication. See the end of this section for additional notes.

- *BUBL Information Service, an Internet-based Information Service for the UK higher education community <URL: http://bubl.ac.uk/>*
- *Central Library & Documentation Bureau*
- *CNPIEC Reference Guide: Chinese National Directory of Foreign Periodicals*
- *Combined Health Information Database (CHID)*
- *Current Awareness Abstracts of Library & Information Management Literature, ASLIB (UK)*
- *Educational Administration Abstracts (EAA)*
- *FINDEX, a free Internet Directory of over 150,000 publications from around the world www.publist.com*
- *Herbal Connection, The "Abstracts Section" http://www.herbnet.com*
- *IBZ International Bibliography of Periodical Literature*
- *Index to Periodical Articles Related to Law*
- *Information Reports & Bibliographies*
- *Information Science Abstracts*
- *Informed Librarian, The <http:www.infosourcespub.com>*
- *INSPEC*
- *Journal of Academic Librarianship: Guide to Professional Literature, The*
- *Konyvtari Figyelo-Library Review*
- *Library & Information Science Abstracts (LISA)*
- *Library and Information Science Annual (LISCA) www.lu.com/arba*
- *Library Literature*

(continued)

- *Microcomputer Abstracts can be found Online at: DIALOG, File 233; HRIN & OCLC and on Internet at: Cambridge Scientific Abstracts; Dialog Web; & OCLC*
- *National Clearinghouse on Child Abuse & Neglect Information http://www.calib.com/ncanch*
- *Newsletter of Library and Information Services*
- *NIAAA Alcohol and Alcohol Problems Science Database (ETOH)*
- *PASCAL, c/o Institute de L'Information Scientifique et Technique http://www.inist.fr*
- *REHABDATA, National Rehabilitation Information Center (NARIC) http://www.naric.com/naric*
- *Social Services Abstracts http://www.csa.com*
- *Sociological Abstracts http://www.csa.com*

Special Bibliographic Notes related to special journal issues (separates) and indexing/abstracting:

- indexing/abstracting services in this list will also cover material in any "separate" that is co-published simultaneously with Haworth's special thematic journal issue or DocuSerial. Indexing/abstracting usually covers material at the article/chapter level.

- monographic co-editions are intended for either non-subscribers or libraries which intend to purchase a second copy for their circulating collections.

- monographic co-editions are reported to all jobbers/wholesalers/approval plans. The source journal is listed as the "series" to assist the prevention of duplicate purchasing in the same manner utilized for books-in-series.

- to facilitate user/access services all indexing/abstracting services are encouraged to utilize the co-indexing entry note indicated at the bottom of the first page of each article/chapter/contribution.

- this is intended to assist a library user of any reference tool (whether print, electronic, online, or CD-ROM) to locate the monographic version if the library has purchased this version but not a subscription to the source journal.

- individual articles/chapters in any Haworth publication are also available through the Haworth Document Delivery Service (HDDS).

Readers, Reading and Librarians

CONTENTS

Introduction:
Remembrance of Things Past–and Future

Whether you want to translate Proust's masterpiece as *In Search of Lost Time* or *Remembrance of Things Past*, reading it can truly change your life. Alain DeBotton explains why in his cruise through the delight and distress of the twentieth century's greatest novel.[1]

Among any list of twentieth century novels, it should come first, along with *Ulysses* and Ford's *The Good Soldier.* Add your own winners. The multiplicity of possible "best" and "better" is the stuff of every reader's day. Fortunately there is no universal answer, but assistance can come from other readers, from librarians. And that's what this volume is all about.

In times past there was no question that the role of the library was to provide the choice books for both pleasure and for education. Before Charles Babbage conceived the notion of a computer, librarians were busy with helping readers. A library was there as a cultural center, not as an extension of Microsoft.

How much have things changed? Has the focus on electronic wonders really shifted the basic mission of the librarian? Is, for example, the readers' advisory service still a viable aspect of public library hopes and goals? Are librarians avid readers, or more concerned with loading paper into computer printers? Does the public come to the library for reading material or for instruction in software?

One response comes from a skeptical journalist: A story in *Time* makes the insupportable claim that "more knowledge comes down a wire than anyone could ever acquire from books." More data, perhaps, but knowledge? That a journalist could mistake one for the other is telling.

"I find today's library literature strangely infatuated, unquestioning, reflecting a kind of data panic, and filled with dire fantasies of patrons left behind–woebegone hitchhikers on the information superhighway. A press re-

[Haworth co-indexing entry note]: "Introduction: Remembrance of Things Past–and Future." Katz, Bill. Co-published simultaneously in *The Acquisitions Librarian* (The Haworth Information Press, an imprint of The Haworth Press, Inc.) No. 25, 2001, pp. 1-3; and: *Readers, Reading and Librarians* (ed: Bill Katz) The Haworth Information Press, an imprint of The Haworth Press, Inc., 2001, pp. 1-3. Single or multiple copies of this article are available for a fee from The Haworth Document Delivery Service [1-800-342-9678, 9:00 a.m. - 5:00 p.m. (EST). E-mail address: getinfo@haworthpressinc.com].

lease from the U.S. National Commission on Libraries and Information Science says that communities without library Internet connections will become 'information have-nots'. The emblematic image, continually evoked as reason enough, is the 'schoolchild doing research', who shouldn't be stuck with stodgy print encyclopedias or forced to browse through the stacks and read books."[2]

Add the insult of name change. Libraries are now information centers, palaces of electronic data. Librarians are information scientists or media experts. Some, to be sure, are labeled webmasters. The jargon would be alarming were it not so fatuous. Descriptors, which appear and disappear as rapidly as trends in diet, are the work of professional demeanors of language. None sees the humor, more or less the irony, in the conspicuous foolishness of it all. Why? Because they cannot tell Proust from prudence. They desperately need a little of both.

The scouts along the information trail mean well enough. They are to be credited for making life at a reference desk considerably more civilized. One must give them credit for sometimes tedious, yet welcome solutions to housekeeping problems such as storage of information. The problem is their total self-confident trust in technology. This can result in more misery than pleasure. Try to solve computer commands that presuppose a vast interest in the theory of relativity and medieval mystics.

How many really understand a common computer search? Few. The result is another contribution to the dumbing down of Americans. Infatuated with the mouse and keyboard the innocents enter a word or two, arrive at full text answers from, say, the *Reader's Digest* and go forth happy with a solution to the meaning of life. What they left behind, what they missed for lack of true understanding of online searching will never be known to them.

Computers for the majority are masters, not servants. The masters are too rapidly substituting casual bits of data for knowledge.

Without proper training or understanding of the electronic miracle (and how many can truly claim that?), the average person would be considerably ahead with a good magazine article carefully selected by an involved librarian. A well-chosen book might be even better.

A false computer printout is perhaps not a dangerous thing, but it is a poor substitute for a fastidious, intellectual choice of a book. Fortunately, librarians realize the problem and battle the stereotyped ideas about the glories of modern technology.

The majority of librarians are avid readers. Why else go into the profession? Some wish to become computer experts, which is fine and necessary; and others turn to management, but the majority are as involved with books as were the keepers of papyrus rolls and cuneiform some 5,000 or so years ago.

A casual visit to a bookstore will make the argument that a vast number of laypeople love books. Who will quarrel with statistics that even put "Amazon.com" at the top of the list of favorite sites on the Web for considering the joys of reading?

Regular readers of the champion of common sense and intellectual heat can turn to much of the so-called "library literature" without apology. Whether it be *The New York Review of Books* or *The New York Times Book Review*, there is confirmation that the reader is not alone out there. At another entry level, look at any issue of *Library Journal, Choice, Booklist*, and, yes, *Kirkus* for inherent, enthusiastic support of readers and books. That portion of the library press with the greatest number of faithful readers never can be accused of deserting reading or books. Their editors are a credit to the profession. They represent the finest tradition associated with librarians. Some may rightfully trespass into the territory of databases, yet only to support the basic notions of reading and research.

The contributors to this volume refute the idea that reading is a thing of the past. All believe it is not receding, but, if anything, increasing in importance. Read on and you, too, will find that to remember things past about reading is, in truth, to see the future.

Come, let's reaffirm the enthusiasm for books and readers. Give the clique around the computer honors, but keep them at a distance.

Instead of complaining, the true librarian must line up and cheer for the true library.

Bill Katz
Editor

NOTES

1. Alain DeBotton, *How Proust Can Change Your Life*, New York: Pantheon Books, 1997.
2. Sallie Tisdale, "Silence Please," *Harper's*, March, 1997, p. 65. An attack on libraries where too much emphasis is put on computers, this makes some valid points. It is more interesting for the mirror it holds up to exaggerated claims about the computer.

READING, BOOKS, AND LIBRARIANS

Making Choices:
What Readers Say About Choosing Books
to Read for Pleasure

Catherine Sheldrick Ross

SUMMARY. This paper analyses 194 open-ended interviews with committed readers who read for pleasure, focussing in particular on interviewees' responses to questions about how they choose and how they reject a book. The analysis suggests that a comprehensive model

Catherine Ross is Professor, Faculty of Information and Media Studies, at The University of Western Ontario, London, Canada, where she teaches graduate courses in reference, research methods, reading and genres of fiction and information needs and uses (E-mail: Ross@Julian.uwo.ca).

The research reported in this paper was conducted with support from a research grant from the Social Sciences and Humanities Research Council of Canada. An earlier version of the paper was presented at the 1998 Canadian Association for Information Science conference and was published in Elaine G. Toms et al., editors, *Information Science at the Dawn of the Next Millennium: Proceedings of the 26th Annual Conference of the Canadian Association for Information Science*, Ottawa: CAIS, 3-5 June, 1998, 107-124.

[Haworth co-indexing entry note]: "Making Choices: What Readers Say About Choosing Books to Read for Pleasure." Ross, Catherine Sheldrick. Co-published simultaneously in *The Acquisitions Librarian* (The Haworth Information Press, an imprint of The Haworth Press, Inc.) No. 25, 2001, pp. 5-21; and: *Readers, Reading and Librarians* (ed: Bill Katz) The Haworth Information Press, an imprint of The Haworth Press, Inc., 2001, pp. 5-21. Single or multiple copies of this article are available for a fee from The Haworth Document Delivery Service [1-800-342-9678, 9:00 a.m. - 5:00 p.m. (EST). E-mail address: getinfo@haworthpressinc.com].

for the process of choosing books for pleasure-reading must include five related elements that are examined in the paper: the reading experience wanted by the reader; alerting sources the reader uses; elements in a book that the reader takes into account in making book choices; clues on the book itself; and costs to the reader in getting access to a particular book. The paper concludes with implications of this research for librarians in the intermediary role of matching reader to book. *[Article copies available for a fee from The Haworth Document Delivery Service: 1-800-342-9678. E-mail address: <getinfo@haworthpressinc.com> Website: <http://www.haworthpressinc.com>]*

KEYWORDS. Fiction, selection factors, readers' advisory, popular reading

In the so-called 500 channel universe of expanding choices among multiple media, attracting the attention of the reader is increasingly difficult. Conversely, as one committed pleasure-reader put it, "Selecting one book out of the many, many thousands available seems almost impossible when you think about it." It is therefore not a trivial concern how a reader goes about making the series of choices that ends up, if all goes well, with a compatible match of reader and book. Indeed the successful encounter of a reader with a book that gives pleasure or instruction is the end-point toward which an enormous number of institutional activities converge: family structures that foster reading; the education system that teaches literacy; publishing houses that select certain authors' work to publish and promote; publicity and reviewing structures that focus attention on certain books; and finally the bookclubs, bookstores and libraries that acquire the physical book and make it accessible to readers. The purpose of this paper is to report what committed readers say about how they negotiate the complex chain of choices that ends in their reading a particular book for pleasure. In addition to the fundamental decision to spend time reading rather than doing something else, there are two further stages of choice: the set of choices that gets a particular book home from the library or bookstore and makes it available for reading; and the choice to read one book rather than another at any given time. For many, the opportunity to choose is valuable in itself, an aspect of the freedom that is a crucial part of the enjoyment of reading:

> That's my thing–this business of freedom. When I go to the library, I'm completely engrossed in what I'm doing. . . . It's a very personal choice and nobody can make it but me. . . . Choosing books is wonderful. I enjoy that. In fact, it's hard to restrain myself without ending up with the whole library and transferring it to my house. . . . I'm a browser. For me, it's an adventure. I don't know what I'm going to find and I don't

want to be anticipated. (Sarah, age 40, graduate student/library assistant–Code names are used throughout in identifying interviewees)

ABOUT THE STUDY

Evidence concerning readers' book choices comes from a transcribed set of 194 intensive, open-ended interviews with adult readers, undertaken as part of a larger study on reading for pleasure. The interviewed subjects were not randomly chosen but were deliberately selected as individuals who read a lot and read by choice. The goal was not to investigate the 95% of the North American population who can read or even the 55% who say they have read a book in the past six months. Rather the study focussed on committed readers who said that reading for pleasure is a very important part of their lives. This criterion means that most of the interviewees studied fall within the 10% of the North American population who show up in national reading surveys as "heavy readers"–those who read upward of a book a week (Cole & Gold 1979, 63; Book Industry Study Group 1984, 84). Unlike non-book readers who read primarily for information, heavy readers tend to say they read for pleasure (Cole & Gold 1979, 61-2). And because they borrow and buy far more books than their proportionate share, their impact on the world of literacy is far greater than the 10% figure their numbers would predict.

The demographic profile of the interviewees in my study resembled that of heavy readers, as consistently described in reports of reading surveys based on large-scale national samples. Previous studies conducted in Canada and the United States have found that heavy readers are more likely to be female than male; to be younger rather than older; and to have achieved a higher educational level than the population at large (Book Industry Study Group 1984, 69-84; Cole & Gold 1978, 49-52; Gallup Organization 1978; Watson et al. 1980). Of the 194 people interviewed for my study, 65% were female and 35% were male. Interviewees ranged in age from 16 to 80, distributed as follows: age 16-20–3.6%; age 21-30–44.8%; age 31-40–18%; age 41-50–14%; age 51-60–11.3%; age 60-80–8.2%. The level of education was generally high, although the study included some readers, especially older readers, who had received little formal education.

I interviewed 25 of the readers, and the other 169 readers were interviewed by graduate students enrolled in successive offerings of my course on Genres of Fiction and Reading in the Masters Program of Library and Information Science at The University of Western Ontario. The student interviewers each picked as an interviewee someone whom they knew to be an enthusiastic reader for pleasure. Before they conducted and transcribed their interview, the student interviewers were trained in using open-ended questions and follow-up probes and were provided with a schedule of interview questions to be used as a guide for the interview. Using a chronological approach that started with the first thing the reader remembered reading as a child and worked forward to the present, the interviews explored, from the reader's perspective, the whole experience of pleasure-reading including the following: factors that fostered or hindered reading in childhood; how the reader goes about choosing or rejecting a book; rereading; ways in which a particular book has helped; and so on. The analysis presented in this paper focusses on the issue of reader's choice and depends primarily upon interviewees' answers to the following questions:

> How do you choose a book to read for pleasure?

> Are there types of books that you do *not* enjoy and would not choose?

Since the topic of choice was so basic and so salient, interviewees did not limit their discussion of choice to their answers to these two questions but tended to include commentary on choice throughout the entire interview. Therefore relevant data from the 194 interviews coded under themes related to choosing were derived, as appropriate, from the entire interview.

"I'M CALLING THE SHOTS NOW":
LEARNING TO CHOOSE BY CHOOSING

At every stage, choice permeates the topic of reading for pleasure, starting with the initial development in childhood of competencies in literacy. In order to achieve the bulk of reading practice that creates confident readers, beginners must be motivated to choose the activity of reading over any number of other activities that compete for their time. Then there is the question of what particular text gets read and who chooses it–is it freely chosen or is it assigned? In *The Power of Reading,* Stephen Krashen summarizes research on factors that encourage success in reading and emphasizes the crucial role of "free voluntary reading." Free voluntary reading, he says, "means putting down a book you don't like and choosing another one instead. It is the kind of reading that highly literate people do obsessively all the time" (1993, ix-x). The connection between voluntary reading and powerful literacy is that people learn to read by reading. They choose reading over some other competing activity because of the inherent pleasure in the reading experience itself. That pleasure is enhanced when readers are reading something that they themselves have selected. As one late-comer to pleasure-reading explained, contrasting her previous reluctance to read required school books with her current enjoyment of leisure reading:

> [I find reading enjoyable now] only because I have the freedom to choose which kinds of books I read. As a child I was not a good reader.

I didn't understand what I read, and I found that in order to understand I had to read *so slowly* that I lost the flow. It was like pulling teeth–one word at a time. . . . But once I got to the point where I could pick and choose what I wanted to read, I found I was enjoying what I was reading much more. I get more of a kick out of it because I'm calling the shots now. (Adrienne, age 32, elementary school librarian)

Being able to choose successfully among materials is an important skill that is never directly taught but is learned by readers who teach themselves, beginning in childhood. Each successful book choice makes it more likely that the beginning reader will want to repeat the pleasurable experience by reading something further. Each book read contributes to the bulk of reading experience that enhances the reader's ability to choose another satisfying book. Conversely, each unsuccessful choice decreases the beginning reader's desire to read, which in turn reduces the likelihood of further learning based on interaction with books. Most of the 194 readers have taught themselves strategies for choosing enjoyable books that less practiced readers may never discover. When asked how they go about choosing a book to read for pleasure, most interviewees launched into an elaborate description, involving many interrelated considerations, often starting with their own mood at the time of reading and going on variously to how they find new authors or what clues they look for on the book itself. Fewer than 10% of the readers said they were currently dissatisfied with their ability to select enjoyable books. But this minority is worth considering because the problems that these readers experience in finding enjoyable books to read are probably also faced by average readers. Average readers are less intensively involved with reading than readers chosen for this study and are likely to have developed fewer successful strategies for choosing books. One reader who was dissatisfied with her way of choosing books was Amelia, a former non-reader who started reading for pleasure after her marriage. The first book she read for enjoyment was Steven King's *The Shining,* following which she went on to read other horror novels, including the Halloween series and Anne Rice. Her main strategy for choosing books has been by author and genre, but at the time of the interview she had exhausted her stock of known authors and had difficulty in finding new books of interest:

[Disgusted] I go to the library and, like, stand there for hours. So I end up picking just at random. I pick some books up, bring them home, and end up taking them all back. You read the first couple pages, and then the author *goes on and on about some medal,* or, you know, describing [something at length] . . . . It's just so boring and you don't really get any excitement out of it. (Amelia, age 45, housewife)

Barbara had a longer history of successful interactions with books and more strategies for identifying enjoyable books, but she was also at a dead end because two of her ways to find out about books were no longer available:

> Lately I've been having trouble finding a book because I haven't been talking to people who have been reading. . . . The last three times I went to the library, I have taken out five books and I've returned them unread. I start the first page and then I know. I can tell the author's style and the kind of book by the first page. I know whether or not I'm going to enjoy it. . . . I've just been in a kind of dead end lately. At the library, they used to have all the new books out, so you could get an idea. They've stopped doing that and I miss it. (Barbara, age 28, speech language pathologist)

In contrast, an overwhelming majority of the 194 readers expressed confidence in their ability to make successful book choices. This confidence is likely to be both a result and a cause of their prolonged and continued engagement in reading. In this respect, they differ most decidedly from non-book-readers and reluctant book-readers. For many of these experienced readers, the process of selection seemed almost intuitive because it depended on a broad familiarity with books:

> I feel books. I get a feel for a book. I am sometimes wrong but rarely. Ninety percent of the time–95% of the time–I know before I read it that a book is going to be good or enjoyable, that I'll get something out of it–whatever the experience is that I'm looking for. (Paul, age 42, librarian)

> I have a whole shelf of books to be read. This year I've worked through them in a fairly random way. When I finish one, there might be a day or so and then I would say, "What am I really feeling like?" I pick something–sometimes it's intuitive. I'm pretty good at telling what will work out. Maybe because of all these years of persisting through books. (Rebecca, age 34, social worker)

> I just choose from some inner stimulus. I don't know what prompts me to choose. . . . If I start to read plays and it's a satisfying experience, I will continue to take out some plays until I find some that make me feel a little jaded or disappointed and then I might stop. . . . And you read a really good book review and think, "I can't wait until I can read that book," and to me that's the whole aura of reading. Some of it is retrospective because you deliberate on what you have read; it's current because you're experiencing; and also it's anticipatory because you know what you want to read. (Jean, age 44, teacher-librarian)

Not surprisingly, most of the readers in my study described themselves as avid readers in childhood. Their current familiarity with books and authors was based on a long apprenticeship in reading. Only 20 of the 194 readers, or a little more than 10% including Amelia and Adrienne quoted previously, identified themselves as reluctant readers as children. Typically the interviewees described themselves in childhood as voracious and indiscriminate readers who "read everything they could get their hands on": books in their own home, including their parents' and grandparents' childhood books; books in classrooms and in the school and public libraries; books received as birthday and Christmas gifts; and books borrowed and exchanged among friends. Reading series books, a practice disparaged by reading experts and librarians, was nevertheless a successful strategy used by 60% of the readers as a way of reducing the risk of choosing books and maximizing the likelihood of reading pleasure (Ross 1995, 217). When reading experts such as librarians or teachers challenged the choices of these self-confident readers, these readers as children generally wrote off, ignored, or worked around the reading experts and followed their own choices. Initially the opportunity for the child reader to choose books from a small, limited but readily available collection or from a favorite genre or series conferred an advantage, since it minimizes the problem that Sharon Baker calls "overload" (Baker 1986) while reducing the work needed to get physical access to books. Once readers outgrow the somewhat protected field of children's books, the process of choosing books becomes far more difficult and risky as the number of possible choices expands exponentially. Readers reported times, especially when they were adolescents or when they were moving to a new stage in their reading, when they were dissatisfied with their method of finding and choosing books. With practice and persistence, however, most by adulthood had arrived at a system that worked.

BEHIND THE EYES OF KNOWLEDGE

So what have these practiced readers taught themselves about choosing books that other people don't know? Notably the systems they described for choosing books usually depended on considerable previous experience and knowledge of authors, publishers, cover art, and conventions for promoting books and sometimes depended on a social network of family or friends who recommended and lent books. We can consider this to be "behind the eyes" knowledge that the reader can draw upon when considering for selection or rejection any particular book that comes to hand. Past experiences with books and remembered information from reviews or from word of mouth are carried in the reader's head and available to be called upon when the reader is browsing in a bookstore or library. In order to be alerted to the existence of new books that will provide the reading experience they want, committed readers typically put out antennae that scan their everyday environments for clues. They tuck away for future use in memory or on lists the names of books and authors mentioned in magazine and newspaper reviews; books given currency because they have been made into films or television productions; and authors and titles that come up in conversation. Recommendations are important, but only from a trusted source with tastes known to be compatible, such as certain reviewers, family members and "friends that know my taste," selected bookstore staff and librarians, and more recently Internet acquaintances. Each instance of a reader's engagement with a particular book takes place within a personal context that includes the following: the reader's literary competencies derived from previous experiences reading books; the reader's preferences developed during a lifetime of reading; and events going on in the rest of the reader's life at any particular time, which in turn relate to the reader's mood and time available for reading. Derek emphasized prior experience as a factor in enjoying a book: "Sometimes you have to be ready for a book. There are some books it's not your time to read, or it's not their time to be read by you. Sometimes a book just has nothing to say to you, and that's probably because you have to have had some prior experience." All these personal factors interact to determine what the reader means at any given time by "a good book."

Marsha was typical in using an array of cues in concert with each other when choosing books: previous experience with the author (" It's very safe to know that you've got an author that you like, and there are more books sitting there waiting. . . . I like the fact that LeCarre is still writing"); the reputation of the book ("I always thought I should read important books"); the reputation of the publisher ("I decided that Penguins . . . were important books"); recommendations of friends and family ("So it's important for someone to recommend a book. I very rarely pick up a book that I've never heard of"); and clues provided by the packaging of the book itself ("I always read the blurbs on the back. I'm easily put off or become very cynical of something that's too glowing"). Taking this amount of care to avoid unsatisfying choices was worth the trouble because a bad reading experience threatened her pleasure in reading in general. Readers explained how they read their way into reading, following up a successful experience with an attempt to repeat the pleasurable experience by reading something else. Successful choices are therefore part of a self-reinforcing system that sustains the pleasure of reading itself, while disappointing choices kill the desire to read:

> I think that's why I'm so careful about [choosing a book]. I don't just pick up any book and read it. Because if I get disappointed, then I get put off, and I get really mad. I get mad at myself for wasting my time. I get mad at the hours I spent reading. (Marsha, age 26, student)

STRATEGIES FOR SELECTION

The bedrock for choice is the reader's mood: What do I feel like reading now? What will I want to read in the future (that I should borrow or buy now to have on hand)? Readers overwhelmingly reported that they choose books according to their mood and what else is going on in their lives. Short books, easy reads, and old favorites are picked when the reader is busy or under stress. At such times, rereading a childhood favorite is the quintessence of comfort reading (Ross 1994). More demanding and unfamiliar material is chosen when the reader's life is calmer. Wendy said, "It depends on my mood. . . . Some days you don't want a book that reaches too deep into you and other days you do." And moods can fluctuate over time, as Larry explained: "As my mood fluctuates from day to day and even within the day, I'll want to read one book as opposed to another." Readers variously identified moods, each of which required its own kind of book: "A very pensive and solitary mood" is appropriate for reading poetry, said Edward; "If I'm feeling a bit down" Lisa picks up a humorous book; Ivor had to be in "an almost somber mood" to read Lillian Rubin's *Worlds of Pain*, but if he's "very, very tired" he reads "something a little lighter, something that you don't have to struggle with." Tess said, "When I'm really stressed, I will try to find a writer or a book that is really gentle, that has a gentle plot–like Barbara Pym or Jane Austen or early Trollope." On the other hand, Anna said, "If my life is going through a calmer phase . . . I might set an external stimulus for myself and pick up something new." In each of these cases, readers were quite specific about the kinds of books that would suit their mood, and often specified a dimension along which variation might occur: stressed out vs. relaxed; tired vs. rested; sad or somber vs. upbeat; wishing comfort and sameness vs. wishing novelty:

> Sometimes I want nothing but escape and then I like a big romance like *The Far Pavilions.* Other times I want something that offers a little intellectual stimulation such as *The White Hotel* by D. M. Thomas . . . And if I'm *really* tired, I read mystery stories like Agatha Christie. Agatha Christie's for when I'm so tired I can hardly see. . . . You see, this D. M. Thomas–I can't predict what might happen and I like that. That's exciting. But it isn't exciting if I'm tired. Then I wouldn't read it. (Diane, age 37, social worker)

When readers wanted safety, reassurance and confirmation, they often reread old favorites or read new books by known authors that they can trust. At other times, they wanted to be amazed by something unpredictable, unexpected or new. At such times, readers reported that they might pick books on sheer impulse to introduce novelty into their reading and discover new authors or genres. One reader said she always checks the just-returned section of the public library first because "I place faith in people having chosen the popular novels and returning them." Another described how she would occasionally "just walk along an aisle in a library, run my finger along the spines of the books and just go, 'Stop now' and pull it out"; unless she can tell it's going to be something completely unappealing "like a war story," she'll read it, just as an experiment. Other tactics used to produce serendipity included randomly picking a different letter each time and examining fiction with authors' names beginning, say, with A or S. Readers in the study adopted various strategies to establish the right balance, for each individual reader, between safety and the certainty of success on the one hand and novelty and surprise on the other. Since readers are reluctant in bookstores to indulge in what one person called a "cold buy," libraries are a resource that supports readers in taking risks with new and unfamiliar authors, genres, or subject areas.

The single most important strategy for selection that readers used was to choose a book by a known and trusted author. This pattern is consistent with David Spiller's finding that, of 500 persons that he interviewed returning books to British public libraries, 54% choose novels by known authors. Readers in my study elaborated: "I follow authors that I like and I keep up with what they are writing"; "It's like finding a gold mine and following a vein when you find a good author like Salman Rushdie"; "I'll walk along the shelves and authors will come past me in a sort of parade and I'll think, 'Oh, yes, I feel like a little bit of Atwood today'"; "An author string is a very common way for me to read"; "You have to trust your author. If you've read everything by your favorite author you have to try to reproduce the same satisfaction and enjoyment in another author"; "I choose primarily in terms of authors. I think first of authors and then, when I have exhausted those possibilities, I'll think of types. If a library has books divided into genres, then that makes it easier for me." Genre was second only to the author in providing clues as to the kind of experience the reader can expect from a book. In fact, genre was often used in conjunction with author: "If I am looking for something light to read like a mystery novel, I will look at the authors–I have certain authors I like and if I see something I haven't read before."

Once the reader starts to browse within a range of books, then the cover and the clues provided on the book itself become important. As Charles explained, "When you're as genre-specific as I guess I am, and read as voraciously as I do, you're looking for some quick identifiers on what's a good book. It'll take me ten minutes to go in [to the science fiction section], get five books, and leave because I'm just so familiar with the genre in general." The most frequently mentioned "quick identifiers" were the cover, the blurb on the back, and the sample page. This finding is similar to the

Book Industry Study Group survey result that 29% of readers indicated that the description or synopsis on the book jacket or cover was "very important" in making choices (1984, 133). Titles are also important–readers said they were drawn both to an unusual, catchy title (in the case of an unfamiliar book) and to a familiar title that they had heard about before. Charles stressed that "the cover actually does play a really important role in the choice," but was not an overriding factor: "If Margaret Weiss was wrapped in a brown paper bag, I'd still pick her book."

A feature that strongly attracted one reader equally strongly put off another, but in each case the information was helpful in matching book and reader. For example, a die-cut mauve cover with a title in swash lettering or a black cover spattered with gore each advertise themselves to their respective genre readers while at the same time warning off others who dislike romance or horror ("Those gold things with women with their shirts half ripped off, that kind of thing, is a definite turnoff"). One reader said, "Another way that I choose books is if they have won prizes," while another said he is *less* likely to pick prize-winners because the basis for awarding prizes is usually "a type of literary excellence that doesn't particularly make for enjoyable reading." Readers stressed the need to evaluate cues critically and skeptically, reading between the lines. Covers can be deceptive, as a number of readers pointed out: "I'm suspicious of covers" and "Covers are so misleading sometimes that they have no real connection with what's inside . . . I've learned that very good books can be hidden behind lousy covers." Regarding cover blurbs: "You read the back of the Harold Robbins' books–'It's spellbinding'–and you get into it and they have this F-word. I quit reading them." A final test for many readers is to read a sample paragraph or page, which was considered a good indicator of the writing style and level of literary competence demanded by the book: "You see a title of a book that sounds interesting, open it up and scan random pages, just to make sure that the writing is at a fairly decent level." In short, the majority of readers resembled Paul in reporting that they put a book through a series of tests and filters:

> I read the first few pages, look at the back cover, look at the front cover, read what I can about the author, and get an impression of the book. . . . The cover is important. The title. What I know about the author. What other people have said about it. Who it was that said that–is it *The Times Educational Supplement* or it is *The Kodiak Daily Fishwrapper?* I read all the information that is designed to make you interested in the book. Then I'll open it just at random and read one paragraph on each page and then open it again. Maybe three or four times I'll do that and just dip in. So the book is auditioning for me. It's like an audition: The book reads a very small part but it's only got that one chance to succeed. (Paul, age 42, librarian)

The interviewed readers were emphatic about what they *don't* like in a book, and used cues on the book itself as a warning. When asked what they *wouldn't* choose to read, readers had no trouble being specific, as in these examples: "Books that deal with fad diets, fad exercise programs, anything that was written in California by somebody with long hair and little round glasses. Anything that consists of navel gazing by some pretentious writer"; "I'm not going to read a depressing book . . . I don't like foul language in books. I get enough of all that in real life. I don't think it's necessary"; "Maybe I'm elitist, but I don't like mass market fiction–the sort of books like *Scruples* that feature some incredibly wealthy woman on the cover. Someone who goes from the Lower East Side [of Manhattan] to the top of the cosmetic industry in about two years." The most frequent response to the question about books that would *not* be chosen was to specify a particular genre, especially romance, westerns, and horror. For example, Maurice said, "There are some words on the back cover that turn me off–you know like 'psychological thriller' or 'horror'. If I see that, it goes straight back on the shelf." In addition, readers mentioned certain characters as unappealing–drippy heroines, violent heroes, and alpha males. Other readers variously ruled out books with particular content (too much, or "unnecessary," sex and violence; too much gore or horror); books with an undesired emotional effect ("makes me depressed"; "makes me feel like a patsy, taken for a ride"); and books written in a style that the reader dislikes. The frequently-given explanation that the rejected category of book is "poorly written" requires interpretation. "Poorly written" often seems to mean successfully written to achieve an effect that some readers admire but that this particular reader dislikes, finding it too sexually arousing, too scary, too sentimental, too full of verbal effects, too descriptive, or too literary.

A MODEL FOR THE PROCESS
OF CHOOSING A BOOK FOR PLEASURE

In summary, an analysis of readers' statements suggests that a comprehensive model for the process of choosing a book to read for pleasure must include five related elements that come into play in concert with each other (see also Smith 1996, 48-49 for a summary of previous research studies that examine dimensions of a book found important to readers). Anyone wanting to promote free voluntary reading can help less practiced readers by making it easier for them to make the complex discoveries, discriminations, and judgments involved in negotiating these five categories. Anything that reduces uncertainty in any of these categories provides what Gregory Bateson has defined as genuine information–"differences that makes a difference" (Bateson 1979, 110).

1. Reading Experience Wanted: The "What Mood Am I In?" Test

Familiarity vs. novelty

Safety vs. risk

Easy vs. challenging

Upbeat and positive vs. hard-hitting, ironic or critical

Do I want to be reassured/stimulated/frightened/amazed?

Do I want my beliefs and values to be confirmed or to be challenged by an uncomfortable but stimulating new perspective?

Readers tended to say that mood at the time of reading was more important for choosing fiction than non-fiction.

2. Alerting Sources that the Reader Uses to Find Out About New Books

Browsing in bookstores or libraries, including looking for genre labels, limiting searching to certain subject or genre areas, and monitoring displays of new books and "just returned" shelves

Recommendations from friends, co-workers or family members

Reviews or advertisements in newspapers, magazines, Internet, radio and television

Viewing dramatized productions of an authors' work in stage-plays, television or films

"Literary log-rolling" (books highlighted by trusted, favored authors, either within their own books or on publicity blurbs, e.g., "Pynchon writes jacket blurbs for DeLillo")

Lists (prize-winning books; books made familiar on course curricula; lists of recommended books produced by libraries, literary critics, or other readers)

Serendipity

Because of their high degree of commitment to reading, the readers in this study were themselves apt to be a key alerting source for others, passing on recommendations derived from reviews, choosing books at the library and bookstore for family members, and buying books as gifts for others.

3. Elements of a Book that Readers Take Into Account in Order to Match Book Choices to the Reading Experience Desired

Subject (related to genre in fiction and to topic in non-fiction)

Treatment (popular vs. literary or serious style; conventional and familiar vs. unpredictable; upbeat vs. negative or pessimistic in tone)

Characters depicted (e.g., presence of strong female characters or sympathetic characters or depressing characters; use of schematized black and white characterization)

Setting (the kind of world that the reader enters in reading the book)

Ending (happy or sad; predictable or unexpected; resolved or open-ended)

Physical size of the book ("thick books" vs. "quick reads")

For the majority of readers, for each particular instance of choice, a single factor was given precedence as an overriding consideration. Hence one reader might be looking primarily for a mystery story, with the secondary requirement being the presence of a smart female detective. Another might say that the major requirement is "nothing depressing or frightening" but she also wants to be "transported, moved into a world that's different from the everyday one." For others the size of the book is a key factor: "And the third thing I look at [after author and the description on the back cover] is the thickness. I will reject a book even if it's a book by an author that I know if it's a small, little book." In narrowing down choices, readers are strongly guided by what they *don't* want, so that they can quickly rule out whole categories ("nothing too long") and entire genres ("the psychological thriller").

4. Clues on the Book Itself Used to Determine the Reading Experience Being Offered

Author

Genre

Cover

Title

Sample Page

Publisher

The more experienced the reader, the greater his or her ability to use these clues to make subtle discriminations about the anticipated reading experience. A problem faced by beginning readers is that it takes a long apprenticeship in reading to build up the depth of knowledge needed to interpret the cover information that provides valuable clues to experienced readers. Series books such as Harlequins simplify the process of choice by highlighting genre, publisher and cover in one easily identifiable logo.

5. Cost in Time or Money Involved for the Reader in Getting Intellectual or Physical Access to a Particular Book

Intellectual access (previous knowledge of content or of literary conventions needed by the reader to make sense of the text)

Physical access (time and work required before the reader can lay hands on the book itself)

Length of time required or degree of cognitive and emotional commitment required by the book itself (easy quick read vs. long demanding read)

The likelihood of a reader's choosing a particular book can be regarded as a ratio of the degree of pleasure expected from the book divided by the degree of work needed to appropriate, physically and mentally, the book. Some readers said that they often read "books lying around" or they would "read what's around me" or "books I find at home." "I will not go out of my way to read this book," one reader said, but did in fact read it, because the book came easily to hand. Conversely, readers reported being willing to put themselves on waiting lists, special-order, or pay hard-cover prices to read a book that they expected to yield a high degree of pleasure. It follows that people who want to promote a particular book choice can either increase the reader's expectation of pleasure from a book or decrease the work needed for the reader to acquire the book.

IMPLICATIONS FOR LIBRARIES

This picture of the way that avid readers go about choosing books to read for pleasure has direct implications for library staff who function as intermediaries between the reader and the book.

1. Confident readers learn to read by reading–by reading a lot. The long apprenticeship in reading, which begins in childhood, is supported by public libraries, primarily by rich collections of books of all kinds that can be taken home, read aloud by parents and siblings, and read independently. What keeps children reading is the pleasure of the reading experience itself. This means that children's librarians should use a broad definition of "excellence" when developing children's collections. Books that win awards for literary or artistic superiority certainly need to be made widely available, but so do books, such as series books, that foster the love of reading and encourage the repetition of the reading experience. In "Serious about Series," Silk Makowski

(1994) argues YA series books are a genre unto themselves and should be judged by criteria that take into account what these series are really about: the continuity of the experience that keeps readers reading book after book. Repetition is a key part of the apprenticeship in learning how to read continuous text, which is why series books for children and young adults are allies in the making of confident readers.

2. Developing a strong fiction collection requires, among other things, an understanding of the genres of popular fiction–especially the specific satisfactions that each genre offers to its readers. What do readers look for in a good work of fantasy/speculative fiction, horror, detective fiction, or romance? A useful way to build up professional expertise is deliberately to read a popular example of a genre that you normally would not choose to read as part of your own pleasure reading. The two genres that librarians know *least* about and value the least happen to be among the genres most widely read by readers: teen series and romance. Ethnographic studies of reading such as Janice Radway's *Reading the Romance* (1984) and genre studies such as John G. Cawelti's *Adventure, Mystery, and Romance* (1976) can be indispensable guides for getting a handle on genre readers and their reading experiences.

3. The successful matching of book to reader requires a lot of meta-knowledge about books, genres, authors, publishers, etc., that inexperienced readers lack. At every stage from the acquisition of the book to the readers' advisory process of getting the book into the hands of the reader, libraries can help novice readers by supplying the meta-knowledge. In practice, this means creating scaffolding devices that make it easier for readers to recognize the nature of the experience offered by particular books: displays and other alerting devices; annotated lists of the "If you like N, you might enjoy X, Y, Z" sort; bulletin boards or web pages that make available other readers' recommendations; genre labels; separation of fiction collections by genre. The more information about books is made visible by the arrangement and display of the books themselves, the less information the reader needs to have in his/her head. Unless it is stripped off by library processing, the packaging information on the cover of the book itself offers readers clues they can use as "quick identifiers."

4. Trying to change readers' book preferences doesn't work. Readers know what they want to read and find presumptuous any suggestion that they should be reading different/better/more challenging/or more diverse materials. The role of the library is to acquire a variety of books for every reading taste and mood and then help readers in the tricky process of finding those books that match their own preferences.

REFERENCES

Baker, Sharon L. 1986. "Overload, Browsers, and Selections." *Library and Information Science Research* 8: 315-329.

Bateson, Gregory. 1979. *Mind and Nature.* Toronto and New York: Bantam Books.

Book Industry Study Group. 1984. *1983 Consumer Research Study on Reading and Book Purchasing: Focus on Adults.* New York: Book Industry Study Group.

Cawelti, John G. 1976. *Adventure, Mystery, and Romance: Formula Stories as Art and Popular Culture.* Chicago: U of Chicago Press.

Cole, John Y. and Gold, Carol S., eds. 1979. *Reading in America: Selected Findings of the Book Industry Study Group's 1978 Study.* Washington: Library of Congress.

Gallup Organization. 1978. *Book Reading and Library Usage: A Study of Habits and Perceptions.* Conducted for the American Library Association. Princeton, NJ: Gallup Organization.

Krashen, Stephen D. 1993. *The Power of Reading: Insights from the Research.* Englewood, CO: Libraries Unlimited.

Makowski, Silk. 1994. "Serious about Series: Selection Criteria for a Neglected Genre." *Voice of Youth Advocates* (February): 349-351.

Norman, Donald A. 1988. *The Psychology of Everyday Things.* New York: Basic Books.

Radway, Janice. 1984. *Reading the Romance: Women, Patriarchy and Popular Literature.* Chapel Hill: University of North Carolina Press.

Ross, Catherine Sheldrick. 1994. "Readers Reading L. M. Montgomery." In *Harvesting Thistles*: *The Textual Garden of L. M. Montgomery,* ed. Mary H. Rubio. Guelph: Canadian Children's Literature, pp. 23-35.

Ross, Catherine Sheldrick. 1995. "'If They Read Nancy Drew, So What?': Series Book Readers Talk Back." *Library and Information Science Research* 17: 201-236.

Smith, Duncan. 1996. "One Reader Reading: A Case Study." In *Guiding the Reader to the Next Book,* ed. Kenneth D. Shearer. New York: Neal-Schuman, pp. 45-70.

Spiller, David. 1980. "The Provision of Fiction for Public Libraries." *Journal of Librarianship* 12, 4: 238-66.

Watson, Kenneth F. et al. 1980. *Leisure Reading Habits: A Survey of the Leisure Reading Habits of Canadian Adults with Some International Comparisons.* Ottawa: Infoscan.

The Book's Remarkable Longevity in the Face of New Communications Technologies– Past, Present and Future

Kenneth Shearer

SUMMARY. The circulation of popular books, especially novels, has been the dominant role played by public libraries since the founding of the Boston Public Library in the middle of the 19th Century. The attraction of stories that libraries collect is powerful and continues to serve a genuine, widespread need in the face of the respective debuts of film, radio, TV, and the Internet.

But the circulation of human stories–in print, audiocassette, and videocassette formats–without attendant advisory services and related value-added contributions by librarians, fails to realize the potential that libraries can serve for users who want to answer the call of stories, but are not quite sure which ones would serve them best. *[Article copies available for a fee from The Haworth Document Delivery Service: 1-800-342-9678. E-mail address: <getinfo@haworthpressinc.com> Website: <http://www.haworthpressinc.com>]*

KEYWORDS. Circulation, popular reading, Boston Public Library, multi-media

---

Kenneth Shearer is Professor, School of Library and Information Sciences, North Carolina Central University, Fayetteville Street, Durham, NC 27707.

[Haworth co-indexing entry note]: "The Book's Remarkable Longevity in the Face of New Communications Technologies–Past, Present and Future." Shearer, Kenneth. Co-published simultaneously in *The Acquisitions Librarian* (The Haworth Information Press, an imprint of The Haworth Press, Inc.) No. 25, 2001, pp. 23-33; and: *Readers, Reading and Librarians* (ed: Bill Katz) The Haworth Information Press, an imprint of The Haworth Press, Inc., 2001, pp. 23-33. Single or multiple copies of this article are available for a fee from The Haworth Document Delivery Service [1-800-342-9678, 9:00 a.m. - 5:00 p.m. (EST). E-mail address: getinfo@haworthpressinc.com].

DEWEY PREDICTS THE DEATH OF PRINT

American librarians at the turn of the third millennium are neither the first nor the last of their tribe to read that books are unlikely to survive the onslaught of the latest technology. Nearly three quarters of a century ago, in 1926, Melville Dewey, the most important of the founders of modern librarianship, weighing the impact of movies on reading books, concluded,

> . . . I am not at all sure that the library of fifty years from now will not have outgrown the book and that it may go back into the museum like inscriptions on clay. For the enemies of the book: the radio, the movies . . . are working a short cut . . . to give the public in the quickest and cheapest way information and inspiration and recreation on the highest plane. [1]

He continued, "If the movies are teaching the many millions a week not to read, let us utilize that great means . . . " [2]

It is instructive to notice how Dewey was right and how he was wrong in his predictions. Did radio and movies and later TV and personal computers come to absorb vast amounts of the time and attention of the public? Of course! It is the seeming implication that when and if the other communications technologies absorb more and more time, then the use of books will atrophy, which has proven wrong time after time. Dewey was correct in one respect in this prediction: film came to be an important medium in libraries, especially after the invention of film in the videocassette format. However, the book was not relegated to the museum as a consequence.

Even earlier, one hundred and fifteen years ago in 1883, the other most important founder of modern librarianship, Charles Cutter, wrote a charming library science fiction story in which he predicted what the public library would be like a century into *his* future and 15 years in *our* past. Because he had no reason to anticipate the invention of the radio, he predicted that in listening-rooms located in library branches, there would be "fonographic editions prepared by the best readers, . . . read by machines, often to crowded audiences. . . . The reading machines have reached such a pitch of perfection that it is as if one were listening to an agreeable elocutionist."[3] His guide in this future library preferred "to do [his] own reading [by himself] but there are many whose eyes are weak or who do not read with ease, or prefer to listen in company."[4] Cutter predicted that listening-rooms would create huge increases in library use. Why did those increases fail to materialize?

The reason listening-rooms failed to be the wave of Cutter's future is that privately accessible radios, and later TVs and VCRs rendered obsolete that role of the library. As these machines for listening to stories became available in homes, each of these potentially explosive new uses for the library took place, or now takes place outside the library and in the home.

How many public, school and academic libraries still collect 16 and 8 mm film for common use? I am old enough to recall when the 16 and 8 mm film were the "enemy" of the book, as well as the "best hope" for the library to survive and thrive in the future.

In 1876, the dominant communications media were the book, periodical and newspaper. What remains constant during the development of changing communications technologies since the founding of modern librarianship in 1876–the rich period of the inventions of the telegraph, telephone, phono-graph, motion pictures, radio, television, photocopier, compact disc, telefac-simile, audiocassette, videocassette, satellite, big, medium and personal com-puters and Internet–is the staying power of the book and its role in libraries. The print forms of newspapers and scholarly serials do appear to be in some decline as a consequence of competition with newer communications media, especially the computer in its role in provision of access to the Internet, but the book does not.

An analogy from medicine to what appears, at least to a degree, to be the situation in librarianship may help to make the point: as catscans, chemother-apies and microsurgical techniques emerge, the need for obstetricians to attend to the delivery of children remains. Books remain a major reason for public, school, research, and academic library use. The delivery of in-depth development of ideas, instruction, and deeply engaging, value-shaping sto-ries is handled best by books.

During the remainder of this article, I will confine my remarks to the *public* library because to extend it to all types of libraries would necessitate a different structure, many more qualifications and more space than allocated here. The public library is the one that Cutter wrote his library science fiction story about and to it we return.

CUTTER PREDICTS FICTION USE WILL DECLINE IN THE FUTURE

Cutter's tale reveals his strong bias against fiction and for non-fiction. He has his guide to the library of the future remark with pride that, "We have not yet escaped the preponderant use of fiction though we have diminished it since your day. It used to be 75 percent. Thanks to our training the school children in good ways it has fallen to forty. I doubt if it goes much further."[5] Later in the story the guide amplifies on the theme of reducing fiction reading so that children grow up "as real inquirers instead of being desultory amuse-ment-seekers. The ordinary novel-reader is not done away with, though his tribe may be diminished. But the novel-readers come from a different class, and read for a different object. We never can convert them, and often cannot intercept the taste in youth."[6] (Was the "different class" from which novel-readers came drawn from cultural and/or possibly socioeconomic inferiors to the librarians Cutter was addressing?)

Carrier explores in detail the attitudes of librarians, literary critics and the general public toward fiction during 1876-1900. Most library spokespersons of the period held negative attitudes but even so some reasons were expressed that supported the inclusion of novels in public libraries, i.e.,

> . . . since libraries were supported by taxation, they should provide for the needs of every member of the reading community; even reading books of little literary worth had some value, in that it kept many from worse literature, not supplied by libraries at all, and worse activities; reading for relaxation only was valuable, especially for the over-worked; and the belief that censorship often imposed a cure worse than the disease . . . [7]

Cutter's hope in 1883 that a century later fiction circulation would be reduced from 75% to 40% was an understandable wish. It was in the spirit of the times of the ruling classes. Altick pointed out the difficulty of public librarians in Victorian England who wished to be viewed as contributors to society when,

> Sharing this feeling as they did, the proponents of free libraries were ill equipped to face what became, if not the gravest, at least the best-publicized charge against libraries once they were established: namely, that far from encouraging habits of study and self-improvement, they catered to the popular passion for light reading, above all for fiction. [8]

Fiction in those days had much the reputation of commercial TV today, a passive waste of time. And, of course, something women tended to do.

HIGHLY-WROUGHT ROMANCES THOUGHT TO BE INJURIOUS TO GIRLS

The following excerpt is drawn from an influential book on obstetrics and gynecology by a French physician whose work was translated into English and went into many printings for an American market, both the medical community and general public. It gives an insight into the connection between females and novel reading as depicted by males in the Victorian age:

> . . . . it is of the highest importance to remove young girls from boarding school, when they approach the age of puberty in order to exercise a constant watch over them. We should prevent, as far as possible, the false emotions produced by the reading of licentious books, especially

of the highly-wrought romances of the modern school, which are the
more injurious, as all the faculties become, as it were, overpowered by
the desire to experience the sentiment which these works always represent in an imaginary and exaggerated strain . . . [9]

The shift in librarians' thinking from a general view of fiction as largely a
time waster or actually injurious to the health of some readers to its better
reputation today seems to emerge, in part, from the desire of educators and
society in general to have children read books instead of watch television.
Furthermore, feminist scholars have sensitized us to the tendency to characterize whatever is more common among women as less valuable than the
parallel activity among men. Men are more likely than women, in the aggregate, to read non-fiction. Therefore, non-fiction was seen as intrinsically
better in more patriarchal societies.

Janice Radway, a professor of English and a reader-response theorist,
examines the role of reading romance fiction in contemporary women's lives
and finds a complex tapestry that includes rebellion against norms restrictive
to women. She concludes, and this is only one of many points, "Reading is
not a self-conscious, productive process in which they collaborate with the
author, but an act of discovery during which they glean from her information
about people, places, and events not themselves *in* the book." [10]

READERS IDENTIFY NOVELS AND OTHER STORIES AS BOOKS THAT MAKE A DIFFERENCE

The role of books in the lives of individuals has received attention in
Books Made the Difference by Gordon and Patricia Sabine sponsored by the
Center for the Book. The Sabines identify such reasons as (1) books are
potentially life-changing in their impact, including a source of satisfying
career choices, (2) they change for the better how one views life, (3) they
offer models to hold in mind as one pursues goals, (4) they provide ways to
getting away from it all so that one comes back refreshed, (5) they reinforce
one's deeply held beliefs, and (6) they foster a love of the art and craft of
writing. It is noteworthy that the much maligned novel is often the kind of
book cited by individuals as the book that made the greatest difference for the
better in their lives. In fact, a quick count indicates that nearly as many of the
titles chosen were novels, plays or poetry as were any other categories: the
ratio was about seven novels, plays and poetry to an aggregate of nine for all
others. [11]

As one examines the categories occupied by the other titles chosen, it is
apparent that story-telling, often with a moral or the story of a life in the form
of a biography or autobiography dominates the non-fiction choices. Like

novels, these stories clearly have a great power over the moral imagination of large numbers of people. Values, beliefs, commitments, meaning are all well expressed by the written word. Story-based tales are a kind of non-fiction often circulated in public libraries in 1876, 1926, 1976 and now.

This discussion raises the question of just how much circulation from public libraries today (115 years after Mr. Cutter hoped that fiction would drop from 75% to 40%) is actually contributed by fiction. The answer, amazingly enough, appears to be unavailable anywhere. We cannot help wondering why this, the most common category of use during all public library history, is a statistic not collected *on the national level*. Could it be that librarians once felt ashamed of the dominance of fiction circulation and now their descendants have forgotten to add it back to the arsenal of statistics collected on public libraries? Or is it that librarians still prefer to suppress the fact that an enormous amount of usage and resources is accounted for by the circulation of novels in public libraries?

CUTTER PROVEN WRONG:
FICTION STILL IS MAINSTAY OF LIBRARY CIRCULATION

Fortunately, the state of North Carolina does systematically collect data on the relative incidence of fiction and non-fiction circulation. During 1996, of approximately 36,000,000 book circulations from North Carolina public libraries, 67% was accounted for by fiction.[12] That is correct, two thirds of the tenth most populous state's *total* book circulation in 1996 was accounted for by fiction. Sixty percent of *adult* circulation was fiction; 76% of *children's* circulation was fiction.[13] There is evidence that North Carolina is reasonably typical of circulation patterns elsewhere and none found to indicate otherwise.

Mr. Cutter would have been disappointed; of that, it seems we can be certain. Nonetheless, Cutter, notwithstanding his Victorian value system and his advocacy of non-fiction, could not picture a future in which fiction circulation ever accounted for much less than 40% of total circulation. He was too well in touch with the underlying motivations for leisure reading.

We need here to insert another thread into the argument of this article: large numbers of books are on audiocassette and far more are made into movies available in a videocassette format. Just as avid readers can rarely afford the expense and space which would be required to buy all the books of interest to them, most avid film buffs and audiocassette listeners have the same logistic and financial problems; this gives rise to a very important practical reason for the public to finance public libraries. Until and unless very large videocassette and audiocassette collections are available at home on-line or on terminal/consoles, the public library will increasingly include these book-like items, along with the book itself, as a mainstay for its future.

Public librarians, trustees and the public involved in the Public Library Association's Planning Process recognize the role of popular material provision in the *ranking* of essential services they perform. In their choice of prioritized roles for public libraries, the one most often emphasized is that of Popular Materials Center (94%). It is chosen more often than the next two most popular choices, Reference Library (78%) and Door to Early Learning (78%), and far above the roles of both Informal Learning Center (44%) and Formal Education Center (34%), with the other roles falling below these.[14]

It would paint a less than complete picture of the Popular Materials Center role in public libraries to neglect non-fiction merely because it appears to be in the minority of popular materials circulated from public libraries. A look at recent best seller lists reminds us that such books as stories of the life and death of Princess Diana, the story of John D. Rockefeller's rise to a titan of industry, along with novel-like non-fiction such as the phenomenally successful books *Midnight in the Garden of Good and Evil, Angela's Ashes,* and *A Civil Action,* are not the purely utilitarian items that their textbook and university press non-fiction brethren usually are.

LIBRARIANS HAVE CONFLICTED FEELINGS ABOUT FICTION USAGE

We see a field with a history of conflicted feelings about the role of the Popular Materials Center, especially as it applied to the facilitation of the reading of fiction, even to the point of not collecting national statistics on this mainstay of service. And if that were not neurosis-inducing enough, the general public seems to hold a similarly conflicted value system. For in a poll that George D'Elia conducted, he found that the general public placed roles of the public library with "education" and "learning" in their names above the Popular Materials Center as "very important" roles for the public library to serve. The general public rated Formal Education Support Center first with 88%, Independent Learning Center second with 85%, and Preschooler's Door to Learning as third (83%), well above their ranking of Popular Materials Center (51%). It is worth noting that a slight majority of respondents did view this role as "very important."[15]

If it is correct to believe that the most common role for public libraries will remain that of a Popular Materials Center, will the value of the institution be perceived as marginal by the general public, by librarians and by the politicians who determine the extent of their financial support? Or is there a way to advance its enthusiastic support? While Americans are no longer quite the Puritans they were in Cutter and Dewey's time, the defense of the use of tax money is still fought in terms of the serious public purposes that it serves, whether for fire prevention, education, police protection, garbage removal or the provision of library materials. The issue needs to be dealt with directly.

The crux of the question is this: Does the reading of popular materials serve an important public purpose which deserves the community support? Does it contribute to the educational, or any other important, goal of society?

It would seem that how public librarians perceive what they are doing, present what they are doing, and do what they are doing intelligently will go a long way toward improving the support of libraries that disseminate popular materials, and advancing librarians' professional standing. Public librarians must themselves view leisure reading as a worthwhile activity deserving full professional service. Do they have good reasons to do that?

It is a thesis of this article that they do have good reasons and that they have to be invested in the fact that life-altering experiences are produced by books–just as the Sabines discovered. But what of the soothing balm, stimulating excitement and meaningful speculation that novels, including romances, mysteries, and science fiction and other genres, bring to the leisure time of so many Americans? Is that also well worth the cost?

READING NOVELS IS A CREATIVE ACT

Smith addresses this issue about as persuasively as anyone writing today. He has begun to develop a rationale for librarians to explain to themselves and others why the bedrock circulation of fiction is valuable:

> . . . the reading of fiction is a very creative act that is connected in significant ways to the reader's life. Fiction readers are not really running away from anything. Readers read to see themselves and their worlds in a new way–or sometimes to reconnect with a memory of themselves in a different world. . . .
> Fiction readers have long been a core user group . . . , but we have always been uneasy about them.[16]

Ross, in her prize-winning research on possibly the most denigrated of all publicly-mentionable reading–series books like Nancy Drew and the Hardy Boys–learns something rather surprising given the reputation series books have. She concludes from her extensive efforts, including 142 interviews, that "series books teach beginning readers about the process of reading itself–strategies for making sense out of extended text . . . far from being harmful, [they] might be for some readers an essential stage in their development as powerful literates."[17]

Ross shows that reading series fiction may even be utilitarian. Perhaps, generalizing her findings about series readers, we may hypothesize that just as writers learn to be good writers by writing, readers learn to become good readers by reading. The fact is that hundreds of millions of novels and over a billion books of all types are being circulated by public libraries to Americans annually and may very well keep up and advance their literacy and attention span skills, surely public goods even in the narrowest sense. We call ours the "Information Age," a time when more and more occupations require literacy skill at a higher and higher level.

Public librarians must promote the value of reading, auditing and viewing stories to funders, politicians and the general public. Wayne Wiegand raises the question, Why don't we have any schools of library and reading studies? Why are they all called schools of library and information studies, or given similar names? Certainly a school of library and reading studies would be an appropriate name for a program to prepare public librarians and school media coordinators. Is the answer to Wiegand's question that librarians feel obliged to present libraries as exclusively and relentlessly utilitarian? Does that account for the absence of fiction circulation figures in the nation's public libraries?

Wiegand points out that the scholarship on which to base reading studies is plentiful, as is ample evidence of the need for a reading studies knowledge base for librarians. He notes that "67% of Americans used public libraries in 1994, and of that number 80% went to borrow a book." "What," he asks, "do these numbers suggest to you about the value 140 million library patrons place on the act of reading?"[18]

The historical basis for the reluctance of public librarians to publicly acknowledge that what they handle much of the time is popular reading is explored by Altick. He digs into the arguments for and against the founding of–and support for–public libraries in 19th Century Britain where he notes that what is missing from the dialogue,

> is any sense of the intellectual and spiritual enrichment–or the simple relaxation–that an individual man or woman, boy or girl, may derive from reading, quite apart from any benefit that may accrue to the community. The Victorians' silence on this matter is quite understandable, for an institution to be supported by public funds must be justified first of all in terms of the common good. Although the principle that a community might tax itself to provide facilities for recreation had been fairly well accepted in the case of parks and museums, for example, it was still generally denied when libraries were in question. The old religious and utilitarian prejudices against reading for entertainment still persisted; if the nation were to subsidize the reading habit, it should only do so for serious purposes.[19]

Public librarians add value to leisure time and make a difference in the quality of life of those who love stories. Leisure time is becoming a very valued and hard to acquire asset. Librarians make it easier for people to find stories–in print, audio, and video formats–that are fulfilling and that reward their expenditure of leisure time more than competing means can. Librarians can speak with them as individuals about their reading interests and relate books to their personal needs. As we enter the twenty-first century, it is enough to improve individuals' lives; we can worry a bit less than our ancestors did about narrowly serving "the public good." If librarians serve to improve the quality of life for great numbers of people, surely in the aggregate they have served the public good.

LIBRARIANS ADVISE INDIVIDUALS IN THE ART OF LIVING MORE FULLY

We started out this article with a quote from Melville Dewey's address to the 1926 meeting of the American Library Association in which he posed the possibility that by 1976 the American public would outgrow books and turn to radio and movies instead to meet the needs once met by books. Since Dewey spoke, the audiocassette and videocassette versions of stories were born and now flourish. These newer versions of human stories–stories that are told to us or visualized for us–are selected, acquired, organized, circulated, used, and discussed just as books are. They fit into the Popular Materials Center role, the role opted as a major use of resources by nearly all public libraries in the country today, at least insofar as those that have undertaken the Public Library Association's Planning and Role-Setting Process are representative.

It is time to acknowledge and embrace this core function and to focus our collective energies much more fully on doing it in earnest. Helping to fill in hours of quality leisure time is as valuable as answering information questions. It is time to stress the educational roles that reading, auditing and viewing play in the lives of the individuals who enjoy them. It is time to assist them with meeting these needs as professionally and thoroughly as librarians answer reference questions or compile information and referral directories or support informal education.

Answering the universal human hunger for stories in a personalized manner is a difficult and valued art. The field is developing some research strategies to study the practice of this art in librarianship and it is developing a literature on how to establish this service on a firmer basis.[20] Many useful readers' advisory tools in print are being published to supplement the standbys. Amazon.com, Webrary, Fiction_L, NoveList, and other computerized aids are making the job more feasible. To do it well, librarians need first to rid themselves of the residual patriarchal and Victorian baggage that has stood in their way. An essential part of lifelong learning is to learn how to live well and how to realize one's potential. Librarians are helping and, in the future, will help individuals even more skillfully to a better life and a better chance to realize their potential by guiding them to the stories that speak uniquely to them.

NOTES

1. Dewey, Melville. "Our Next Half-Century." *Library Journal* (1926): 888.

2. Ibid., p. 889.

3. Cutter, Charles A. "Buffalo Public Library in 1983," *Public Libraries* (1982): 134-135. (Originally published in *Library Journal* (1883: 215).

4. Ibid., p. 135.

5. Ibid., p. 133.

6. Ibid., p. 135.

7. Carrier, Esther Jane. *Fiction in Public Libraries, 1876-1900* (New York: Scarecrow Pr., 1965), 364.

8. Altick, Richard. *The English Common Reader; A Social History of the Mass Reading Public, 1800-1900* (Chicago: Univ. of Chicago Pr., 1957), 231.

9. An excerpt from Marc Colombat's *Treatise on the Diseases and Hygiene of Females*, tr. Charles Meigs (Philadelphia: n.p. given, 1850) In *Victorian Women; A Documentary Account of Women's Lives in Nineteenth Century England, France, and the United States*, eds. Erna O. Hallerstein, Leslis P. Hume and Karen M. Offen (Stanford, CA: Stanford Univ. Pr., 1981), 93.

10. Radway, Janice A. *Reading the Romance: Women, Patriarchy, and Popular Literature* (Chapel Hill, NC: Univ. of North Carolina Pr., 1984), 190.

11. Sabine, Gordon and Patricia Sabine. *Books That Made the Difference; What People Told Us* (Hamden, CT: Library Professional Publications, 1983). Ratings are based on an analysis of the list of titles on pp. 5-9.

12. Shearer, Kenneth. "Readers' Advisory Service: New Attention to a Core Business of the Public Library." *North Carolina Libraries* (Fall, 1998), in press.

13. Ibid. These figures are based on further analysis of information taken from the table in this article.

14. Shearer, Kenneth. "Confusing What Is Most Wanted with What Is Most Used: A Crisis in Public Library Practice Today." *Public Libraries* (1993): 195.

15. D'Elia, George. "The Roles of the Public Library in Society; The Results of a National Survey. Final Report" (Evanston, IL: Urban Libraries Council, 1993), 31.

16. Smith, Duncan. "Writers & Readers: Valuing Fiction." *Booklist* (1998): 1095.

17. Ross, Catherine. "If They Read Nancy Drew, So What? Readers Talk Back." *Library & Information Science Research* (1995): 201.

18. Wiegand, Wayne. "Out of Sight, Out of Mind: Why Don't We Have Any Schools of Library and Reading Studies?" (1997): 323.

19. Altick, Richard. Op. cit.

20. A book devoted to research on readers' advisory in the public library is *Guiding the Reader to the Next Book*, ed. Kenneth Shearer (New York: Neal-Schuman, 1996). A work that outlines good practice in readers' service in the public library is Saricks, Joyce and Nancy Brown. *Readers Advisory Service in the Public Library*, 2nd. ed. (Chicago: American Library Association, 1997). Another recent contribution to this effort is *Serving Readers*, ed. Ted Balcom (Atkinson, WI: Highsmith Pr., 1997).

Some Speculation
on the Future of the Book

Lee Shiflett

SUMMARY. The continuing debate over the future of the book is a highly charged one that is too frequently driven by prophecy rather than evidence. The introduction of technological change rarely completely displaces older technologies especially when the older technologies are as much a part of the fabric of the culture as the book. The major direction of the competing communication technology is seen as an evolving process where the electronic forms of materials will eventually find a form that realizes their potential among the functions traditionally associated only with the book. *[Article copies available for a fee from The Haworth Document Delivery Service: 1-800-342-9678. E-mail address: <getinfo@haworthpressinc.com> Website: <http://www.haworthpressinc.com>]*

KEYWORDS. Future of the book, books, hypertext, electronic communication, multi-media

Since the Christians gained ascendancy over the pagans, the shape of the book has been the codex. During the half millennium since the invention of printing in the western world, the book has taken the form of sheets of paper, printed, folded, and held together at one end. With some variations, this artifact has served the world of readers well for the past 1,500 years. It is convenient, usually portable,

Lee Shiflett holds a BA at the University of Florida; MLS, at Rutgers University; and PhD in Library and Information Studies, Florida State University. Currently, he is Professor, School of Library and Information Science, Louisiana State University, Baton Rouge, LA 70803.

[Haworth co-indexing entry note]: "Some Speculation on the Future of the Book." Shiflett, Lee. Co-published simultaneously in *The Acquisitions Librarian* (The Haworth Information Press, an imprint of The Haworth Press, Inc.) No. 25, 2001, pp. 35-49; and: *Readers, Reading and Librarians* (ed: Bill Katz) The Haworth Information Press, an imprint of The Haworth Press, Inc., 2001, pp. 35-49. Single or multiple copies of this article are available for a fee from The Haworth Document Delivery Service [1-800-342-9678, 9:00 a.m. - 5:00 p.m. (EST). E-mail address: getinfo@haworthpressinc.com].

and requires only that the user be literate. At its basic level, the book requires no arcane technology to produce and no unnatural equipment to use.

The debate over the future of the book reached its majority years ago. The lines have been drawn between those who defend the form of the book as central to western civilization and those who maintain that the book has outlived its usefulness. It is unfortunate that those who defend the book ultimately are forced to do so not from the inherent technical superiority of the form over other alternatives, but from a less arguable nostalgia for a passing era, from sentimentality, and from their emotional reaction to the other alternatives. If the assumptions underlying the attack on the book are accepted, then it almost inexorably follows that as a manifestation of information technology, the book will be marginalized at best, and perhaps obsolete in the opening decades of the 21st century. We must face it. For what it does do, electronic access to information is more effective, cheaper, and in most cases easier to accomplish than the production and use of paper artifacts. Electronic media are more versatile in their presentation, more varied in their usability, and more capable of offering a far greater range of displays for the communication of information to the reading public than the traditional book has ever been.

But, this assessment rests on the acceptance of the notion that the main purpose of the book is to communicate information. This role has, of course, been one of the principal purposes for the form from its inception, but it is not the only one and, in many cases, not even the principal one for many people who use, read, cherish, and delight in the relics of human ingenuity on our shelves. We value books only partially for the information they contain. They have been cherished for their fine paper, presswork, illustrations and, of course, their bindings. For the collector of books, the content is frequently irrelevant to the purpose of collecting. English book collector Richard Heber mandated that everyone should have three copies of every book he owned; one to show, one to use, and one to lend.[1] Of course, Heber refers only to the text. One would only show a pristine Caxton. Later reprints of the text would serve for reading and lending. People collect fine press work, the productions of particular book designers, examples of typographic excellence and excess, and fine bindings. There are antiquarian shops in major cities where sections are devoted to elegant bindings from which the book blocks have been removed, presumably for other purposes, and the hides of the books sit awaiting a customer to carry them off to a biblio-taxidermist for finishing. The book is valued for information by some, but for many the artifact is the true object of the collector.

Further, whatever information is found in books is so diverse that the concept itself almost ceases to have real meaning in the context of books. Information implies some relation to truth. In the natural sciences, truth is obviously central to the progress of knowledge. The accumulation of facts about the universe in essence accumulate to either affirm or, when sufficient, to overturn the paradigms through which scientific knowledge is created and understood. Even facts that have lost the status of truth in the scientific world retain a secondary truth as part of the historical record of science. In the social sciences, the picture is more problematic. Truth is at best ambiguous and, at least in the branches of the social sciences that aspire to scientific reputability, the notion of truth only exists in the context of various competing paradigms. In the humanities, especially those arenas that diverge from the purely factual, the whole concept of truth is irrelevant. Unless one wants to strain the Keatsian equation that beauty is truth to its ultimate nonsensical conclusion, the idea has no meaning.

No one would doubt the value of fiction, but the question of what sort of knowledge or truth it contains is nonsense within the context of information transfer. Clearly, the whole concept of information within the context of books is one that needs serious attention if the debate over the future of the book is to become meaningful within the concept of the book as an instrument of information transfer.

The complexity is compounded by the ways in which the terms *data, knowledge,* and *information* are thrown about in an almost interchangeable manner without a clear distinction as to their meanings or to their contexts. Added to this is the problem of relevance to the user of the whatever it is called–one person's data is another's information and a third's knowledge. One of the most perceptive analyses of the problem is found in Fritz Machlup's work in which he distinguishes among different kinds of the phenomena he calls *knowledge.* He made a series of distinctions that rest on user perception rather than any inherent characteristic of the things themselves. Machlup divided the world of knowledge into five major groups. The first he called *practical knowledge*–that which enables us to do something. The second, *intellectual knowledge,* forms part of the common cultural experience of a group and is related to the values of the social and intellectual aspects of human experience. *Pastime knowledge* consists of the constant barrage of gossip, news, and trivia that assails us without beneficial lasting effect and is the third grouping. The fourth major division is *spiritual knowledge* which addresses the religious needs of humanity. The last category is one that in most exhaustive classifications is given the heading, *other,* but Machlup prefers to call *unwanted knowledge,* acquired accidently, retained without plan of purpose, and which emerges at unexpected moments.[2] These are not exclusive categories. What one person would consider *spiritual,* a minister would call *practical* and others would dismiss as *unwanted* or *pastime.* But the distinctions can be useful in a gross way to provide a handle on the phenomenon of the book and books themselves, as "containers" of information, can be classified accordingly. The central issue here is that the book itself is used as a vehicle for all types of knowledge though it has become increasingly inappropriate for these multi-utilitarian purposes. One can hold and carry water in cupped hands, but a tarred basket or fired pot makes a more useful container for the purpose.

The entire notion of the book is almost inexorably tied to the form. It is obvious that in whatever format, content is not a crucial issue. The same content can be realized in a myriad of formats. Microforms are common, but are nothing more than pictures of books. Information can and is inscribed in stone. Texts can be presented in video, and audiotape is commonly used by the visually impaired and more recently for people engaged in activities such as driving in which reading would be an obviously inappropriate collateral activity.

Advances or changes in technology virtually never result in the complete replacement of one set of forms for another. While the scroll was effectively replaced by the codex in the western world by the fifth century, the scroll has persisted for certain religious works and has even been reintroduced by new technology with the commonly used microfilm reel. It is not so much the change itself, but the fear of the change that seems to sustain the debate on the future of the book. The introduction and widespread adaptation of any new technology frequently has that effect. John Philip Sousa railed against the phonograph in 1906. The idea that mechanically reproduced music would replace amateur musicians and, worse, live performances was anathema. It threatened to reduce the world of music to a few professional executers whose work could be universally reproduced and distributed. For Sousa, this development was the end of live music turning "the expression of music to a mathematical system of megaphones, wheels, cogs, disks, cylinders, and all manner of revolving things, which are as like real art as the marble statue of Eve is like her beautiful, living, breathing daughters."[3] Of course, it is difficult to determine what effect the widespread acceptance of sound recording has had on the music industry, but the simple fact that it is now called the *music industry* would indicate a profound change in the musical world of Sousa. One might make a forceful argument that the proliferation of garage bands, blues clubs, and even the resurgence of municipal brass bands has disproven the argument that recording meant the end of live music and amateur musicianship in America. The form itself is still alive, though not in a way that might be recognizable to Sousa.

A perhaps more crucial episode was the introduction of sound to the movies. *The Jazz Singer,* released in 1927, is generally credited with marking this advance in technology, but it was only the first commercial success of such productions. In 1895, Edison had developed the Kinetophone which synchronized sound and pictures, but its use was limited. Attempts to merge sound and film were considered by movie makers to be nothing more than a novelty until Jolson burst into song and movie studios rushed to add sound to movies they had already released to the public or that were already in production. The technology had existed for three decades before *The Jazz Singer,* but Hollywood movie makers had no enthusiasm for films with sound. Jesse Lasky, a founder of Paramount, explained his own unwillingness to alter the form: "a cool, peaceful theater was a relief from the turmoil of life outside and people wouldn't go into a boiler factory to rest."[4]

Lasky deplored the lost artistry of the silent films, but their continued success in the realm of serious film and the resurgent interest in restoration of this lost world of entertainment demonstrate that the form has not totally been overwhelmed by the tintinnabulation of the talkies. The continued popularity of early silent films in local festivals and through cable television demonstrates some continued interest in the art form. The archival interest in preserving and restoring these artifacts is another evidence of continued interest. The traditional showing of silent films to piano accompaniment is an area which has always troubled serious viewers and attempts are being made to resurrect the films as they were originally released by their creators. Many of these films were first shown to the public with full orchestration for musical ensembles which Gillian Anderson and others of the Library of Congress have been attempting to reconstruct.[5] Further, there are experimental films still being made without sound and even a few commercially successful productions such as Mel Brooks' 1976 *Silent Movie* and even an episode of the television series *77 Sunset Strip,* "The Silent Caper," that astonished everyone who saw it and did not realize until afterward that there was no dialogue.[6]

Two more recent innovations in format have had ambiguous results. In the 1980s, the CD gained ascendancy over the vinyl record and the VHS over the Beta format for films. The triumph of the CD over the vinyl disc can, in one sense, be viewed as the replacement of a crude technology by a superior one. But, in other senses, the transition has not been complete. There are a number of companies still pressing vinyl, frequently in new releases, and there are numerous older artists whose records are only available in the older format. The industry has been good with the Beatles, the Weavers, and even Harry James. But, Dorothy Shay, Ed McCurty, and Jonah Jones are grossly underrepresented on CD. And, of course, there are listeners who simply prefer the sound quality of the analog recording over the digital recording on CD.

The ascendancy of VHS over Beta was, it appears, more a function of marketing than the emergence of a superior technology, but VHS itself seems to be in danger of replacement by digitized formats in the near future. In both cases, those of recorded music and of video, it is unclear that the new technology available has any advantage to the listener or viewer. Indeed, the only clear advantage has been to the producers of CD players and VHS video players and of CDs and VHS format video tapes who have profited from the new markets in equipment and products. Clearly change for the sake of change or change for the sake of profit may well have been the driving force in many of the recent technological innovations. But, it must also be added, the new forms–particularly in digital recording–have had some advantages in access to particular portions of the "text" embedded in the music or films and certainly have made many obscure recording artists and films, at least those for which there has been perceived to be a commercial potential, more widely available to the public.

In the realm of textual material, the hegemony of the book and its variant, the periodical, has been complete, though problematic in the 20th century. As early as the 1920s it had become apparent that the limitations imposed by the form rendered it inadequate for certain types of information transfer, and new methods were crudely devised to deal with the problem. The publication of things that looked like books and behaved like periodicals by Commerce Clearing House, Prentice-Hall, and other specialists in tax law created a hybrid form that disconcerted acquisitions librarians who dealt with books–not information services or the more unfortunate neologism that is now used by the Census Bureau, *information products.* These bastardized forms upset librarians who could no longer mark and park things on the shelves, but had to revisit them on a weekly and sometimes daily basis to insert the updated text and delete the superseded pages and, when all was over, had neither a usable book nor a back run of magazines, but a loose leaf binder with paper that represented nothing so much as the record of a library's failure to maintain a subscription.

The rise of the mass market paperback in the 1930s represented a similar failure of the book to adequately fill the demand for a form that was inexpensive, convenient, and disposable. Though it looked like a book, felt like a book, and talked like a book, it was never considered a book by either its producers or its consumers. Designed to supply an ephemeral demand, sold through newsstands in train and bus stations to provide light reading to travelers, and intended to be discarded after a single reading, paperbacks were not of great concern for most libraries and indeed were not normally available from the channels of the book trade through which libraries operated. That is, they were not important until the 1960s when it became apparent that the tradition under which the mass market paperback was simply a cheap reprint of a trade edition was no longer true and that a great number of titles were published in only that incarnation.

But the greatest failure of the form of the book has always been its inability to adequately convey meaning. The entire history of book illustration is in one sense an attempt to overcome the limitations of the form–a linear exposition utilizing text as the prime means of communication. From wood cuts to steel engraving to the use of transparencies as overlays to illustrate complex substructures of automobile engines and anatomy in the encyclopedias of the 1950s, the publishing industry has attempted to grapple with the need to convey material in a method that has usually been a compromise between the inherent limitations of the book form and the need to enhance the text itself.

Many subterfuges have been undertaken to accomplish this end with varied degrees of success. The costs of printing art illustrations, for example, have always been one of the problems in publishing art books. Relying on small black and white reproductions of paintings is probably better than nothing, but it does little to convey to the reader the complexity of color, composition, or texture. Kandinsky lies flat on the page and Rembrandt is nothing more than a dark blob. While it is technically possible to produce adequate illustrations, it is commercially unfeasible to undertake this on any large scale except in the most lavish and expensive books. The solution of at least some art publishers was to engage in what could only be described as multi-media approaches. Rather than reproduce the paintings in the book itself, a pocket was constructed on the cover of the book containing a set of slides keyed to the text.[7] It is not an adequate solution, since it leaves the reader to find a projector or devise some other means to view the slides. While the slides were a poor substitute for adequate reproductions, a further innovation–another attempt to cut costs, perhaps, by the publishers–made them seem almost ideal. When art books were produced that used microfiche inserted in the pockets, it was mandatory that the user have access to equipment far beyond that available to most readers.

Art books are only one prominent example of this problem with the form of the book. In many other arenas of human activity, books are produced in which the graphic conundrum reveals itself. One interesting example of a novel solution to the problem is found in the *Stereoscopic Atlas of Mastoido-tympanoplastic Surgery* published by Mosby in 1966.[8] The problem in ear surgery, as in other types of surgery, is, of course, that the layering of tissues is complex and even such an obvious solution as transparent overlays fails to adequately convey the complexities of the object itself. Mosby solved this by including, in a pocket on the inside back cover, a Viewmaster compact viewer and a series of circular stereoscopic reels. Again, an ingenious if not totally adequate solution to the challenge.

The problem here is, of course, that the linear narrative form that the traditional book does accomplish so well is not universally suited to all kinds of information needs. While audiovisualists have been arguing this point for decades, it is a telling one. American humorist H. Allen Smith addressed the difficulty in 1972 when he based one of his pieces for *The Chicago Tribune*. As a starting point, he took an observation he attributed to Hilaire Belloc to the effect that to describe the process of tying a knot without recourse to diagrams is the highest test of one's ability to write. Smith attempted this feat but, characteristically, abandoned the attempt for a description of local folk remedies for arthritis and finally concluded, "I can't write!"[9]

The narrative form has limitations that can be overcome but only by a vastly superior writer. Unfortunately, there are only a few of these around in any generation and those few are not usually the ones writing for the Boy Scout *Handbook*. These limitations derive from the nature of the varying forms of media, their limitations, and their strengths. While there have been numerous attempts to distinguish among the media of communication, none in this century has been as incisive, provocative, or as useful as that of Gotthold Ephraim Lessing, expressed in his *Laocoon*, first published in 1766.

Lessing, of course, only addressed the distinction between the narrative and the plastic arts when he observed that the poet must, perforce, ignore that which is filled in by the reader while the sculptor or painter must include the details.[10] The novelist, historian, or anyone else involved in creating a narrative can not supply the details of an individual moment in the narrative with the completeness of the visual artist. When the writer describes someone sitting in contemplation, it is, perhaps, sufficient to note that her brow was furrowed or his hands rested on the open pages of a book. It is to the reader to envision the room, the furnishings, the lighting, the clothing, and all the other elements that define that space at that particular moment unless these elements are of particular importance to the writer's purpose. The visual artist, though, must include the entire spectrum of detail that makes the picture "real" including details that, perhaps, the reader would not think to envision. It is no wonder that the almost universal reaction of the reading audience to a film that has been made out of a book they have read is shock. The movie is never our vision of the book we had read.

The new forms of the book represent a technology that, in many ways, circumvents the limitations of the traditional codex and offers potentials that have only been partially realized through other methods of presentation. The principal advantage is, of course, the ability to interpolate a wide variety of textural, non-textural, and other material into the text at appropriate points in the narrative. While this is an obvious asset for certain types of treatments, the full potential seemingly has not been explored to any considerable extent. At present, what we are offered are products emanating out of the audiovisual education tradition that attempt to meld sound, sight, and text into an educational package with a few attempts to utilize the format as a multi-dimensional art form. What has been lacking to a considerable extent has been the serious attempt to explore the potential of the medium to integrate the narrative argument with evidence.

The problems associated with documentation have plagued scholars since the age of scholasticism. In historical and literary studies, writers note their sources so that a persistent reader can follow the train of logic and argument. It is a tradition that is sanctified by academe and institutionalized in the style sheets produced by the professional associations and ossified in the scholarly journals. Unfortunately, the materials too often are inaccessible to average readers who, even if they wished to follow the foundation of evidence which supports the narrative, would find it impossible to retrace the steps of the author from archive to archive across the country. Primary sources in history exist in limited copies, usually found only in archival collections and most scholarly works are based on the holdings of more than one repository.

In other disciplines, the problem is similar, even though not on the same order. Literary criticism frequently forces the author to reproduce the text or a significant portion of the text itself in order to provide the reader with a context for the argument being propounded. The circumlocutions encountered in this process bog down the flow of the narrative argument. Literature, though, is not usually so awkward as the convolutions that are engaged in by historians and critics of non-textural material. Film criticism and history are one arena in which the process approaches the ridiculous. The late Chris Farley used to do a sketch on *Saturday Night Live* in which he interviewed the guest hosts of the evening, usually movie actors, and attempted to engage them in a critique of their latest films. Farley, after bumbling around in the conventions of an interviewer without a real response from the interviewee, finally had to resort to blurting out: "Remember the bit in the movie where you . . . " which he followed by describing a series of car crashes, a fight, or some other bit of action designed to excite the fancy of the adolescent male, concluding lamely, "that was neat!"[11] All writers are forced to resort to such techniques in discussing movies to let their audience know what they are talking about. It is, at best, a clumsy convention that probably has done much to inhibit the full realization of film scholarship.

Musicology suffers from a similar and, perhaps, more serious problem. At both the popular and scholarly levels, those who write about music are forced to use poor substitutes for the actual text (i.e., the music itself) in order to present evidence or examples. In most narratives, you find, at best, a few bars of a condensed score or, perhaps, simply a short melodic sequence which, if you do not read music, is not particularly informative within the context of the narrative. It is even more disconcerting to encounter entire books on popular music, rock, country-western, and folk music in which the author offers only the lyrics. It is a context within which the descriptive phrases, "the crescendo at the end of the first movement" or "the delicate horn work at the bridge" have much less significance to the reader than would the actual passage played for the reader in the proper point in the narrative. The confines of the traditional book have, to a great extent, hindered the development of argument and exposition.

The utilization of hypertext for such circumstances is both possible and intriguing as an alternative to the cumbersome forms of scholarly citation that have been part of the rituals of such writing. The potential value to historical work which depends on the evidence provided by archival collections of letters, diaries, photographs, or any other primarily textual material could be greatly enhanced by the actual reproduction of the documents themselves in the work. We rely on the historian's word as to the phrasing, intent and import of the evidence to an extent that places almost total weight on the historian's reputation. The potential of the media to provide a full textual context for such a narrative would mean a significant step forward in the ways in which scholarship and research can be presented.

Fiction poses a particularly interesting problem for the future of the book. As one of the dominant "subjects" of the book, it may be the canary in the mines for the health of the form itself. At present, fiction accounts for approximately 12.5% of the trade books published in the United States.[12] This, of course, means only the number of titles. When the discrepancy between the average press run of an academic or university press title and the average novel is factored in, the tonnage of fiction produced probably outweighs all other genres of publication.

Charles Meadows has written what is, perhaps, the most thoughtful recent critique of the future of the book in which he addresses the particular problem this form presents. *Ink into Bits* is the highly personalized essay of an icon of information science on the future of his discipline and, particularly, on the future of the book. While he generally concludes that the usurpation of the book by electronic media is inevitable, he is not overly pleased with the prospect of hypertext fiction which allows the reader to chose among different narrative developments throughout the text, thus enabling the reader to be a direct participant in creating the art form. Meadow would have none of it, concluding that, "Possibly, hypertext fiction appeals more to professional critics and literary scholars than to just plain readers" and Meadow as a "plain reader" does not find the form appealing.[13]

What Meadow misses is that the hypertext novel is no more a novel in the traditional sense than the movie, *The Ten Commandments,* was *Exodus.* Hypertext is a new entity that represents a radical departure from the form that the novel has had since the eighteenth century. A great writer, as Meadow goes on to note, can realize much the same effect as achieved by hypertext, but there are few writers that accomplished. One can only wonder what a writer such as Laurence Sterne, author of *The Life and Opinions of Tristram Shandy,* the great English anti-novel, might have done with the format.

The defender of the book as a form must balk at defending the plethora of half-articulate, ill-conceived, and crudely fashioned fiction that clogs the commerce of American publishing. The reading of fiction is probably as healthy in the United States as it ever was[14] even though we are not and have never been a nation of readers, and it is probable that the widespread availability of new types of entertainment to directly compete for the readers' time will have an effect on the demand for fiction. But, it must be noted that the same competitors for the readers' time have become major consumers of the kind of writing that used to find sole outlet in the book. The gaping maw of the television and the film industry has already consumed a large portion of the talent that could previously find an outlet only in print. The number of writers employed by the movie and television industries must detract from the number of capable producers of fiction, if not literature, that is potentially publishable. Even such a talented writer as Stephen King seems in his later work to have a focus more on the screen than the book. Much of his work, at least in recent years, reads more as though they were drafts of screenplays than literary efforts.

Many critics dismiss King as a genre writer and, in doing so, fall into a pernicious trap. The difference between generic novels and literature is a distinction that is based not on something inherent in the form, but on a perceived judgment about the quality of the writing and the author's intention. It parallels the distinction frequently made in libraries utilizing the Dewey Decimal Classification between literature and fiction. These were distinctions that, at their best, are too subjective to be sustained and seem to miss the obvious point that literature does not compete with other forms in the way fiction does. The works of Danielle Steele have more in common with *Days of Our Lives* than with *Ulysses* or *Pride and Prejudice.*

One of the major problems associated with the book has been the tremendous proliferation of the form from its beginnings. Within the masses of books produced since Gutenberg there are volumes that should have remained unwritten, efforts that would have been better received as magazine articles, and books that could have been better presented in another form. We even now have a sub-genre of books made from movies and television shows. The remainder houses are filled with the corpses of books that have, for good or bad reasons, failed to find a place on anyone's shelves.

Until recently, the written record, most frequently in the form of a book, has been the customary and, in most cases, the only means by which someone with an idea, information, or even nonsense could communicate to the world at large. Indeed, the word *publish* has come to be almost entirely associated with the act of producing books to the exclusion of all other forms of public communication.

In 1845, Edgar Allan Poe commented on what he saw as one of the great tendencies of the age–the increase in the production of magazines. Poe viewed this as a positive sign. There were more people who could "put the greatest amount of thought into the smallest compass and disperse it with the utmost attainable rapidity."[15] While Poe was sanguine about the prospect, the proliferation of periodical literature through the twentieth century has left most of us desperate for relief. Rather than concentrating treatises into articles, we see scant ideas puffed up into "least publishable units" in the journals.

The traditional book and its periodical partner, the journal, no longer form a manageable element of the communication process for librarians, scholars, researchers, or even casual readers at any level. Acquisitions budgets, physical facilities, and systematic users of any subject literature are hard pressed to cope with even a small percentage of what is produced in even the major literature of any subject. The dream of comprehensive collection development in any arena except for the most specialized libraries has faded under the strain of increasing prices, increasing output, and declining support to the point where librarians have been merely hanging on to the railing and trying not to fall off during the hard plunges in the ride they have been on the past three decades. There is little prospect that this will cease in the foreseeable future.

Against what is a dismal future, the prospect of electronic access is increasingly seen as a means by which access to and dissemination of information can be accomplished. For the most part, electronic forms of the book have been viewed as simply that–the same content with different means through which to access it. For scholarly and research literature, this view is selling the potential for the new media short. Simply to place the content of a journal or even a monograph into an electronic environment might well accomplish the intentions of the effort–to make the text widely available in a less expensive manner than through the distribution of paper–but it also denies the potential of new formats to transform serious scholarship in a wide array of disciplines.

The new forms of communication offer the distinct potential to reduce the glut of publication that continually undermines the ability of libraries to adequately represent the array of knowledge, opinion, and speculation available through traditional books and magazines. Freedom of the press has only been a right guaranteed in the United States to those who own one. The widespread availability of websites has made this truism obsolete. The jumbled array of information, misinformation, fact, opinion, trivia, and truth available on the World Wide Web at present signifies more anarchy than freedom and undoubtedly, as disturbing as it may be to many, is a sign of health in the American psyche.

Past predictions that movies, radio, television, and, more recently, videotape would consume the leisure time of Americans to the point that the publication of books would cease have been made, but it is abundantly clear that these have not taken place. At present, the American book publishing industry is healthy even though publishers are concerned about its future. It may well be true that the publishing industry would be much more robust had it not had direct competition from alternative outlets for consumer time and money, but this would be a difficult thesis to demonstrate in any convincing way. The fact is that books thrive in an environment that is laden with information. No review increases the readership of a book or its sales more than the author appearing on a late night talk show and if Oprah mentions it, it is sure to become a best-seller.

It is probable that the book–the paper codex–will remain the standard of publishing and of readers for at least the first few decades of the next century. It has too much heritage for abandonment and is too useful a form to be dropped without compelling pressure. Indeed, what pressures there are would seem to be pushing toward its retention. The shelves of the large chain book stores are lined with books about television shows, movies, and interestingly enough, books on computing and accessing the internet. The competing media have, in a sense, contributed significantly to the popularity of the book as a form. In the conservative world of colleges and universities, pressure to produce research that is publishable in a traditional form will ensure that the book will prevail for at least the next generation of academics.[16]

While there have been remarkable advances in the technology that would enable a reader to download one or two or even five or ten titles into a small, versatile, convenient reader, the degree of user acceptance remains in question. The idea of a consumer spending $500, $400, or even $100 on a device that could provide them with a few texts that would also be available in a mass market paperback format for less than $10.00 each tests economic credulity.[17] The ultimate question here is would the user of these electronic texts be willing to put them to the same uses that they would put a book picked up at the airport or drug store. They probably would not be willing to take them to the beach, use them to save their seats in restaurants or bus terminals, or pass them on to a friend after they were finished.

The electronic book cannot be used in the same way as the traditional book and, consequently, will probably never completely replace it. The electronic book can be and should be a new form that will generate its own social and intellectual conventions of use. The electronic format will undoubtedly replace the traditional paper codex form for certain types of uses to which it is more suitable. Few libraries attempt to maintain collections of telephone books or college catalogs and the whole genre of directories would seem to be better served by non-traditional means. Web sites are usually more current, more detailed, and can be more accurate than printed sources. Pastime knowledge also seems to be an area where the internet or world wide web has the advantage. While trivia encyclopedias have been standards of publishing for years, the remarkable array of multiple sites available on the web make many of them redundant except for coffee table compilations. From "Alf" to "Zena," television is covered, frequently by multiple sites. And, of course, for those who have the misfortune of having to use the search engines to prowl for topics and retrieve the first thousand hits prioritized by relevance on some unfathomable scale, the area of unwanted knowledge is one in which the format obviously excels.

But, the strength of the book remains in its ability to deliver a linear narrative and to develop an argument through the logical sequence of postulates, instances, and events. For this, the book will prevail and remain the preferred form of communication device. What the electronic form can do for the book is to be celebrated rather than deplored. It can liberate the book from carrying a burden that is far greater than that which could have been envisioned at its creation. It frees the book to do what it can do best: to inform, to persuade, and to delight.

NOTES

1. Nicholas A. Basbanes. *A Gentle Madness: Bibliophiles, Bibliomanes, and the Eternal Passion for Books* (NY: Henry Holt, 1995), 110-111.

2. Fritz Machlup. *Knowledge: Its Creation, Distribution, and Economic Significance*, 3 vols. (Princeton, NJ: Princeton University Press, 1980), 1: 108.

3. John Philip Sousa. "The Menace of Mechanical Music," *Appleton's Magazine* 8 (September 1906): 278.

4. Jesse L. Lasky. *I Blow My Own Horn* (Garden City, NY: Doubleday, 1957), 212-3.

5. Connie Cass. "Music Matcher Returns to Silent Films: Lost Scores Pieced Together," *The Times-Picayune* (New Orleans) (5 September 1994), A-4.

6. Episode #69 aired 3 June 1960: Larry James Gianakos. *Television Drama Series Programming: A Comprehensive Chronicle, 1959-1975* (Metuchen, NJ: Scarecrow Press, 1978), 177, 179.

7. See, for example, Daniel Robbins. *Painting Between the Wars, 1918-1940* (NY: McGraw-Hill, 1969).

8. Harold F. Schuknecht, Werner D. Chasin, and John M. Kurkjian. *Stereoscopic Atlas of Mastoidotympanoplastic Surgery* (St Louis: C. V. Mosby, 1966).

9. H. Allen Smith. "How to Tie a Matthew Walker" in *Low Man Rides Again* (Garden City, NY: Doubleday, 1973), 179-84.

10. Gotthold Ephraim Lessing. *Laocoon: An Essay upon the Limits of Painting and Poetry.* Trans. Ellen Frothingham (NY: Noonday Press, 1957), 20-1.

11. Obviously, this illustration would work much better if this journal was capable of providing a clip of the *Saturday Night Live* episode or episodes in which the sequence occurred.

12. *The Bowker Annual: Library and Book Trade Almanac,* 43rd edition (New Providence, NJ: R. R. Bowker, 1998), 522.

13. Charles T. Meadow. *Ink into Bits: A Web of Converging Media* (Lanham, MD: Scarecrow Press, 1998), 79.

14. Nicholas Zill and Marianne Winglee. *Who Reads Literature?: The Future of the United States as a Nation of Readers* (Cabin John, MD: Seven Locks Press, 1990), 7-22.

15. Edgar Allan Poe. *Marginalia* (Charlottesville, VA: University Press of Virginia, 1981), 91.

16. Jim Lichtenberg. "UPs Wonder: Will 'Publish or Perish' Perish," *Publishers Weekly* 244 (October 13, 1997): 14.

17. Paul Hiltz. "Portable E-Books Hit Market, with Bertlesmann Backing." *Publishers Weekly* 245 (June 15, 1998): 11.

The Meaning of Reading:
Fiction and Public Libraries

Kathleen de la Peña McCook
Catherine Jasper

SUMMARY. With the widespread advent of access to digital collections via schools, universities, public libraries, and home computers there sometimes comes a sense of a perceived dichotomy between "real" reading which involves the codex book, and "virtual" reading which takes place on a video display terminal. Reading, both basic literacy and recreational reading for experienced readers, is a significant aspect of librarians' roles and of the public's perception of the library's role. Therefore, the act of reading and the role of reading in people's lives is a topic that warrants study and reflection. *[Article copies available for a fee from The Haworth Document Delivery Service: 1-800-342-9678. E-mail address: <getinfo@haworthpressinc.com> Website: <http://www.haworthpressinc.com>]*

KEYWORDS. Electronic communication, future of the book, reading levels, virtual reading

Reading as a human activity engenders powerful emotions. With the widespread advent of access to digital collections via schools, universities, public libraries, and home computers there sometimes comes a sense of a perceived

Kathleen de la Peña McCook is Professor and Director, University of South Florida, School of Library and Information Science, 4202 East Fowler Avenue, CIS 1040, Tampa, FL 33620-7800 (E-mail: kmccook@chuma.cas.usf.edu). Catherine Jasper is Research Assistant, University of South Florida, School of Library and Information Science (E-mail: cjasper@helios.acomp.usf.edu).

[Haworth co-indexing entry note]: "The Meaning of Reading: Fiction and Public Libraries." McCook, Kathleen de la Peña, and Catherine Jasper. Co-published simultaneously in *The Acquisitions Librarian* (The Haworth Information Press, an imprint of The Haworth Press, Inc.) No. 25. 2001. pp. 51-60; and: *Readers, Reading and Librarians* (ed: Bill Katz) The Haworth Information Press, an imprint of The Haworth Press, Inc., 2001, pp. 51-60. Single or multiple copies of this article are available for a fee from The Haworth Document Delivery Service [1-800-342-9678, 9:00 a.m. - 5:00 p.m. (EST). E-mail address: getinfo@haworthpressinc.com].

dichotomy between "real" reading which involves the codex book, and "virtual" reading which takes place on a video display terminal. In spite of the fact that human intake of words is reading, be it on a printed page or computer monitor, discussion now ensues that, to some degree, pits the vehicles of transmission (book versus monitor) against each other.

This strife is rooted in the attention and resources demanded by the computer as a vehicle for access. The sets of skills required to maintain Internet access to virtual collections has siphoned library staff from work with more traditional library activities; has meant the decision to cancel physical subscriptions in favor of electronic; and has required a seemingly never-ending succession of expensive upgrades to equipment, often times causing new hires to be delayed to pay for new hardware.

Additionally, schools of library and information science accredited by the American Library Association that educate librarians have expanded their inventories of technology-based courses to the perceived detriment of the profession's core values.[1] It is seldom the act of reading that is studied in the curricula, but the act of using technology to organize and access materials which may or may not be physically located in the library or selected by a local librarian. To some extent, however, this newer emphasis on networking and mastery of the web mirrors the older activities of organizing a collection for use through cataloging and classification–the difference is that the collection is now universal rather than local. For instance, the Universal Library Project located at the Carnegie Mellon University embodies the concept of universal collection-building in its most extreme and idealistic form. Its mission, which its creators admit has many large but surmountable challenges, is "to spark a lasting movement, in which all of the institutions responsible for the collection of mankind's works will place these works on the Internet to educate and inspire all of the world's people."[2] To make everything available to everyone via Internet access is an admirable goal, but where does that leave the public library? With the traditional role of acquisition subsumed, what and who will drive the selection process, if a process is even still necessary?

What seems to be missing, and what causes dissension, is the apparent disassociation of the current work of libraries with the content provided. Where once librarians reviewed items for acquisition and retention and were valued for their knowledge of history, literature and culture, the Internet now provides access to unevaluated resources. Position announcements are far more likely to call for experience with automated systems, knowledge of online database searching, and competency with Internet search engines than a broad and rich education in the liberal arts. Librarians now focus on *access* to the world's documents rather than their evaluation. One of the deepest concerns expressed by the profession today is the lack of review of all that is now available.

The information literacy movement addresses this concern, but results in the teaching of evaluation to users rather than the presentation of an evaluated collection. In *Information Literacy Standards for Student Learning,* prepared by the American Association for School Librarians and the Association for Educational Communications and Technology, the standards state that the student be able to assess, evaluate and use information effectively.[3] Where once users could come to a library confident that a certain level of care had gone into assembling the collection therein, now the burden is on the user to evaluate the material accessed electronically.

The act of assembling any set of materials, ideas, or artifacts which results in museums, archives, libraries, concerts, or journals, sets up a relationship of trust between user and provider. People subscribe to magazines because the content and tone are congruent to their needs. Museums guarantee through the hiring of scholarly curatorial staff, that exhibits demonstrate historical verity. Libraries have meant to people a collection of quality and cultural retention. In the brave new library world, librarians are expected to provide the gateways, but are now more in charge of the directional signs than the goal. In the new world a sense of connection between the user and the librarian is disappearing. This is at the heart of the friction over what our profession should be; this is what needs to be explored.

READING

The literature about reading has not moved to address reading done via computer monitor. This is not to say that the design of the video display has not been a topic of study. See for instance, Lynda and William Weinman's *Creative HTML Design.*[4] While the act may require the same optical engagement, the metaphors that adhere to the monitor are of a conduit to a virtual world of 3-D graphics simulating life–real or imagined. An examination of the literature about reading, critical knowledge for librarians, demonstrates a long heritage of reverence for an act much written of, but not fully understood.

It is helpful to turn to the work done on the process of reading as a foundation. For this the research reported by the International Reading Association, *Theoretical Models and Processes of Reading* is most useful.[5] Topics addressed include language acquisition, literacy development, comprehension, reader response theory, metacognition, and cognitive processes. The basis for the promotion of reading, the conceptual analysis of what brings the reader to the book, provides the librarian with the background to work with young readers and new readers of all ages.

While these frameworks of reading theory might seem outside the purview of many librarians, those working in media centers, with literacy programs or

serving populations of new readers will find this sort of theoretical understanding of reading processes to be central to their work. The "Public Library
Service Responses" identified in the *Planning for Results* guidebook issued
by the Public Library Association ReVision Committee in 1998 includes
"Basic Literacy" as one of thirteen suggested responses of libraries to their
communities.[6] Staff, it is noted, should have formal training in reading instruction as well as training programs for literacy volunteers.

But beyond the service response of basic literacy, for which public librarians should have formal training, comes the library role of serving the general
reader. An excellent introduction to the processes that inform the general
reader may be found in the writings of Louise M. Rosenblatt who discusses
the "reader's stance." This, she notes, reflects the reader's purpose which
falls somewhere on the "efferent-aesthetic continuum." By efferent, Rosenblatt denotes "the kind of reading in which attention is focused predominate-
ly on what is to be extracted and retained."[7] By aesthetic is meant "the kind
of reading where the reader adopts an attitude of readiness to focus attention
on what is lived through the reading event."[8]

When all is said and done it is service to the aesthetic reader, the fiction
reader, that undergirds the larger portion of library activity relating to fiction
selection and acquisition. The history of libraries and reading research has
been well summarized by Stephen Karetzky who provides a solid intellectual
summary of the work of Leon Carnovsky, Charles H. Compton, Gilbert
Ward, and Joseph Wheeler.[9] Knowledge of the early investigations of reading
provides an intellectual basis for public library collection development. Key
works like *The Reading Interests and Habits of Adults* by Gray and Munroe,[10] *What People Want to Read About* by Waples and Tyler,[11] *Living With
Books* by Haines,[12] and *The Geography of Reading*[13] by Wilson are classic
studies necessary for an appreciation of the role of librarians in the promotion
and support of reading.

Understanding reading as an adult activity can be enhanced by reviewing a
number of recent studies. These include Graubard's *Reading in the 1980s,*[14]
Nell's *Lost in a Book,*[15] Appleyard's *Becoming a Reader,*[16] Howell's *Beyond
Literacy: The Second Gutenberg Revolution,*[17] Manguel's *A History of Reading,*[18] and Radway's *A Feeling for Books.*[19] These works examine reading
and try to distill the meaning of the act of reading–what McCook has characterized as "the first virtual reality"[20] or as Manguel has observed, trying to
describe the variety of mood:

> We read in slow, long motions, as if drifting in space, weightless. We
> read full of prejudice, malignantly. We read generously, making ex-
> cuses for the text, filling gaps, mending faults. And sometimes, when
> the stars are kind, we read with an intake of breath, with a shudder, as if
> someone or something had 'walked over our grave', as if a memory had

suddenly been rescued from a place deep within us–the recognition of something we never knew was there, or of something we vaguely felt as a flicker or a shadow, whose ghostly form rises and passes back into us before we can see what it is, leaving us older and wiser.[21]

An effort to understand the act of reading deepens and strengthens librarians' appreciation of their relationship to the reader and the book.

FICTION AND LIBRARIES

The importance of reading as described above should leave little doubt that the selection and acquisition of fiction continues to be an important aspect of public library service. While today the competition for resources between cyber access and physical access seems at the forefront of concern, we should take note of the long-standing debate as to fiction's worthiness for inclusion at all. A substantive history of the debate appears in two books by Esther Jane Carrier, *Fiction in Public Libraries, 1876-1900* and *Fiction in Public Libraries, 1900-1950.*[22] Carrier provides a comprehensive summary of the debate between adherents of quality fiction and those who felt fiction of all types should be included in collections. This debate continues today as described by McCook in "Considerations of Theoretical Bases for Readers' Advisory Services."[23]

In spite of the compelling and edgy techno-hype that many posit as the new context for library service, there are frequent signals that the library as it has been provides a compelling model for continuance. In a 1998 article, "Apostles of the Faith that Books Matter," Vivian Gornick writes, "I cannot help thinking, 50 years ago in the Bronx, if the library had responded to my needs instead of shaping my needs, what sort of reader would I have become?"[24] To what extent should public librarians shape needs? This question is central to the future of the librarian's work. Abdication of this responsibility–the "Give 'Em What They Want" contingent[25]–while on its face is more responsive to the public's needs, is hardly different than dropping Internet terminals for unfettered access. The art of librarianship–the acquisition of the right materials–is at issue.

But a central activity of most public libraries will still be service to the general reader. A 1994 survey of the users of three large library systems by D'Elia and Rodger investigated patrons' ability to describe their reason for using the library in terms of the roles suggested by the Public Library Association's 1987 planning manual, *Planning and Role Setting for Public Libraries.*[26] Their study concluded that library customers could in fact identify which of the seven defined roles the library was filling for them. In all three systems, "Popular Materials Library" was the most selected role and the role most often designated as the most important reason for visiting the library.[27]

In the 1998 Public Library Association's *Planning for Results,* the library responses to efferent reading are best characterized by "General Information," "Business and Career Information," "Community Referral," "Consumer Information," and "Government Information."[28] Programs of education for librarians have focused on the needs of efferent readers and new librarians demonstrate an ability to develop work-styles that respond well to these needs.

The aesthetic stance is most clearly reflected in the *Planning for Results* guidebook by the response, "Current Topics and Titles," for which staff are directed to be knowledgeable about popular culture and literature. "Staff will need to spend a significant amount of time keeping current with what's *in* and what's *out.*"[29] However, this response as described does not really grapple with the needs of the general reader beyond the reader's desire for what is popular. Other "responses"–such as "Cultural Awareness" and "Lifelong Learning,"[30] allude to general reading, but general reading is not a focus of these responses. Now, with the issuance of this new approach to planning by the Public Library Association, *Planning for Results,*[31] it is possible to use Rosenblatt's reader's stance typology to see how the needs of efferent and aesthetic readers might be met.[32]

Unfortunately *Planning for Results* makes but passing reference to Readers' Advisory Services[33] though these services have been broadly and recently addressed in the professional literature.[34] It is through Readers' Advisory Services that librarians activate the collection for readers. As Duncan Smith has noted:

> What is needed for readers' advisory work is a balanced perspective, one which focuses not only on reference sources and the contents of today's popular literature but one which focuses on the reader, the reader's experience, and the advisor's understanding of that experience. In order to achieve this balanced perspective, readers' advisors must learn to hear their readers' voices. Hearing their readers' voices means that readers' advisors must not only learn how to listen to their readers talk about reading, they must understand the context in which their readers are reading and indeed how reading fits into their lives.[35]

Smith's work as a consultant to Novelist, an online readers' advisory tool, is an excellent example of the use of technology to enhance a traditional service.[36]

At the broader levels, the importance of books and reading has been cherished by the now 20-year-old Center for the Book and State Centers. The Center for the Book in the Library of Congress works to foster understanding of the vital role of books, reading, libraries and literacy in society. The 1997 *Handbook* for State Centers identifies activities such as awards, book festivals, community of the book projects, exhibits and reading promotion.[37] Clearly these Centers will enhance the importance of books in our society and circularly, as described by Kenneth E. Carpenter, the library:

> Just as book historians are keen to capture the experience of reading, so should library historians seek to capture the library experience. The effort to capture the library experience from the angle of vision of users and others involved with libraries can make clearer the role of libraries in the life of the individual and in American intellectual, cultural, and social life. For instance, examining the library experience will further increase understanding of the extent to which librarians have attempted to mediate between the reader and the book in order to lead the reader to "high" culture.[38]

The transcendent meaning of carefully developed library collections, expert readers' advisory service, and the importance of books in our society has been recently reenforced by a passionate new study of the power of the humanities. In *New American Blues: A Journey Through Poverty to Democracy,* Earl Shorris presents a revolutionary idea to ameliorate poverty.[39] He tells the story of the poor in the United States; he shows how the poor are much like everyone else; he shows that the difference between a comfortable life and a life of poverty is often the failure of the poor to enter the political life–a life which requires reflection. Shorris observes, "human beings become political by cultivating their inborn humanity."[40] His call for a study of the humanities as an answer to poverty is rooted in reading. An experiment in teaching humanities to the multi-generational poor called the Clemente Course (named after the Roberto Clemente Family Guidance Center), demonstrates the power of reading to change lives.

CONCLUSION

To read *New American Blues* is to renew a commitment to the power of libraries in concert with those who value reading. According to the Benton Report, *Buildings, Books and Bytes,* "Americans support their public libraries and hold them in high esteem. They support a combined role for libraries that links digital and traditional book and paper information resources. And they accord equal value to libraries and places where people can read or borrow books or use computers to find information and use online services."[41] An entire issue of *Library Trends* was devoted to discussion of the Benton Report with the general response of writers somewhat negative as to the Report's methodology and leap to conclusions. In his introduction Herbert Goldhor observes, "The future of the book has been pronounced dim so many times in the last century that we are all advised to be skeptical of this latest threat . . . against this is the fact that the circulation of American public libraries is today at an all-time high."[42] The Benton Report provided a widely distributed vision of the public library future, but failed to address the needs of people at the margins of society.[43] For these people the acquisition of fiction well-selected and available in public libraries is a means to encourage participation in the democratic life envisioned by Shorris. Building a solid collection of real value to a community requires the informed expertise of a librarian regardless of format or means of access.

NOTES

1. Georgina N. Olson, "Fiction Acquisition/Fiction Management: Education and Training," in *Fiction Acquisition/Fiction Management.* Georgina N. Olsen, ed. (New York: The Haworth Press, Inc., 1998), pp. 2-3.

2. *The Universal Library.* http://www.ul.cs.cmu.edu/faq/mission.htm. Accessed 8/28/98.

3. American Association for School Librarians and the Association for Educational Communications and Technology, *Information Literacy Standards for Student Learning* (Chicago: American Library Association, 1998).

4. Lynda and William E. Weinman, *Creative HTML Design* (Indianapolis: New Riders, 1998).

5. Robert B. Ruddell et al., *Theoretical Models and Processes of Reading,* 4th ed. (Newark, DE: International Reading Association, 1994).

6. Ethel Himmel and William James Wilson, *Planning for Results: A Public Library Transformation Process* (Chicago: American Library Association, 1998), pp. 58-61.

7. Louise M. Rosenblatt, "The Transactional Theory of Reading and Writing," in *Theoretical Models and Processes of Reading.* Robert B. Ruddell et al., eds. (Newark, DE: International Reading Association, 1994), p. 1066.

8. Ibid., p. 1067.

9. Stephen Karetzky, *Reading Research and Librarianship: A History and Analysis* (Westport, CT: Greenwood Press, 1982).

10. William S. Gray and Ruth Munroe, *The Reading Interests and Habits of Adults* (New York: Macmillan, 1929).

11. Douglas Waples and Ralph W. Tyler, *What People Want to Read About: A Study of Group Interests and a Survey of Problems in Adult Reading* (Chicago: University of Chicago Press, 1931).

12. Helen E. Haines, *Living with Books: The Art of Book Selection* (New York: Columbia University Press, 1935).

13. Louis R. Wilson, *The Geography of Reading: A Study of the Distribution and Status of Libraries in the United States* (Chicago: University of Chicago Press, 1938).

14. Stephen Graubard, *Reading in the 1980s* (New York: Bowker, 1983).

15. Victor Nell, *Lost in a Book: The Psychology of Reading for Pleasure* (New Haven, CT: Yale University Press, 1988).

16. J.A. Appleyard, *Becoming a Reader: The Experience of Fiction from Childhood to Adulthood* (Cambridge: Cambridge University Press, 1990).

17. R. Patton Howell, *Beyond Literacy: The Second Gutenberg Revolution* (San Francisco: Saybrook, 1989).

18. Alberto Manguel, *A History of Reading* (New York: Penguin, 1996).

19. Janice A. Radway, *A Feeling for Books: The Book-of-the-Month Club, Literacy Taste, and Middle Class Desire* (Chapel Hill: University of North Carolina Press, 1997).

20. Kathleen de la Peña McCook, "The First Virtual Reality," *American Libraries 24* (July/August, 1993): 626-628.

21. Manguel, 303.

22. Esther Jane Carrier, *Fiction in Public Libraries, 1876-1900* (New York: The Scarecrow Press, 1965); *Fiction in Public Libraries, 1900-1950* (Littleton, CO: Libraries Unlimited, 1985).

23. Kathleen de la Peña McCook, "Considerations of Theoretical Bases for Readers' Advisory Services," in *Developing Readers' Advisory Services: Concepts and Commitments.* Kathleen de la Peña McCook and Gary O. Rolstad, eds. (New York: Neal-Schuman Publishers, Inc., 1993), pp. 8-9.

24. Vivian Gornick, "Apostles of the Faith That Books Matter," *The New York Times,* 20 February 1998, sec. B, p. 40.

25. *Give 'Em What They Want* (Chicago: American Library Association, 1992).

26. Charles R. McClure et al., *Planning and Role Setting for Public Libraries: A Manual of Options and Procedures* (Chicago, IL: American Library Association, 1987).

27. George D'Elia and Eleanor Jo Rodger, "Public Library Roles and Patron Use: Why Patrons Use the Library," *Public Libraries 33* (May/June 1994): 135-144.

28. Himmel and Wilson, pp. 98-102; 62-66; 72-76; 77-81; 103-107.

29. Ibid., p. 88.

30. Ibid., p. 82-86; 113-117.

31. Himmel and Wilson.

32. Rosenblatt.

33. Himmel and Wilson, pp. 87-89.

34. Joyce G. Saricks, *Readers' Advisory Service in the Public Library,* 2nd ed. (Chicago: American Library Association, 1997).

35. Duncan Smith, "Reconstructing the Reader: Educating Readers' Advisors," in *Developing Readers' Advisory Services: Concepts and Commitments,* Kathleen de la Peña McCook and Gary O. Rolstad, eds. (New York: Neal-Schuman Publishers, Inc., 1993), p. 21.

36. NoveList: Electronic Readers' Advisory, <http://www.carl.org/nl/about.html>, accessed 9/1/98.

37. Maurvene D. Williams, *The State Center for the Book Handbook* (Washington, DC: Library of Congress, 1997).

38. Kenneth E. Carpenter, *Toward a History of Libraries and Culture in America* (Washington, DC: Library of Congress, 1996).

39. Earl Shorris, *New American Blues: A Journey Through Poverty to Democracy* (New York: W.W. Norton & Company, 1997).

40. Shorris, 342.

41. Benton Foundation, *Buildings, Books and Bytes: Libraries and Communities in the Digital Age* (Washington, DC: Benton Foundation, 1996), p. 4.

42. Herbert Goldhor, "Introduction," *Library Trends 46* (Summer 1997): 2.

43. Kathleen de la Peña McCook, "The Search for New Metaphors," *Library Trends 46* (Summer 1997): 117-128.

Books Are for Use?
Keeping the Faith in Reading

Jim Dwyer

SUMMARY. Although reading remains a popular leisure activity and reader's advisory is experiencing a resurgence in public libraries, encouragement of independent reading and the culture of the book have declined in academic libraries. This paper is a personal perspective on the reasons for this decline, a few exceptions to the trend, and possible strategies and resources to reemphasize independent reading. Subtopics include book reviewing, popular or browsing collections, reader's advisory, cultural and institutional changes, the relationship between bookstores and libraries, the relationship between print and electronic resources, and the changing role of the bibliographer. *[Article copies available for a fee from The Haworth Document Delivery Service: 1-800-342-9678. E-mail address: <getinfo@haworthpressinc.com> Website: <http://www.haworthpressinc.com>]*

KEYWORDS. Academic libraries, reading, popular collections, reader's advisory, bookstores, bibliographers

"Throughout the years librarians have transformed their concept of function into a dynamic faith. This faith has sustained the men and women who have built and operated American public, as well as university and research, libraries and the men of wealth and political position who have provided for their financial and legal support. It consists of a belief in the virtue of the

Jim Dwyer is Head of Bibliographic Services, Meriam Library, California State University-Chico, Chico, CA 95929-0295.

[Haworth co-indexing entry note]: "Books Are for Use? Keeping the Faith in Reading." Dwyer, Jim. Co-published simultaneously in *The Acquisitions Librarian* (The Haworth Information Press, an imprint of The Haworth Press, Inc.) No. 25, 2001, pp. 61-79; and: *Readers, Reading and Librarians* (ed: Bill Katz) The Haworth Information Press, an imprint of The Haworth Press, Inc., 2001, pp. 61-79. Single or multiple copies of this article are available for a fee from The Haworth Document Delivery Service [1-800-342-9678, 9:00 a.m. - 5:00 p.m. (EST). E-mail address: getinfo@haworthpressinc.com].

printed word, especially of the book, the reading of which is held to be good in itself for from its reading flows that which is good."[1]

Reading continues to be a popular public activity, books sales are increasing, book discussion groups are popular in many communities, and the reader's advisory function is experiencing a resurgence in public libraries. One would scarcely guess that this was the case, though, if his or her experience were limited to academic libraries. While the role of independent and pleasure reading was once an "article of faith" in university libraries, today there are few contemporary or browsing collections, few "noncurricular" purchases are made, and the reader's advisory service seems to take place primarily in the staff lounge.

Some critics of electronic information systems are quick to blame this state of affairs on the computer or even the demise of the card catalog. While there may be a shred of truth to this argument, beating an electronic straw man is a pointless activity. To paraphrase Shakespeare "the fault is not in our databases, but in ourselves." This paper provides one perspective on the recent history, current role, and the future of reading in the academic library. Topics covered include book reviewing, popular collections, reader's advisory, types of reading, the changing role of the bibliographer, the relationship between libraries and bookstores, and the dynamic relationship between print and electronic media. Because reading is an intensely personal experience to me, I find it impossible to completely separate my personal and professional concerns.

SO WHY DID YOU BECOME A LIBRARIAN?

When librarians get together to do something other than complain about budgets or eat chocolate, the conversation sometimes turns to how we happened to become librarians. School or public librarians often influenced us. In my own case, it was Mr. Barner, a kind soul who was not even a librarian per se, but a bookmobile driver. While the parents would talk to the librarian on board, most of the kids would gather around Mr. Barner. He obviously loved kids and books, and we loved him for it.

As a relatively idealistic English major making a career choice in the early seventies I told a friend in library school that libraries appealed to me because they were a "people's university" where reading and intellectualism were cultivated. "You mean you like books and you like people and you want to make connections between them?" When I answered in the affirmative, she sighed deeply. "Well that's how I feel, too, but when I said that to an advisor she smirked and practically laughed out loud. She told me that I was being very naive, and that I didn't need a library degree to do that. If I wanted to talk to people about books I could do that for minimum wage in a bookstore."

Upon applying to library school I stressed that I had worked at a computer center and thought that libraries would benefit from using computers for transactions such as circulation, inventory, and cataloging. I also mentioned that I had no desire to work on a Master's and PhD in literature ad infinitum. If I had proclaimed that I felt the "library faith" I would have been an object of derision. By declaring that library school was sort of a default choice and that I had some familiarity with computers I was welcomed with open arms. Good thing Mr. Barner didn't apply!

Hey, Did You Actually Read That Book?

I was fortunate to have an opportunity to write book reviews early in my career, initially for a newsletter for Yankee Book Peddler customers. Since then, I have written a few hundred, primarily brief reviews of fiction for *Library Journal.* Reviewing parlays the knowledge of literature, critical thinking, and writing skills obtained as an undergraduate with a librarian's expertise in publishing, libraries, and their clienteles. Like most reviewers, I happily do it at home in my "free time." The only material compensation is a copy of the book and a nice reception at ALA. On the non-material side it's highly rewarding, fun, totally engaging, and if you encounter a snob at a cocktail party you can take them down a notch or two by referring to books which are not yet even in print. "Oh, you haven't read it yet? Didn't you get a review copy?"

Want to earn literally a few bucks for a review? Try Amazon.com. Otherwise there's the satisfaction of occasionally seeing yourself quoted on a dust cover identified only as *"Library Journal."* Would you like to see your name at the end of that quote? Then become a member of the teaching faculty, a scholar without portfolio, or perhaps the person who groomed the biographee's dog, anything but a librarian. This is not necessarily *LJ's* policy, but a hoary practice of publishers who are only too happy not to bite, but merely to disdain the hands of a profession that supports them. Might there be a touch of sexism in marginalizing a "women's profession" via lack of acknowledgement?

HOW POPULAR IS "POPULAR" LITERATURE IN ACADEMIC LIBRARIES?

Unlike some of my fellow students, the library school experience did not extinguish or even diminish my love of libraries and reading. Indeed, my internship at the University of Washington Undergraduate Library under the inspiring supervision of Carla Rickerson strengthened those feelings. Although my primary assignment was as a reference librarian I was also assigned to work in the Popular Collection. It featured contemporary fiction, "hot topic" nonfiction, newspapers, and a few periodicals. Silence may have been golden in the research collections, but the Popular Collection was a site of convivial conversation. A lot of informal reader's advisory took place as librarians and students discussed books that were germane to their interests, curricular or not. Perhaps it was only the tenor of the time, but the works of Herman Hesse, for instance, were considered valuable even if you weren't an English, comp lit, or philosophy student. As it turned out, my first experience as a professional librarian was one of the two I derived the greatest sense of service and satisfaction from. The other was a sabbatical project.

Janelle M. Zauha notes that "Today's browsing rooms are vestiges of the 1920s and 1930s, developed in an era when academic libraries vigorously promoted recreational reading interests of students . . . For example, by 1939, there were no less than four recreational reading collections throughout the University of Iowa campus . . . The 1949 edition of [Guy Lyle's] text, *The Administration of the College Library* devotes a lengthy chapter to the encouragement of reading, including a section on 'Reader's Advisory Service in the College Library.'. . . In his 1974 edition Lyle speaks of browsing rooms as things of the past . . . Evan Farber in his 1988 discussion of why today's students don't use libraries for reading, suggests that recreational reading is 'not just not encouraged, but hardly given a chance' in academic libraries."[2] Other journal articles from years past indicate that libraries are simply following their universities' leads, that after World War II universities de-emphasized independent reading programs and campus clubs.

Including separate popular or browsing collections in academic libraries was still fairly common as late as the nineteen-sixties and seventies, but they are now relatively rare. This is largely but not entirely a result of economic retrenchment in American universities over the past quarter century. As staffs and acquisitions budgets dwindled administrators faced difficult decisions about mitigating the negative effects of the cuts and were forced to prioritize essential activities and supplemental ones. Do you cancel subscriptions, reduce the book budget, fire staff, or close the popular collection and reduce the purchase of "popular" materials? As the old saying goes "It's hard to remember that your original objective was to drain the swamp when you're up to your ass in alligators."

The seventies also saw the widespread implementation of library automation systems. Salespeople were sometimes able to bamboozle administrators into believing that library automation would save them money. Given the initial and ongoing costs of systems, some libraries found themselves reducing acquisitions budgets or laying off staff in order to pay for automation. I remember an ALA conference program where one of the participants (I think it was Marvin Scilken) said "Library X spent a million dollars on an automation system so it could circulate its book."

Over time, libraries have taken the more reasonable approach that automation can help do certain things better and can also provide new services. Unfortunately, many of those slashed book budgets have never been restored to their previous level, let alone increased to cover inflation. Then there is that ego devil called "prestige." The size of a collection was once the source of prestige in university libraries. Now it is who has the newest and most expensive system. This is not meant to imply that computers and print are inherently inimical. The problem is that decisions are often made on an "either/or" basis; it's easier to argue over crumbs than it is to win a bigger piece of the pie.

Zauha provides some powerful arguments for restoring browsing collections: "there must be some reiteration of the original conception of the browsing room as a low-cost, high-benefit means of readers' guidance, and as a center of intellectual and cultural activities for individuals and groups. It must once again be tied to the library's mission. There are a number of ways this can be done."[3] These include:

a. The browsing room as public relations tool. (How about naming that collection after a major donor?)
b. Intellectual stimulation "by encouraging the exploration of current and popular works, and by juxtaposing select fiction, non-fiction, and periodicals in an interdisciplinary collection."[4] (As in the sixties, interest in interdisciplinary study and research is increasing.)
c. A smaller browsing collection is an antidote to information overload.
d. This collection can serve as a bridge to the larger collection.
e. ". . . new fiction, poetry, and current events materials can be used to support or augment curriculum in contemporary fiction, writing, current events or popular culture courses."[5]

In a more recent article the same author provides some strategies for supporting and promoting browsing collections.[6] They include funding by Friends groups or student organizations, imposition of low user fees, better display methods, pamphlets, web sites, student newspaper articles, tie-ins to the curriculum, creating bridges to the public library, using the terms Current or Popular Collections rather than Recreational and Leisure Collections, etc.

Zauha's first article concludes with a challenge: "Why shouldn't the library participate in the student's self-discovery by developing and promoting browsing collections that entice, stimulate, and entertain? It is through these collections that the habit of reading will be nurtured in students who enjoy reading and developed in those as yet unconverted. It is in the spaces of the browsing room that the student's humanity will be remembered and addressed."[7]

READ ANY GOOD BOOKS LATELY?

Do you hear this question at social events more often than you do at work? If so, you might just be an academic librarian. Or perhaps you've been told "You're a librarian so you must read a lot." If you were an inhalation therapist would that mean you must breathe a lot? How does one respond to such a question?

a. Sure, especially computer screens for five to ten hours a day.
b. Compared to the average orangutan, plenty.
c. Absolutely. I only rent subtitled foreign movies, never dubbed ones.
d. Twenty to forty thousand citations per year. If I were a speed-reader I'd have even more speeding citations.
e. The minute I retire.
f. Pretend to be Bill Clinton. "It depends on how you define 'read.'"

Gary Rolstad notes that "As librarians contemplate the growing complexity of their institutions and the demands on their time, they often wish they could get back to books and reading, and have the chance to suggest books to library users. That used to be so much fun. It felt so good to feel like you were keeping up with the publishing world and your favorite area of literature, and it felt even better to keep track of your readers and hear their thanks when they were pleased with your suggestions . . . A few years ago, one might have suspected that reader's advisory was one of the fatalities of the dynamics in libraries. But it has survived very well in the hearts and hopes of most librarians."[8]

Indeed, the literature shows a resurgence of interest in reader's advisory in public and school libraries, but in academic libraries it seems to have little room outside our hearts. An online search of "reader's advisory" retrieved hundreds of articles, but the number dropped to four when I qualified the search with the word "university." Two of them appeared because ALA President Barbara Ford, a university librarian, was visiting public libraries, while the third was about reader's advisory in academic library children's collections. The fourth was "The Social Science Reference Librarian as Reader's Advisor" by Peter B. Allison. He argues that information overload mandates evaluative services: " . . . we must reject such an unhelpful stance of neutrality and seek to assist our patrons to make what are inevitable choices as intelligently as possible . . . We must be ready to suggest not just sources of bibliography, but particular books and articles to our students and patrons. . . . we have perhaps tended to overemphasize the use of indexes and abstracts in our reference work. In doing so we have lost sight of the proper role of textbooks, encyclopedias, handbooks and reviews of research."[9]

Ritual and Actual Knowledge

A distinction is often made between two kinds of knowledge, actual and ritual. Actual knowledge is knowledge about a subject while ritual knowledge is knowing how to find out about something one knows little or nothing about. To limit the first kind of knowledge to teaching faculty and the second to librarians seems self-defeating, particularly if one agrees with Allison about the need for evaluative services. Unfortunately, it is very difficult today for a librarian to possess both kinds of knowledge for at least three reasons:

   a. Information overload due to rapid development and change in disciplines.
   b. Understaffing, resulting in each librarian serving many disciplines.
   c. The time required staying current with rapid changes in computer applications and constant software "upgrades."

In my own case, I resisted seeking a Ph.D. in literature partly because I enjoy and understand the value of being a generalist in an increasingly overspecialized world. A quarter century later I'm writing papers about the use of metafictional techniques in contemporary Native American and Australian Aboriginal literature and ecofeminist detective novels. I barely have the time to stay current in those narrow sub-specialties!

In my first cataloging job, before I ever even met a fictional ecofeminist detective, I also worked at the reference desk a few hours each week. One day a student asked for assistance on a paper about the psychological aspects of trench warfare. After guiding her through the morass of cards beginning with "World War, 1914-1918" and a few periodical indexes, I suggested that she also read *All Quiet on the Western Front,* a classic war novel which provides a powerful personal perspective on the subject.[10] After the student left, the other librarian on duty harrumphed that recommending novels was "something public librarians did." She did not particularly appreciate my observation that students and faculty were our public and that we were their librarians.

Terry Plum notes that "At their service desks, reference librarians abandon knowing anything and officially claim only the ritual knowledge how to find information . . . The danger of permitting knowledge to bleed over into ritual knowledge is implicitly recognized at an institutional level. It is safely contained and bureaucratized in the role of subject bibliographers, special librarians, and, to a much lesser degree, liaison librarians. . ."[11] It might be "dangerous" of me to provide direct medical or legal advice or guess at the correct answer to an engineering question at the reference desk, but how much "containment" of knowledge in a veritable babushka doll of specialists is a good thing? Suppose a student requests information on Australian Aboriginal rituals and you find five titles in the catalog, the most recent being Marlo Morgan's *Mutant Message Down Under.*[12] Even if you are not a cultural anthropologist or even a social sciences librarian you may know that the book is a hoax. HarperCollins didn't suppress its publication or issue a published disclaimer, but at least it released the book as fiction. The problem is that it *reads* like nonfiction and non-critical readers might take it as such. What's so darn professional, or even ethical, about being *nonevaluative* in our service?

This is reminiscent of attempting to provide "values free education" in the 1980s. It wasn't long before the "recent classroom experience free" administrators who dreamed it up realized what real teachers realized all along: that "values free" also tended to be free of having any value. What good is imparting either actual or ritual knowledge without tempering it with critical thinking skills? Value judgments are at the very heart of critical thinking. The traditional gatekeeping functions of editors, peer review, etc., shift a great deal of this burden away from librarians, but the largely unrefereed electronic world of the Internet shifts it right back. There is currently a debate about whether public and school libraries should include filtering software on public terminals, but the amount of porn on the net pales compared to the amount of pure crap.

Beyond the old ritual vs. actual knowledge argument, there are other good reasons that reader's advisory work is unpopular to many academic librarians. First, it is hard and time-consuming to do it right. Good reader's advisory presupposes not only knowledge of academic subjects and general fiction, but also of the backgrounds, interests, and needs of readers. Although reference work also requires us to gauge the requestor's background and needs, reference interviewing tends to be more perfunctory than in-depth reader's advisory. How much time do you have at the reference desk for such service?

Second, only after decades of pressure from other librarians has the Library of Congress begun applying subject headings to adult fiction. Only a few headings are typically assigned compared to the five to ten assigned by Hennepin County Library (and its cadre of activist catalogers led by Sandy Berman) or amazon.com, a giant online bookstore. LC's goal is to process the books as rapidly as possible while Hennepin County follows the "books are for use" adage. Amazon.com clearly realizes that they will sell more books, including fiction, if people are aware of their subject matter and content.

"The third reason for the relative inattention to reader's advisory work is a widespread bias in America's earlier political rhetoric toward work and against play . . . This we believe is an attitude which has shifted materially in American society . . . Indeed, we anticipate that one very urgent step for public librarians to take in order to thrive in the new information market place is to help people make better use of their highly valued leisure time . . . "[13] Shearer notes that the "strong match" between public libraries and the public is a shared love of reading, with reading defined broadly to also include listening and viewing.[14]

But that's in a public library. Over the course of a quarter century working in four different university libraries I have noticed that the percentage of students coming to the reference desk looking for books on a given subject has dropped relative to the percentage seeking only periodical articles or, more recently, web sites. Fewer still request a *good* book on a subject. Whatever gets the paper written with the least effort is the path of least resistance. The trends seem to be away from larger, sometimes more authoritative sources to shorter ones and from longer to shorter historical perspectives. Our faculty and students often seem to inhabit the world of the thirty-second sound bite and short attention spans, and we tend to go with the flow. Could it be that we academic librarians love reading more than our clientele does?

Ours Not to Reason Why?

Please allow me the folly of suggesting three fundamental reasons why university students are less likely to seek reading advice than the general public. The primary one goes back to the library as a "people's university." A significant number of students in the sixties and seventies had very different priorities regarding their education than the narrow (and fundamentally anti-intellectual) goal trumpeted by the dictum "to get a good job get a good education." That phrase was popularized in the fifties and is back in vogue today. When the boomer generation couldn't find much relevance in our classes, an alternative place to find it was the library, a virtual intellectual smorgasbord for the self-directed student. Today's student is more likely to be career oriented, grudgingly jumping through the minimum number of standard academic hoops with as few intellectual "obstacles" between matriculation and graduation as possible. In the words of Barbara MacAdam: "Faculty and students clearly hold differing views toward reading. Faculty, including librarians, have chosen to serve a discipline and its literature, while college students generally expect that the discipline and the literature must serve them and their different, perhaps job- or career-related objectives."[15]

The agenda (syllabus, assignments, and tests) is set by the faculty. They are under pressure from university administrators to produce as many "units" of job-ready students as possible. If a professor assigns his or her students to write a "research" paper based on three periodical articles, many students will read the bare minimum. No matter that in some cases books may be a better choice. A public library client is far likelier to be responding to a personal need or a simple desire to read. Today the public library and the bookstore are more likely to serve as "people's universities" than real universities are.

The second is a cultural shift away from print to a variety of media. This began in the fifties and has accelerated greatly over time. Some of the parents who may have read to their children in the past now employ the plug-in babysitters of television and the PC. The teaching of fine literature is less common, with even introductory English classes in universities often being essentially literature free or "literature lite" at best. Retired marketing professor Stanley Hollander recognizes what now seems to be denied in many freshman English courses: "Historically, drama has been used to convey complex ideas to illiterate and semiliterate people."[16] Sad to say, some college students can be fairly described as semiliterate. While I'm the first to agree that education be relevant, I consider the sort of deep perspective and personal connection that great literature can provide to be highly relevant. By "great literature" I refer not just to the classical canon, but to works of contemporary and historically excluded authors.

The third has to do with the size, complexity, organization, and culture of academic libraries. Many students find them confusing or even intimidating. The Library of Congress Classification does not encourage browsing, particularly in the literature schedules. Just watch the students' eyes glaze over when they ask where the fiction or the poetry sections are and you explain how it's divided by language, nationality, and era rather than by type. I'd go to the public library, too! In my "real life" away from work as performance poet The Reverend Junkyard Moondog I have learned that poetry and fiction are gaining renewed popularity among California college students, but that the academic library is one of the least likely places they might go to find it. In the words of one poet: "They're so tight assed. First they hide the stuff and then they shush you when you try to read poetry aloud or try to discuss it with anybody else."[17] Small, lively, multimedia browsing collections might be just the laxative that the literary doctor ordered.

The long trend away from recreational or enrichment reading in academic libraries seems to be more frustrating to some librarians than to students and faculty. This may be due to differing perceptions of what a library is. As Barbara P. Pinzelik observed at the 1984 ACRL conference, "The faculty member views the library by its collections, the student by its facilities, and the librarian by its services."[18] Many students see the library primarily as a study hall which should be open 'round the clock. As academic libraries place more and more resources and services on the web for twenty-four hour "library without walls" access, they need to remember that many students see those four walls as the most important parts of a library. Likewise, providing faculty members, particularly in the humanities, with various data-bases will not satisfy their desire for a strong collection of scholarly mono-graphs.

It is not uncommon for students or faculty to press for longer library hours or more materials, but it is less common for university administrators to provide the funding to do so. The library director is typically told to do more with less. After all, the perspective of university administrators is not facilities, collections, *or* services. It is "outcomes" in their lowest form: McUni-versities with over one billion degrees sold. The FTE count rose while the library budget dropped so everything's hunky-dory. That'll look great on the Provost's resume as he or she seeks a more prestigious position. (How about a supine position in an early grave?) Zauha refers to "the academic library's present emphasis on accountability,"[19] but our "accountability" is too nar-rowly focused on pleasing administrators, some of whom have not spent much time in classrooms or libraries in years. What about our accountability to the preservation and generation of intellectual life and culture? What about enriching the lives of students?

"The studies cited document years of failure to alter the perceptions of a constantly changing population, in an environment of ever increasing com-plexity, within a climate of diminishing resources. This is an overview that may discourage even the most dedicated, innovative and energetic public services librarian." It may not be possible or even desirable to alter the attitudes of students and faculty, but if we are not more successful in convinc-ing administrators than we have been the future of the academic library seems rather bleak. They may utter platitudes about the library being "the heart of the university,"[20] but we need to convince them that without some new blood from time to time that old pumper isn't going to be very useful.

So What Are We Doing About It?

Despite all the pressures and forces that seem to inhibit any reader's advisory work or cultivation of book loving in universities, a few academic libraries have tried to buck the trend, some more successfully than others. For those who would like to make at least a small attempt to provide reader's advisory services, providing a few reference books is a start. See "Reader's Advisory Tools: A Suggested List of Fiction Sources for All Libraries."[21]

In 1987 Western Kentucky University implemented a small recreational reading collection. Reaction was positive and circulation steadily increased. Encouraged by their success, Linda A. Morrissett surveyed 120 academic libraries in the Southeast. She discovered that 38 of the 75 respondents had at least a small browsing collection. It should be noted, however, that in some cases it amounted to little more than a rack of books. Morrissett concludes by remarking that "A separate leisure reading area spotlights and promotes extracurricular reading, which may be often overlooked in an academic environment."[22]

I did not have time to conduct a survey before writing this article, but had a strong suspicion that leisure collections were more prevalent in the Southeast then than they are nationally now. I called a friend who now works for a major vendor that, among other things, provides browsing collections. On the condition of anonymity, she confirmed that fewer than ten percent of academic libraries have even a small browsing collection and, further, that the purchase of popular and genre fiction by universities has dwindled over the past decade.[23] Zauha's research confirms this trend.[24]

Brigham Young University established a browsing collection in 1972. A study conducted in 1981 revealed that science fiction, fantasy, humor, and romance were the heaviest circulated fiction categories. Westerns were the lowest. Local interest and self-help were the highest circulators in non-fiction while crafts and current issues were the lowest. Fiction was more popular than nonfiction, and paperbacks were more popular than hardbacks.[25] This collection is still in existence and is heavily used by students.[26]

In 1974 the Trenton State College Library established a two- to three-credit Library Reading Program.[27] By 1995, 95 students had completed the course, but the program fell victim to a staff reduction and a decrease in interest by students. The last student enrolled completed the course in 1996.[28]

In the early to mid-nineties the New Mexico State University Library Publications Committee compiled an annual booklet of book reviews by faculty members intended to promote summer leisure reading.[29] When only the same few librarians were willing to serve on the Publications Committee it was disbanded during a library reorganization.[30]

The Bucknell University Library sponsored a series of lunch hour lectures by faculty members on "Books That Made a Difference" for five years in the early to mid-nineties.[31] The inspiration for the program came from the Muhlenburg College Library, which features a small browsing collection of books recommended by the faculty. Dot Thompson, who now teaches a freshman general studies seminar called Reading Changes Lives, organized the Bucknell program.[32]

If you'd like to learn about more former and current efforts along these lines, see Barbara MacAdam's excellent article on "Sustaining the Culture of the Book: The Role of Enrichment Reading and Critical Thinking in the Undergraduate Curriculum."[33]

Last Spring semester (1998) here at Chico State, Lou Bentley of the Associated Students Bookstore organized a committee including Reference Librarian Lakshmi Ariaratnam to create *A List of Unrequired Reading: One Good Book a Month for Four Years*. Faculty and staff notified of the project by e-mail were asked to recommend one book they enjoyed reading and briefly describe why they enjoyed it. "These titles focus on enjoyment and enlightenment, rather than scholarly significance."[34] The top 48 books were not only included in the booklet, but were all placed on a 20% off sale in the Bookstore. Bentley reports that "It's working beautifully. People love it."[35] Sales have been brisk. Bentley also notes that there is a strong overlap between that list and a national list of "The Best 100 Novels Ever Written." And speaking of bookstores . . .

WHAT IF YOU RAN YOUR LIBRARY LIKE A BOOKSTORE?

That was the title of an article in the March, 1998 issue of *American Libraries* that launched a virtual firestorm of controversy.[36] Since most readers of this article are probably very familiar with it and the stream of pro and con letters it inspired I will limit my comments to personal experience and a few articles in *Technicalities*.

To this observer libraries and bookstores are inherently allies, not adversaries. Good bookstores and good libraries promote reading and respect for the intellect. Most chain bookstores do not fit this definition. Crown Books is the most blatant in following an utterly crass, commercial path, with the emphasis being on cheap bestsellers. Would you like a $7.95 book or a $14.95 book? What McDonald's is to cuisine and nutrition, Crown is to the life of the mind. Furthermore, the chains have driven many excellent local bookstores out of business.

The only chain bookstore that really seems to take an interest in the life of the mind or building a community of readers is Barnes & Noble. In a typical month, September, 1998, the Chico branch of B&N hosted the following: three author talks/book signings; the monthly Open Mic Poetry Night, Philosophy Club, and Mystery Book Club; the Butte Literacy Council's Annual Read-A-Thon; ten children's storytimes, and three children's authors book talks.[37] That's more reading promotion than our local university and public libraries do in an entire year! One wonders how many librarians responded negatively to "What If You Ran Your Library Like a Bookstore?" out of embarrassment over our own sins of omission. Dr. John was right when he observed that "If I don't do it somebody else will."

Of course B&N is far from perfect. In his last published column the late and lamented Murray S. Martin had this to say: "Because booksellers like Barnes & Noble use best seller lists as promotional devices, they tend to undervalue other authors–even when there is a continuing interest in their works–because they don't meet the high-volume threshold."[38] Bookstores are not intended to be repositories of culture.

Tom Leonhardt turned the question on its head by asking "Why Can't Libraries Be More Like Libraries?" "If I have any concerns about libraries and change, they have to do with changing too much and for the wrong reasons. When we change because we don't believe in or understand what library services are, then we will cease to exist as libraries and be nothing more than just a bookstore, or just another academic department, or part of a computer center. We must heed Goethe's admonition to seek *Dauer im Wechsel*, changing the way we do things while remaining true to the foundations of librarianship."[39] I strongly agree with Leonhardt, but would take his argument one step further by pointing out that some of our more technologically oriented library administrators have jumped too wholeheartedly on the virtual library bandwagon, abandoning the books and intellectual climate that many library users seek. When I hear the words "paperless library" it sounds like crying "Wilf," Wilf Lancaster that is.

BOOKS AND BYTES: "WHY CAN'T WE ALL JUST GET ALONG?"

If Gilbert and Sullivan were alive today a new verse of a "A Punishment to Fit the Crime" might go: "A medium to fit the text/A medium to fit the text/Librarians seem so perplexed/Which medium to fit the text?" Just as the printed book did not completely destroy the oral tradition, nor television kill radio, neither do television and computers supplant print. Part of our job as librarians is to make the connections between people and ideas as contained and expressed in a variety of media.

Some would argue that time spent on the Internet is time spent not reading books, but that assumes a zero sum game with only two variables. A great deal of Internet use is in the workplace, and how many people get to read books on the job? Internet use from home isn't always taking time from pleasure reading, but from other tasks, from other recreational activities, and even from watching television. You can go online for book discussion groups or to correspond with authors or critics around the world, to revel in the delights of the Booklover's and similar web sites, to enjoy digitized rare manuscripts and books that you would otherwise not have access to, or even to order books. For practical advice on using the Internet to promote reading see Robert Burgin's "Reader's Advisory Resources for Adults on the Internet."[40]

Barbara MacAdam expresses a more serious concern: "We hold a dangerous illusion that an abundance of information equates with knowledge. . . . Stories are still an extraordinarily powerful way to organize what would otherwise be isolated bits of information (data); and more, they convey ideas and feelings that actually convey more truth than just the information (more real meaning.) But, as a civilization, are we becoming increasingly data rich and story poor."[41] Further, "A world dominated by electronic media may ultimately deprive people of the ability to engage in reflective thought."[42]

Indeed, data rich and wisdom poor with a pitifully short attention span seems to be a chillingly accurate description of modern society. A major problem with most television programming and the Internet is *how* they have been implemented. Their commercial, consumerist orientation favors scanning, flitting, channel surfing, web clicking. Form takes precedence over content, flash over substance. There is some deep, thoughtful content in both media, but one must search long and hard to find it. Many people seem as content with superficial junk media as they are with junk food or superficial relationships. Can such things truly sustain the heart, the mind, or the soul? It is not different types of media which are inherently inimical to one another, but two different ways of viewing the world and of living, one quick and externally imposed with little context versus one which is deep and personal with the context of historical and literary wisdom. The former creates the herd, the latter the individual. Which are we "turning out" in American higher education today?

This widespread social problem is obviously too large for librarians to solve on our own, but we can contribute to a solution. Part of it is not just to continue to provide historic, literary, and cultural resources, generally in the form of books and journals, but to *champion their use.* Another is to consistently find "the medium to fit the text," e.g., quick electronic sources for fast facts, indexing and full text of articles as well as deeper sources for deeper thought. Then we need to make useful links between different sources of information and knowledge, not just "separate the sheep from the goats."

One of the biggest problems we face is developing collections of both traditional and electronic sources within severe budgetary constraints. Judging from a study performed by Joe Crotts here at Chico State in 1997, humanities and history professors may be our strongest allies in supporting print collections. Crotts analyzed "the relationship of expenditure and enrollment to circulation. The basis of differentiation among the variables is *subject*"[43] (emphasis his). Student enrollment by discipline and number of faculty by discipline are not factors in circulation, but subject definitely is. He also confirmed that the annual average of new books received was directly related to circulation. Extrapolating from his study and other internal evidence we know that history and humanities departments have a high demand for books because they actually use them. The social sciences have some demand for books but more for journals, while the sciences, engineering, and business use more electronic sources. This information allows us to refine our purchasing to fit actual use.

MOMMY, WHEN I GROW UP CAN I BE A BIBLIOGRAPHER?

Historically, a bibliographer combined the skills of a book reviewer, a cataloger, an archivist, a scholar, a reader's advisor, and sometimes a book dealer. While there are still some rare book dealers and archivists who meet this description, they are relatively uncommon. Today's subject bibliographers are more likely to serve as a liaison to an academic department, coordinating collection development and providing specialized reference and bibliographic instruction. As such, they may produce short subject bibliographies for specific disciplines or classes.

Today they may also produce "webliographies" of the best Internet research sites on a given topic or guides covering both print and electronic sources. When library research was based almost exclusively on print sources, the pace of change was much slower than it is in today's environment. Hence, teaching-faculty members lose currency in their fields more quickly than before and may be more likely to turn to the assistance of a librarian to help them find the best sites and teach their students online research skills. Here's a good example of ritual knowledge: I don't really know any Spanish, just un poquito Spanglish for Mexican restaurants or traveling in Mexico. "Mas cilantro, por favor" or "Hey, hombre, no moleste mi dama!" Nevertheless I have created webliographies for Spanish and Latin American Studies classes. Just as in the case of cataloging and reference, it seems that the jobs will continue to evolve rather than just disappearing. Scholarship and bibliography will continue to be closely inter-twined, and bibliography will continue to be an area where the librarian-scholar tradition continues.

My interest in the relationship between fiction with environmental themes and actual environmental activism led me to apply for a sabbatical to write some articles or perhaps a short book on the subject. My request was approved, but delayed for a year, during which time I discovered that there were no research sources for the emerging field of ecocriticism. That delay provided a head start on compiling *Earth Works: Recommended Fiction About Nature and the Environment for Adults and Young Adults,* a five-hundred page annotated bibliography.[44] The project entailed not just the sixty hours per week for a one-semester sabbatical, but an additional twenty hours per week for an addi-tional year and a half. Do not go gently into that good book contract!

While writing *Earth Works* I became a member of the Western Literature Association and the Association for the Study of Literature and the Environ-ment. ASLE's unofficial motto is "We'd rather be hiking," so conferences are held in places like Fort Collins, Colorado or Missoula, Montana where opportu-nities for hiking and whitewater adventure abound. After decades of attending American Library Association programs about automation, cataloging, adminis-tration, and ALA itself ad nauseum, I was finally participating in conferences about books and scholarship! Since my title is Head of Bibliographic Services, other WLA or ASLE members often say something to the effect of "So you're a bibliographer. Cool. I wish our library had one." I do, too!

I'm not suggesting that most librarians write a reference book for fun and profit since there's possibly too much "fun" and very little profit in it, but it seems to me that there is much to be gained by participation in non-library organizations. One gains a different and refreshing perspective on his work and can "fly the library flag" in the process. If that doesn't particularly appeal to you, but you still love books and people despite being a librarian, read on . . . .

IS THERE A POET IN THE HOUSE?

There may be poets in your library right now. Perhaps one is lurking in the P section, perusing *Poetry Index* or *Poet's Market,* logged on to a poetry site, snoozing in a soft chair in a sunny corner, or even answering reference questions, cataloging an electronic journal, or emptying wastebaskets and dusting floors. As I was writing this very paragraph I received a call from the Reference Desk requesting assistance tracking down an obscure poem. (We found it on the Internet.) In our sophisticated, affluent society how many poets, writers, artists, or musicians do you know who *don't* have "day jobs?" There are probably other poetry lovers in your library, too, hmmm, maybe some of the folks you met at that reading over at Barnes & Noble . . . .

As a librarian, performance poet, and poetry lover I am particularly fond of Poets House. Poets House is both a physical place and a membership organization. Stanley Kunitz and Elizabeth Kray founded it in 1985, and today it has a library of over 35,000 volumes of contemporary poetry. It publishes the *Directory of American Poetry,* a two volume annotated bibliography of nearly 3,000 current poetry books. Members receive a copy of the *Directory* and a subscription to their newsletter *InHouse* as part of a $40 membership. Higher membership levels with more perks are also available. Poets House also presents over thirty live poetry programs annually and conducts the Poetry in the Branches program in the New York and Brooklyn Public Libraries.[45]

You may know the name due to their presence at the American Library Association Annual Conference. They collaborate with Small Press Distributors to create a Poetry Showcase of over 1,000 current books. This exhibit is unique because it also features a series of readings by twelve prominent poets over the course of three days. What a relief, a place at ALA where you can sit down and experience a refreshing literary alternative reality for anywhere from a few minutes to three hours at a time! At the San Francisco Conference in 1997 a few California librarian/poets introduced the San Francisco tradition of open mic readings after the featured poets. At the 1998 conference in Washington, Poets House sponsored a reading called "Librarians Out Loud" which was varied, lively, and well attended. For more information about Poets House or to become a member write to 72 Spring Street, New York, NY 10012 or call 212-431-8131.

Belly Up to the Books

It seems appropriate to close with another quote from our emeritus friend in the Marketing Department, Stanley C. Hollander. "Sight-seeing guides to San Francisco's courthouse district used to (perhaps still do) point to a bar called The Library. . . . this name permitted legal secretaries to tell telephone callers truthfully that their boss was 'in the library'. The name was appropriate in another sense, because libraries can be highly addictive . . . Lost weekends of total absorption can occur in the library as well as the bar. Neither will infuse participants with total reality, but the library will come much closer to the mark. Libraries are also less expensive, produce fewer hangovers (library dust has created few cases of silicosis), and in the long run are more hospitable to variety and imagination. Books, periodicals, libraries, and the librarians who staff them are good things."[46] I'll read to that!

NOTES

1. Leigh, Robert D. *The Public Library in the United States: The General Report of the Public Library Inquiry.* New York: Columbia University Press, 1950, 12.

2. Zauha, Janelle M. "Recreational Reading in Academic Browsing Rooms: Resources for Readers' Advisory." *Collection Building* 12:2-3 (1993), 57-58.

3. ibid. 59.

4. ibid. 60.

5. ibid. 60.

6. Zauha, Janelle M. "Options for Fiction Provision in Academic Libraries: Book Lease Plans." *The Acquisitions Librarian* 19 (1998), 52-53.

7. Zauha. "Recreational . . . " 61.

8. Rolstad, Gary O. "Our Kind of Service, Readers' Advisory Is." *Collection Building* 12:2-3 (1993), 5.

9. Allison, Peter B. "The Social Sciences Reference Librarian as Reader's Advisor." *Academic Libraries: Myths and Realities.* Chicago: ACRL, 1984, 350.

10. Remarque, Erich Maria. *All Quiet on the Western Front.* Boston: Little, Brown, 1929.

11. Plum, Terry. "Academic Libraries and the Rituals of Knowledge." *RQ* 33:4 (June, 1994), 496-497.

12. Morgan, Marlo. *Mutant Message Down Under.* New York: HarperCollins, 1994.

13. Shearer, Kenneth. "Reflections on the Findings and Implications for Practice." *Guiding the Reader to the Next Book.* New York: Neal-Schuman, 1996, 170.

14. ibid. p. 177.

15. MacAdam, Barbara. "Sustaining the Culture of the Book: The Role of Enrichment Reading and Critical Thinking in the Undergraduate Curriculum." *Library Trends* 44:2 (Fall, 1995), 249.

16. Hollander, Stanley C. "Lost in the Library." *Journal of Marketing* 62:1 (Winter, 1998), 115.

17. Red, Ruby. Personal conversation. September, 1998.

18. Pinzelik, Barbara. "Conflicting Perceptions of the Academic Library." *Academic Libraries: Myths and Realities.* Chicago: ACRL, 1984, 333.

19. Zauha. "Recreational . . ." 61.

20. Pinzelik. "Conflicting . . ." 335.

21. Readers' Advisory Committee, RUSA Collection Development Section. Diefenthal, Muzette et al. "Readers' Advisory Reference Tools: A Suggested List of Fiction Sources for All Libraries." *RQ* 36:2 (December, 1997). Also see 44 below.

22. Morrissett, Linda A. "Leisure Reading Collections in Academic Libraries: A Survey." *North Carolina Libraries* 52:3-4 (Fall-Winter, 1994), 124.

23. Anonymous. Telephone conversation. September, 1998.

24. Zauha. "Options . . ."

25. Christensen, John O. "Management of Popular Reading Collections." *Collection Management* 6:3-4 (Fall-Winter, 1984), 76.

26. BYU Reference Librarian. Telephone conversation. September, 1998.

27. Fogarty, Ellie A. and Nelson M. Evans. "Helping Students Delve Deeper into Books." *C&RL News* 56:10 (November, 1995), 704.

28. Evans, Nelson M. Telephone conversation. September, 1998.

29. Mayhood, Gary and Karen Stabler. "Reading for Fun Is a Novel Idea." *C&RL News* 54:2 (February, 1993), 69.

30. Mayhood, Gary. Telephone conversation. September, 1998.

31. Thompson, Dot S. and Roberta Laulicht Sims. "Beyond the Book Review." *C&RL News* 53:10 (November, 1992), 646.

32. Thompson, Dot S. Telephone conversation. September, 1998.

33. MacAdam. "Sustaining . . . "

34. Bentley, Lou et al. *A List of Unrequired Reading: One Good Book a Month for Four Years.* Chico: Associated Student Bookstore, 1998, 1.

35. Bentley, Lou. Telephone conversation, September, 1998.

36. Coffman, Steve. "What If You Ran Your Library Like a Bookstore." *American Libraries* 29:3 (March, 1998), 40.

37. *Barnes & Noble Events.* September, 1998.

38. Martin, Murray. "Where Do We Go from Here?" *Technicalities* 18:6 (June, 1998), 5.

39. Leonhardt, Thomas W. "Why Can't Libraries Be More Like Libraries?" *Technicalities* 18:5 (May, 1998), 9.

40. Burgin, Robert. "Readers' Advisory Resources for Adults on the Internet." *Guiding the Reader to the Next Book.* New York: Neal-Schuman, 1996, 185-194.

41. MacAdam. "Sustaining . . . " 244.

42. ibid., 245.

43. Crotts, Joe. *Subject Usage of Library Monographs: A Case Study.* United States Educational Resources Information Center, 1997. ED 422 800. Abridged version submitted for publication in a major academic library journal.

44. Dwyer, Jim. *Earth Works: Recommended Fiction and Nonfiction about Nature and the Environment for Adults and Young Adults.* New York: Neal-Schuman, 1996.

45. *A Place for Poetry.* New York: Poets House, 1998.

46. Hollander, 124.

A Librarian's Thoughts
on Reading

Sherri Kendrick

SUMMARY. Being a reader led me to becoming a librarian. As a librarian I've learned that reading is a very individual pursuit and it's not easy to connect books and readers. I've had to teach myself readers' advisory to find the best ways to connect books to readers. Sponsoring book groups at the library is one of my more successful attempts at sharing the joys of reading. Book groups provide information, fun and a sense of community. Libraries should sponsor as many book groups as possible to spread the fun of reading and the communal aspect of reading in relation to the isolation of computer information. *[Article copies available for a fee from The Haworth Document Delivery Service: 1-800-342-9678. E-mail address: <getinfo@haworthpressinc.com> Website: <http://www.haworthpressinc.com>]*

KEYWORDS. Joy of reading, readers' advisory, book groups

I am a reader, I'm an avid reader. I'm addicted to reading. If I could afford it, I'd spend my life reading and traveling. There is just something magical about books. Reading is like going on a treasure hunt, following the path the writer creates until you come to the end and find yourself and a connection to the world. The books a person reads are clues to the tastes, thoughts and feelings of that person. Reading is one of the most enjoyable pastimes; you can visit so many worlds without leaving your chair.

Sherri Kendrick is Reference Librarian, Cliffside Park Public Library, Cliffside Park, NJ 07010.

[Haworth co-indexing entry note]: "A Librarian's Thoughts on Reading." Kendrick, Sherri. Co-published simultaneously in *The Acquisitions Librarian* (The Haworth Information Press, an imprint of The Haworth Press, Inc.) No. 25, 2001, pp. 81-89; and: *Readers, Reading and Librarians* (ed: Bill Katz) The Haworth Information Press, an imprint of The Haworth Press, Inc., 2001, pp. 81-89. Single or multiple copies of this article are available for a fee from The Haworth Document Delivery Service [1-800-342-9678, 9:00 a.m. - 5:00 p.m. (EST). E-mail address: getinfo@haworthpressinc.com].

I get so caught up in the world of the book that when it ends I feel a sense of loss. Sometimes I'm so affected by a book that I have a time of disorientation and I have to reconnect to my world. Sometimes I want to inhale the books to get through as many as possible, but I also want to go as slow as I can to savor the moment. When I read a newly published book I feel like I'm the first to discover it and sometimes I only want to read new books. Then there are times when I want to read older books, because I want to discover what others before me have discovered, I don't want to miss out on what others know because they've read the book.

I think my love of books is genetic. I'm a third generation librarian, but I never grew up thinking of being a librarian, it feels like I just stumbled along and fell into librarianship. Perhaps it was my early training. Whenever we moved it was my responsibility to help my father unpack the books. He preferred my help because I would hand the books to him alphabetically and help him line them up neatly along the shelves. My mother would just haphazardly put the books on the shelf. I think that is why I found being a page in the library such an easy job, it was what I was trained for since the age of four.

My love of reading can also be seen in my fantasy. As far back as I can remember, it was my dream to be locked up in a library, alone, with the aim of reading every book. As I got older and started visiting more libraries, my fantasy started taking on a fatalistic feeling. I realized my dream to read all the books in the world was an impossible dream, like tilting at windmills. So I amended my fantasy–I wanted to win the lottery so I wouldn't have to work, and could then spend all my time reading and I could hopefully put a dent in the amount of books to be read.

The discovery of bibliographies was an added bonus to my reading. There was nothing like the thrill of reading a book and then finding a bibliography with even more books to be read. I would joyfully copy down titles, in the misguided belief that I would find the time to read all these books. For years I kept lists of books to read, divided by subject, in the hopes I would someday get to read them all. Now I know if I even get one-tenth of that reading done I'll be lucky.

Perhaps it was a combination of these joys that led me to be a librarian. I know it was not something I'd considered as a youngster. For some reason I never made the connection that my love of being with books and being in libraries, could lead to work in a library, even with an aunt and a grandmother as librarian role models. It was only after graduating from college, with no idea of what to do with myself, when my mother said to me–why don't you work in a library. I went to the town library and got a job as a page. From that moment on I was happy, I never thought of it as work, it was fun. It was as a page that I learned that though books bring joy, they can sometimes be a nuisance. How can you have room on the shelf for all these books that seemed to just sit there. It always seemed that more books were coming in than going out, and I never had enough room on the shelf, and who needs three or four copies of each Robert Ludlum book anyway.

Everybody does it, readers' advisory. They may call it something else, may not realize that's what they are doing, and may not realize how hard it is. Recommending a book is more difficult that it sounds. Reading is highly individual, tastes vary with age, with mood and with season. Reading is a highly subjective endeavor and book recommendations should be taken with a grain of salt. What may be interesting to one person or a group, may not be interesting to everybody. When *Angela's Ashes* was a bestseller and everybody wanted to read it, all I heard was how lovely it was, what a beautiful story. One patron came in and said she hated this book. She didn't need to read about his depressing life, she had enough problems, and she seemed mad that she even wasted time with it. Another patron asked a circulation staff member to recommend a book, she did, and he returned it and all but threw it in her face saying he'd never ask her for another book, this was terrible. He was genuinely angry that she gave him a book that he hated.

Book tastes can change over time. I had tried to read Willa Cather's *Death Comes for the Archbishop* two or three times over the years and could never get past the first twenty or thirty pages. Finally I picked it up for one last try, and I fell in love with it, I have since read it three or four times and it is one of my favorite books. Our book group read *Soldier of the Great War* by Mark Helprin and one member said it's one of her all time favorites. I couldn't stand it, never finished it. Even after the discussion I didn't like it.

I was trained to be a reference librarian. I fell into readers' advisory by accident, I didn't even know that's what it's called. My only training was my own interest, and my years at the circulation desk.

At the circulation desk I'd found out about the "popular" authors. I'd listen to what the patrons had to say, I thought I was being polite, but later I found it came in handy. Patrons would come to the desk and ask for a good book, and I would tell them what was going out a lot. It never occurred to me that this was more than a simple–here's a book, read it.

As a page and a circulation desk person, I'd notice that people are very funny about how they choose a book. In spite of the "you can't judge a book by its cover" saying, I noticed that people did. The style of covers could give you a clue to what was inside, and I found that I used this method myself sometimes. One of the quickest methods of book selecting I've seen done is by checking the due date slips in the books. Patrons would open books to check how many due dates were stamped. If there were none, the book would be put back. I guess they were too afraid to be the first to try a book, like a due date stamp was a stamp of approval, that this was a good book. I'd start stamping due dates in the books that had none and then they'd be taken out.

I don't know why but readers' advisory questions are not always taken as seriously as "information" questions. Finding a book to read is a very important job–the wrong book may turn a person off of reading, or turn a person into a reader. At a time when everyone is concerned with literacy, I'd think that turning someone on to reading would be an important job. Perhaps it is not taken as seriously because readers' advisory is not an exact science. For me readers' advisory involves some luck, instinct and a rapport with the patron. Added to this is the training and knowledge of books that comes with the job. Because on the whole, readers' advisory is not a course taught in library schools. Most of the readers' advisors I know gained their knowledge on the job and taught themselves through trial and error.

My own experience was one of floundering, isolation and a struggle to learn what works. As a circulation person I started recognizing the authors that circulated the most. And when asked for a book suggestion could only suggest the popular authors. For the longest time it seemed to me that was enough. When I started library school, there were plenty of classes on children's literature but nothing for the adult librarians, so I learned nothing of readers' advisory in school.

Readers' advisory may not be an exact science but it is one of the fun aspects of being a librarian. What can be more fun than discussing books with patrons and have them come back and thank you for giving them a good book? This is what kept me on the path to learning about readers' advisory. I'd study genres and authors and create reading lists. I'd do book displays and watch which books would circulate. I discovered that these little services were appreciated, but I felt like I was working in a black hole. It was after becoming a member of RUSA's Readers' Advisory Committee that I felt connected to a community of like-minded librarians. I realized that others were providing the same services and my small efforts were a part of a larger trend. Many librarians across the country were focusing on the importance of books in people's lives and we were all trying to find ways to meet the patron's needs.

Recommending books is also sharing a little of yourself with a patron. To be successful you need to relate to the patron, learn their likes and dislikes and then connect them with a book. It's only your love of books, of helping others find the same joy, that gets you into readers' advisory in the first place. Your desire to have others enjoy reading, helps you to find creative ways to suggest books. Your love of books and reading helps you to locate those little gems to pass along, the ones the publishers don't push like Edith Forbes or Elizabeth Berg. Your love of reading encourages you to get past the bestsellers and by word of mouth, publicize the other books sitting on the shelf.

If you didn't have the love of books, I think your readers' advisory service would be limited to suggesting bestsellers, or not even taking the questions seriously and just send the patron off to browse in the fiction area because you've got more "important" questions to answer. But because you love books and love to help others find a "good" book you spend time creating read-a-like lists, and book displays. You take time to learn about authors' styles and what you can do to connect authors and readers. You take time to find what works in your community.

One thing I've learned about reading, as a librarian, is that looking for a book is like looking for a needle in a haystack. Depending on your mood, finding a book can be easy or difficult. Looking at the shelves with so many possibilities, how does one decide what to take a chance on. And that's what you're doing, taking a chance, investing yourself. If a connection is made, the reader feels enriched. If no connection is made, the reader feels annoyed, dispirited, it's been a waste of time.

I think that is one reason why readers rely on word of mouth recommendations. If someone else has read it and enjoyed it, then it must be good. That's another reason people ask the librarian for book recommendations; because we work with books we must have some secret knowledge and so the reader will listen to our suggestions. Unfortunately, this isn't always effective. Tastes vary widely and the key for the readers' advisor librarian is to figure out the requester's taste. This process is similar to a reference interview, except it's not as precise. And sometimes it is hard to know if you've been successful, not everyone comes back to tell you how it worked.

It seems strange that librarians don't do more readers' advisory. To me, it seems like a basic principle of librarianship. Libraries were built to hold books and people continue to read and are always in search of a new book, a new author. Who better than the librarians who thought enough about a book to purchase it, to recommend it. We spend so much time and money on acquisitions, we should be able to recommend our purchases to the patrons. We purchase a particular selection because we believe that someone in our area will want to read it, so it seems natural to link a book with a patron.

Reading is a very individual activity and a very communal one. The act of reading is done individually and sharing it makes it communal. One of the joys of reading is sharing the thoughts and feelings a book has provoked in you with others. The idea of a book group associated with the library seems natural.

I started a book group at the library because I needed a new challenge. I needed something to balance the feelings I had that there was too much information and not enough fun. I saw a book group as a continuation of my readers' advisory services, and I also wanted to find others who share my love of reading. I did a survey to see what kind of interest there was in a book discussion group and I received enough responses to start a group in the morning with retirees, and one in the evening with working people.

I thought, as I'm sure many others have thought, what can be so hard about talking about a book. You read and you talk. But this is not always the case. Some books are easier to talk about than others. Other dynamics exist as well, the chemistry of the members, the room set up. I remember my first meeting where we sat in chairs in a circle, it wasn't the most conducive to discussion. I think all of us felt uncomfortable. Next time I put the chairs around a table and it felt more relaxed. The addition of coffee and cookies gave the group a relaxed air as well; we felt we were here to enjoy ourselves. Being a group of strangers makes it uncomfortable, so in addition to discussing the book, everyone is slowly getting to know each other, to relax and feel safe enough to discuss thoughts. A camaraderie has to be built, a sense of trust, that one can express thoughts without being attacked or thought stupid. Only time brings cohesiveness to a group, time, interest and determination. People have to be interested enough to keep coming back, to work on building a relationship with the group. My groups fluctuated in size, but a core group of about eight people remained. Some people would come for a meeting and for whatever reasons, never return. Sometimes book groups attract one-timers, they come to discuss a particular book and you would never see them again. It felt like a loss when the newcomers would not last, like we had not done our best to welcome them. But sometimes the group would get too big and discussions were hard to handle because everyone would not get a chance to talk, or smaller discussions would start up and it got distracting. We found that ten people were the most we could handle and four would be the smallest for a good discussion.

Being a leader of the group takes a little of the fun out of it. You worry about picking bad books, about keeping the discussion going, keeping the interest up. But you also learn about books and people. Some books just need to be shared. We discussed Laura Esquivel's *Like Water for Chocolate,* even though we had all read it before and watched the movie. But the book was such a delight we had to share it with each other. Some books are easier to discuss than others, and some provoke longer discussions. One year the evening group decided to spend the summer reading *The Brothers Karamazov,* and before we got serious, they wanted to do something light, so we picked *Circle of Friends* by Maeve Binchy. Everyone came into the discussion expecting it to be short, none of us felt like there was much to say about it. But to all of our amazement, we spent over two hours on it. For some reason it sparked a lot of discussion about friendships and growing up and everyone had stories to tell. The age of the reader can make a difference in the enjoyment of a book. The morning group read *Justine* by Lawrence Durrell and everyone loved it. Everyone but me, and I was the youngest member. The opposite happened when we read *So Far From God* by Ana Castillo, that time I was the only member to love it. Once the group was established we would spend time picking the books to be read. Sometimes we would vote and sometimes we would each get to pick a book. This way everyone felt like they were participating and it was really a group effort.

When Oprah Winfrey started her book group it seemed that she started a whole new craze. People all over the country were reading what she told them, and book groups started popping up all over the place. This resurgence in reading just shows that people were starved for the joys of reading, and needed someone to tell them it's o.k. to read and enjoy it; that's what Oprah did, gave reading the stamp of approval. People thought this book group idea was a new phenomenon, but it's not, it's just a new awakening, a new phase. It's not the new fad of the '90s. Book groups have been going on for years in different forms. Traditionally, book groups tend to be women, and I think this is because book groups provided community, provided a place of self-education, a chance to escape from the family for a time for some intelligent conversation.

I never gave being in a book group much thought. It was fun and I learned. I read books with the groups that inspired us and books that divided us. In the five years we've been meeting I can count the books I didn't finish–three. I dutifully read each book whether I liked it or not. That was our responsibility. Some books I ended up liking more after the discussion, one book that I couldn't finish was another member's favorite.

I started thinking about book groups and why people join them. What do they get out of a group? For myself, it's the reading and sharing that goes on. I read books I've always wanted to but never got around to, and I read books I never would have on my own. The discussion is the second part of it. I like the sharing, the little insights, not only to the book but to the people themselves. I have fun with the group. One member is in three groups, she says she can't imagine reading a book and not discussing it. For her the groups give her a chance to catch up on all the reading she never had the time for when she was raising a family. Now she'll read anything, but she feels she misses something if she can't discuss it.

The only male member of the group enjoys the discussions. He wishes he wasn't the only male, but he can't imagine being in an all male book group. He says each man would be so intent on getting their opinions stated that no one would be listening and it wouldn't be a discussion. I'd have to agree with him on this; when I have had more men in the group, the women had to struggle to get themselves heard. Sometimes I wonder if having men in the group inhibits the women. We've had some very personal and thought provoking discussions when there were no men. But the men do add a different perspective and I don't know which, if either, is better.

I have another friend who is an avid reader; she rivals me in reading addiction. Though she loves reading she is not in a book group. She said she loves to talk about books, but she reads where her interest goes and she doesn't want to be obligated to read something she's not interested in. She would feel that her time was being wasted by spending it on a book that's not of her choosing. I think she said it best when she said sharing a book is like sharing your soul and you're giving someone a chance to stomp on it. Being in a group requires some trust. There are some books I don't want to read with a group. I find them too personal and I don't want to share the experience with others. I want to keep it safe, and there is a fear the group won't have the same feelings that I did and it would be a blow against me.

I suppose I should be very interested to know that reading groups have found a home on the internet. That despite the push for getting all our information from computers, reading is still a very important part of people's lives. I should look at it as a positive step, and I do, but I also find it a little strange. For me the enjoyment of reading comes not only from the intellectual discoveries, but from the physical holding of a book, curling up with a cup of tea or coffee, carrying a book, making it a part of myself. Always having a world to go to no matter where I am. When I discuss it, I want to see the other person's reactions, I want the camaraderie, the sense of sharing a moment. Transferring this to the computer just doesn't seem the same. I like the idea of the convenience of it and the idea of discussion going on with people all over the world, but somehow it seems to lack a closeness, a sense of being together. I asked my friend who is not in a book group if she would be interested in an on-line book group. Her response was no, for her it's a trust issue. She would feel more reserved in discussing books on-line because she would feel more responsibility. She would be worried her thoughts would be taken the wrong way, she wouldn't want to be misquoted and she's not sure where the discussion would end. Her statements could be passed on and misunderstood and she wouldn't be able to respond to them. In a live group, she would know who she was talking to and everyone would see who was responsible for the statements in the discussion. To her it seems that the discussion would have a beginning, middle and end, and she would trust the group to be responsible for each other.

Reading groups provide a place for intelligent conversation, a chance to learn without the pressure of tests, an informal classroom. I think with the rush and pressure of work, book groups give people a chance to slow down and connect with others. A chance to take a look at the world around you and share it. It's a chance to bond with other people you might not have met in the regular course of your life. These bonds can be very strong. The act of sharing and discussing books creates a friendship. A safe place to discuss personal thoughts and social issues. A chance to say what's on your mind, other than work or family. A chance to talk about more than daily life. A chance to keep the brain active and have a sense of being involved.

Book groups allow you to connect to others on a surface level or on a very deep level. You can put as much or as little of yourself in the discussion, depending on your reaction to the book. Book groups have grown in popularity. Why? A reaction to computer madness, probably. Computers are wonderful and useful for many reasons. But with the advance of computers and access to all this information, what are we to do with it? Information is great if you have some need for it, but to be deluged with information for the sake of getting it faster, what is the point? Book groups provide information with social interaction.

Reading is an important part of life. It provides information, entertainment and a sense of belonging to the world. Librarians have a major role in connecting books and readers. Librarians should spend more time on readers' advisory, to teach themselves the creative ways to connect readers and books. Librarians should sponsor as many book groups as they can to bring in people to the library and share the fun reading provides. When I started the groups, it seemed very natural to have them sponsored by the library. The combination–libraries and book groups–just made sense. But over the years I have learned that book groups exist in all kinds of places in all shapes and sizes and for various reasons. But all of them exist because of a belief in the power of reading. A belief that reading a book is important, it's more than just escapist entertainment. Books have the power to connect individuals to the world at large. Books can open up new worlds, books can show that we are not alone in our thoughts and feelings. And isn't the act of reading, of finding a connection to your life and to the world, a very moving and important experience?

READERS' ADVISORY

From Reading Words to Reading the World: Readers' Advisory for Adult Literacy Students

Marguerite Crowley Weibel

SUMMARY. This article suggests that the public library offers many books in its general collection that are appropriate for adults who are just learning to read or working to improve their reading. Librarians can play an important role in promoting literacy by recommending books from the poetry, art and photography, literature, and children's collections. Representative titles from all sections are discussed. *[Article copies available for a fee from The Haworth Document Delivery Service: 1-800-342-9678. E-mail address: <getinfo@haworthpressinc.com> Website: <http://www.haworthpressinc.com>]*

Marguerite Crowley Weibel has an MLS from Kent State University and an MA in adult education from Ohio State University. She is Librarian and Assistant Professor at the Ohio State University Prior Health Sciences Library and the author of two books about libraries and literacy.

[Haworth co-indexing entry note]: "From Reading Words to Reading the World: Readers' Advisory for Adult Literacy Students." Weibel, Marguerite Crowley. Co-published simultaneously in *The Acquisitions Librarian* (The Haworth Information Press, an imprint of The Haworth Press, Inc.) No. 25, 2001, pp. 91-111; and: *Readers, Reading and Librarians* (ed: Bill Katz) The Haworth Information Press, an imprint of The Haworth Press, Inc., 2001, pp. 91-111. Single or multiple copies of this article are available for a fee from The Haworth Document Delivery Service [1-800-342-9678, 9:00 a.m. - 5:00 p.m. (EST). E-mail address: getinfo@haworthpressinc.com].

KEYWORDS. Adult literacy, libraries and literacy, books and reading, popular reading, reading levels

INTRODUCTION

All of us who consider ourselves readers can recall certain books and certain reading experiences that started us along that journey from reading words to reading the world. We recall these moments fondly and enjoy sharing our book stories with other readers. For me, it was *Little Women* by Louisa May Alcott. I can still recall sitting on my parents' bed, totally absorbed in the nineteenth century New England world of the March girls, then looking up for a moment and being startled back to reality by the sight of the iron fire escape outside the window and the sounds of summer in the city five stories below. Reading that book gave me my first glimpse of what the reading life was all about. I could not have articulated it then, but at some level of consciousness I began to understand that reading was much more than a pleasant way to pass the time, that it had transformational power, that it could take me to places and times other than my own, that it could introduce me to people I would never otherwise meet and ideas I would not otherwise encounter, that it could fundamentally alter the way I perceived my world.

But what about all those adults who never had these pleasant introductions to the world of reading, or worse, came to associate reading with their lack of skill and their exclusion from a world that seemed to come so easily to others. Statistics reported by the National Institute for Literacy tell us that some 20% of adults over 16 read at less than a 5th grade level.[1] Some of these adults are what I call beginning level new readers, able to read and write perhaps their names and a few common words but not able to use reading to carry on the basic activities of their daily lives. Others among the 20% are at what I would call an intermediate new reader level, able to use reading for minimal functions such as reading menus, filling out brief forms, or reading short articles in the newspaper, but not skilled enough to use reading to advance to a new job or to obtain needed information about topics essential to everyday living such as health care. Beyond this 20%, there is yet another group of students I would call advanced new readers or developing readers who read well enough to accomplish the necessary activities of their lives, but don't have a high school diploma or lack the combination of skill and confidence to seek further schooling.

Is it still possible for these adults, some struggling to learn to read or improve their reading in various adult literacy programs, others just coping on their own, to have that kind of reading experience that makes them see reading, not just as an important skill for everyday life, but an invitation to join in a lifelong conversation about people, places, and ideas? Yes, I believe it is possible, but only with the active involvement of libraries and librarians.

Many public libraries have collections for new and developing readers. These collections usually consist of materials specifically written for this audience, including "life skills" materials that teach things such as learning how to use a checking account or obtain a drivers license, short novels written for adults with limited reading skill, and workbooks preparing students for the GED and other tests. These are all useful materials, but the library has so much more to offer. There are literally hundreds of books within the general collection of any public library that will be accessible to new and developing readers. In some cases, students can read the books on their own. In other cases, books can be made accessible to literacy students with the help of the tutors and teachers who work with them.

I'd like to take a virtual tour through a typical public library collection, pointing out examples of books that adult literacy students can use. To put a discussion of these books in context, however, I'd like to begin with a story.

When I first started teaching adult literacy students, I had a student named Albert. He was a black man who had grown up in the rural south and didn't have much opportunity for education. He had also been a soldier during World War II, an experience which gave him a very different sort of education. Albert was what I call a beginning level reader. He could read and write his name, address, and several basic words. He could make out a few words of a headline in the newspaper, but he would have trouble reading a whole article, even a short one, all the way through. We were using a workbook that was and probably still is fairly common: simple words in simple, declarative sentences about a basic adult experience. Most of the words were repeated several times. I no longer have that particular book, but the sentences were similar to these:

Jim White moved to the big city.

Jim needed a place to live and a job.

Jim met two friends, Jack and Bob.

Jack helped Jim find a place to live.

Bob helped him find a job.

Jim, Jack, and Bob were good friends in the big city.

These sentences were followed by basic comprehension questions:

Why did Jim White move to the big city?

Who helped Jim find a place to live?

Who helped Jim find a job?

We were sitting side by side at a table, Albert to my right. As he read each of the questions, then stopped to consider the answer, I found myself lifting up the page with the end of my pencil to see the original story. I couldn't remember it well enough to answer these simple questions!

Albert, if he noticed, kindly said nothing, but I was embarrassed and irritated by my own lack of attention. The more I thought about this incident, however, the more I understood that the material itself was at least partly to blame. It was boring. It was written in the kind of flat, simplistic language found frequently in texts for new readers but never heard in real speech. There was nothing in the language to please the reader's ear, nor anything in the story to engage the reader's imagination. It was an exercise in reading, not the real thing.

I knew there had to be something better, so I went to the public library. I recalled reading some poetry of Langston Hughes and Gwendolyn Brooks that was easy to understand, yet powerful enough that I remembered it some ten years after the fact. Here is the first stanza of one of the poems that I found and read with Albert:

> The face of war is my face.
> The face of war is your face.
> What color
> Is the face
> Of war?
> Brown, black, white–
> Your face and my face.
>
> –Langston Hughes, *War*[2]

Simple words, as in the story from the workbook, and they are repeated several times, just as words are in most beginning reading exercises. But what a difference! These words are startling in their power. They make you think and ask questions. They even present a sophisticated idea, that the opponents in a war may be countries or ideological forces, but the soldiers are men like us.

These are questions that any reader can grapple with, especially a student like Albert who had been part of the Allied invasion force on D-Day, one of the black soldiers assigned to clear the dead bodies after battle.

This experience with Albert happened twenty years ago, but I remember it so well because it made me a different kind of teacher, as clearly as the experience of reading *Little Women* made me a different kind of reader. It taught me that *what* students read really matters. In their classrooms and tutoring sessions, adult literacy students learn the basic skills of reading, the sight words and phonetic patterns that enable them to recognize familiar words and decode the unfamiliar ones. These skills are necessary, for sure, but unless those skills are framed by the experience of reading texts that engage a student's mind and heart, he is not likely to embrace reading as an activity that contributes to the richness of his life. He may learn how to read, but he will not become a reader.

The public library has the two things literacy students need to become readers: lots of books and the librarians who know the books in their collections and can connect them to individual students. Students need a readers' advisory service attuned to their particular needs because they are unfamiliar with the resources in the library and often intimidated by an institution they perceive as existing for people who read well. Literacy teachers and tutors, on the other hand, may be avid library users on their own, but unaware of the depth of resources in the children's collection, for example, that are in fact appropriate for adults, or the many art, photography, and poetry books that will appeal to a wide audience, including those with limited reading skills.

In my quest to identify appropriate books for new readers, I have found a treasure trove in the library, hundreds of books that students in reading programs can read, some on their own, others with help from teachers and tutors. I'd like to offer some examples of those books by taking a virtual tour of a typical public library collection with one question in mind: What books can adult literacy students, from beginning to advanced new reader levels, use?

Poetry

We've already mentioned poetry, so we'll start our tour in the poetry section. It is most appropriate that we do so because poetry offers so many possibilities for rewarding and enlightening reading experiences for literacy students. Many poems are short and simple to read, but they are also much more. As we saw in the example of *War*, even simple poems introduce students to a more sophisticated language, to the use of metaphor and vivid imagery. They help new readers look beyond the literal and begin to see how words convey meaning on several levels. Poetry is a rich and inclusive medium. It is written in many forms and covers virtually any subject matter imaginable. There are poems that tell stories, poems that make clever use of language, poems that create vivid word pictures, poems that capture the ear and the imagination with memorable rhymes and rhythms, poems which recall memories both bitter and sweet, poems which cry out against pain and injustice, poems which celebrate laughter and living, poems which express our deepest fears and longings. In short, poems communicate across the spectrum of human experience, and there is no better source for the poems that will speak to new and developing adult readers than the public library.

The poem *War*, quoted from Langston Hughes, is contained in the anthology *The Panther and the Lash,* which is available in many libraries. Hughes' poetry is remarkable for its mix of power, simplicity, compelling rhythms, and deeply felt emotions. Two other anthologies of his work that will appeal to new readers are *The Dream Keeper* and *Don't You Turn Back,* with poems selected by Lee Bennett Hopkins. In some libraries, these anthologies will be found in the adult collection, in some libraries in the children's collection, and sometimes in both. *The Dream Keeper* was first published in 1937, but more recent editions have been produced, notably one illustrated by Brian Pinckney and published in 1994.

Three other well known poets whose work is also both powerful and accessible are Gwendolyn Brooks, Lucille Clifton, and William Carlos Williams. Anthologies of the works of these poets will also be readily available in most public libraries.

Many of the poetry books found in public libraries are general anthologies that include the works of several different poets. In some cases, the poems were collected around a theme such as Lillian Morrison's collection of sports poems, *Rhythm Road: Poems to Move to.* On the other hand, for her anthology *Peeling the Onion,* Ruth Gordon chose poems for the clarity of their insight rather than for any thematic similarity. Most of these anthologies will be found in the children's collection, although in most cases the poems collected in the anthologies were originally written for adults.

Some books marketed for children strike me as even more appropriate for adults. Cynthia Rylant's *Something Permanent,* for example, is a collection of poems Rylant wrote in response to the Depression-era photographs of Walker Evans. The poems are easy to read and might well appeal to middle school children, but the depth of insight they reveal can best be appreciated by adults whose own lives have known the sting of hardship and the renewing power of family. Two other anthologies that match simple but evocative poems with compelling photographs are *A Song in Stone: City Poems* and *On Our Way: Poems of Pride and Love,* both compiled by Lee Bennett Hopkins. I have found both titles in the children's collection of the public library as well as in college libraries.

Publishers and educators have always collaborated to introduce the poems of prominent American writers to children, so you will find books such as *You Come, Too, a* collection of the works of Robert Frost, *Rainbows Are Made,* Lee Bennett Hopkins's anthology of the works of Carl Sandburg, and *Poems of Emily Dickinson* collected by Helen Plotz, in the children's section of the library. The poems contained within the anthologies, however, were originally written for an adult audience, and the appearance, content, and format of the books remain appropriate for adults.

READING PICTURES

A public library's collection of art and photography books offers another rich source of materials for adult literacy students. From the dawn of time, people have felt compelled to record their lives in pictures. Even in our modern world, we are fascinated by the discovery of pictures on the walls of ancient caves, or in the tombs of ancient kings. These distant human cousins left no written record, but looking at their drawings, we can "read" some part of their life story. From these pictures, we learn something about the tools they used, the animals they hunted, the clothing they wore. We also sense that they had the same need we do to understand and explain their world and to communicate their ideas to others.

All pictures offer something for a viewer to "read," whether they are paintings of a culture long past, expressionist paintings of one artist's particular vision, photographs of times, places, or people we never knew or photographs of current culture. Looking at pictures, the viewer can describe what he sees, make inferences about the events pictured or the meanings suggested, recognize people, places, or situations familiar to his own life, react to the emotional content, or judge its success in communicating some idea. These are the same critical thinking skills students need to apply to the written word as they develop into perceptive, thoughtful readers.

Pictures are an invaluable tool for one of the teaching methods frequently used among beginning level adult literacy students. The method is called language experience, and it simply means that a student will talk about something of importance to her such as her family, work, or goals for learning to read. As the student talks, the tutor writes down the student's words, reads them back to her, then teaches her to read the words on her own. This method employs an important principle of adult basic education, namely that instruction should be rooted in the student's own interests, needs, and experiences. The method has its limits, however, especially with students who are naturally reticent about talking about themselves. Besides, to read well, students eventually need to read and think about experiences, information, and ideas beyond their own circumstances. Pictures bring the outside world into the classroom, giving students something outside their own circumstances to respond to. This is an important step in moving from reading words to reading the world.

Even the smallest public library will have a collection of art and photography books that will appeal to new and developing adult literacy students and offer them opportunities to describe and discuss the content of pictures. Let's look first at some examples from the art collection.

Art Books

The many art books found in a typical public library encompass a wide range of styles and content. Some present pictures that are almost photographic in their representation of the world they depict. Others express situations, ideas, and emotions in an abstract manner. All have potential uses with literacy students.

Several publishing houses produce series of books focusing on specific artists, and two in particular would be attractive to new readers. The Rizzoli Art Series, published by Rizzoli Publications, Inc., produces paperback books with artwork reproduced on large pages that give viewers a sense of the scale of the original, but the books themselves are thin enough to carry and browse through easily. Each title contains a fairly small sampling of the work of the artist featured, but it is enough to introduce the reader to that artist's style and subject matter. Among the artists included in this series are European masters such as Van Gogh, Monet, and Degas, and twentieth-century American painters Edward Hopper and Roy Lichtenstein. Comparing the works of these last two artists, one somber and representational, the other abstract, a bit playful and often puzzling, would be an interesting exercise for more advanced classes. Watson-Guptill Publications Company is the other publisher whose attractive and accessible series of paperback books highlighting the works of many famous painters, including several Americans, would be appealing to literacy students.

Books depicting the work of two American folk artists whose life stories are truly inspiring may also appeal to new readers. Grandma Moses was already in her sixties when she began to paint seriously, yet she painted images of rural America that have been inscribed on the nation's collective memory. The pictures presented in Margot Cleary's book, *Grandma Moses,* depict times and places long gone, but modern viewers are drawn to the emotional content of the places that Grandma Moses called home. Horace Pippin is another American folk artist whose work continues to speak to viewers. Though his arm was crippled in World War I, he painted powerful images depicting his experiences in the war as well as his experiences as a black man in America in the early part of the twentieth century. Pippin has enjoyed renewed recognition in recent years, and several collections of his work are available, including *Horace Pippin,* published by the Phillips Collection in Washington, DC and *I Tell My Heart: The Art of Horace Pippin,* compiled by Judith Stein and published by the Pennsylvania Academy of Fine Arts. In addition to these collections, Mary Lyons' biography, *Starting Home: The Art of Horace Pippin, Painter,* examines his life in the context of his paintings. Although written for children, the book is also appropriate for adults.

While students who are not familiar with looking at and talking about art may be more comfortable starting out with representational paintings, abstract art can present the kind of mind stretching exercises that are good for all learners. Looking at abstract art, viewers are confronted with images that the conscious mind does not recognize. To make sense of the image, they have to let go of preconceptions, make seemingly illogical associations, let feelings determine a reaction, and try to imagine what an artist might have had in mind when creating the work. Asking students to write all their reactions in response to a work of abstract art would be one way of encouraging them to write creatively, to write whatever comes into their minds rather than what they think a teacher may want them to write.

Georgia O'Keeffe is an American artist whose work might serve as a bridge between representational forms of art and abstract art. In a collection of her work entitled *Georgia O'Keeffe: One Hundred Flowers*, for example, she has painted flowers in such minute detail and vibrant colors that they become almost magical. Describing these pictures will challenge students' vocabularies as well as their powers of observation.

There are hundreds of books produced to introduce children to the world of art, and many of these books will be appropriate for adult new and developing readers as well. Two particularly good collections of art, accompanied by excerpts from works of literature, have been edited by Charles Sullivan and published by Harry N. Abrams. In *Children of Promise: African-American Literature and Art for Young People* and *Here Is My Kingdom: Hispanic-American Literature and Art for Young People*, students will find beautiful and intriguing images matched with excerpts from prose and poetry that are sometimes directly, sometimes only indirectly, related to each other. Imagining why particular words have been paired with particular images will help students look more deeply at both and perhaps see layers of meaning not apparent at first glance.

Photography Books

Collections of photographs offer new readers and their teachers the same kind of opportunities to use words and discuss ideas that collections of art do, but they have the added advantage, at least in most cases, of being a more familiar medium. Teachers can choose from a wide range of photography books to engage students in the intellectual exercises of observing, describing, reacting to, and writing about pictures. Some collections of photography document a particular time and culture. For example, *A Day in the Life of America*, edited by Rick Smolan and David Cohen, presents a montage of pictures taken by more than 100 photographers working in various places across the country on one particular day in 1986. Browsing through such a book, literacy students can find pictures that remind them of their own lives and interests, pictures that suggest other lifestyles and pursuits, and pictures that raise questions of personal values.

Other collections of photographs narrow their focus to a particular place. Bruce Davidson's *Subway* is a good example of this. In Davidson's pictures we find, in the relatively small universe of the New York City subway system, a picture of urban life in microcosm. The pictures depict the ugliness and grit commonly associated with the New York subways, but we also see the buildings, bridges, and waterways that define New York take on an unexpected beauty when framed by the window of a subway car.

Collections of photography examine social structures and movements. Lewis Hine's *Women at Work,* first published in 1938 and reissued in 1981, shows women at work in the rather limited number of fields open to them. The Betty Medsger collection, *Women at Work: A Photodocumentary,* compiled almost forty years later, presents a very different picture of women working in jobs ranging from the traditional to the highly unusual. Extraordinary events are also captured in photodocumentaries such as Leland Rice's *Up Against It: Photographs of the Berlin Wall.* When it divided Germany's largest city, the Berlin Wall was a symbol of oppression, but the many hundreds of messages scrawled across its western face became symbols of hope as well. Rice has preserved many of those messages which were lost when the wall came down, and they still speak across all barriers.

Photographs can also be works of art, as are the photographs in Andreas Feininger's *The Mountains of the Mind.* The rocks, shells, driftwood, and other natural objects pictured are all positioned, illuminated, and in some cases magnified to display the artistic impact of shapes, lines, contours, and contrasts, often masking the object's true identity, as in a work of abstract art. A different kind of artistic photograph appears in Art Gore's *Images of Yesterday.* These pictures reflect the artist's very spiritual response to the beauty and bounty of his rural North Carolina home. Both books will draw many and varied responses from students, opening opportunities for all kinds of discussion and writing activities.

Picture Books

In discussing poetry, art, and photography books, we've mentioned several titles from the children's collection. Let's look a little more closely at this collection, because there are so many treasures here for adults, whether new readers or highly experienced ones. Tutors, teachers, and even some librarians may shy away from suggesting children's books to new readers for fear of offending them. This is an entirely appropriate concern, but upon investigation it turns out that many books written and marketed for children are in fact not only suitable for adults but appealing and informative as well. Take picture books, for example. The best of these books combine beautiful art work with engaging language to tell stories worth listening to. Many of these books will appeal to adults, in some cases even more than they appeal to the children they are intended for. Consider Faith Ringgold's *Tar Beach*, for example. Ringgold is an artist who originally told the story of *Tar Beach* in fabric, creating a "story quilt" which now hangs in New York's Guggenheim Museum. She later adapted her story to picture book form, using illustrations from the quilt to depict her childhood summers in Harlem, where it was common practice for families to spend the hot summer nights on the roof of their apartment building which they laughingly referred to as "tar beach." From that height, young Ringgold could look out at the George Washington Bridge and dream of flying off into a world where she was queen and could right whatever wrongs she encountered. Children will identify with the young girl's fantasy; adults will appreciate the irony of the title and the ability of the adults to create good times in difficult circumstances.

Adults looking back on their childhood experiences is a common theme among picture books for children. Cynthia Rylant's *When I Was Young in the Mountains,* James Stevenson's series of five books beginning with *When I Was Nine,* Judith Hendershot's *In Coal Country,* and Sandra Cisneros' *Hair = Pelitos,* with text in English and Spanish, are but a few outstanding examples.

Picture books for children also deal with many of the problems that contemporary families face. George Ella Lyon's *Mama Is a Miner* is a warm but honest presentation of the conflicting feelings of a mother who faces danger every day she goes down into that mine, but accepts the risk for the financial benefits it gives her family. As she describes her workday to her children, she explains that in the mornings, she looks forward to the respite and camaraderie of lunch, but after lunch, she is "digging for home,"a beautiful metaphor, the stuff of real literature, and an idea that any parent will understand.

Picture books take us into the heart of other cultures as well. At first glance, Rachel Isadora's *At the Crossroads* is a heartwarming story of children joyous at the prospect of their fathers coming home from work, but then you see the underside of the story. The fathers have been away at work for ten months, the children live in corrugated shacks, and they make toys from scraps on the garbage pile. With simplicity and understatement, this selective incident paints a searing picture of life in South Africa under apartheid.

Picture books also teach readers about history. The 1990s have seen several 50-year commemorations of events related to WW II, as well as the release of Stephen Speilberg's award-winning film, *Schindler's List.* Many extraordinary picture books also tell parts of the story of WW II. Chana Byers Abells' *The Children We Remember,* for example, is a simple but stark reminder of the Holocaust. It opens with photographs of Jewish children enjoying the ordinary circumstances of childhood before the war began, then shows us pictures of children suffering unimaginable hardships during the war. It ends with a few pictures of children who survived. Few words accompany these pictures, but then, few are needed.

Picture books also introduce readers to some of the most important words of our culture. Lincoln's Gettysburg Address, for example, is among the most famous speeches in our language, but it is written in a style that readers not comfortable with written text find difficult to grasp. The emotional impact as well as the literal meaning of Lincoln's words come alive, however, if read aloud to the accompaniment of the vivid black and white woodcuts found in Michael McCurdy's illustrations for the picture book, *The Gettysburg Address*. When Lincoln says, "It is for us the living, rather, to be dedicated here to the unfinished work . . . ," we see men and women armed with farming tools obviously and boldly moving forward, and we understand that Lincoln is telling us, even to this day, to carry on the work of mending a nation.

In her many picture books, Eve Bunting has addressed contemporary social issues that are part of the history we are living now. Two outstanding titles are *Smoky Night*, in which Bunting uses the context of recent Los Angeles riots to explore the tension between various ethnic groups struggling to survive in a neighborhood with few resources, and *The Wall*, in which a father and his young son search together for the boy's grandfather's name on the granite wall of the Vietnam Veteran's Memorial.

INTRODUCING LITERATURE

With their delightful marriage of illustrations and stories, picture books appeal to readers of all ages. But as adult new readers gain skill, they will want to read stories that are not just longer but involve additional layers of plot and character development or provide more detailed information. This is a crucial juncture in their literacy development. If students at this level can begin to see reading as a source of pleasure, amusement, and even inspiration, as well as a source of information, then their chances of getting hooked on the reading habit–of becoming readers and ultimately lifelong learners–are greatly enhanced. Introducing students to novels, short stories, memoirs, and nonfiction works that might collectively be called stories from the human family, holds the promise of giving them the experience of deriving personal fulfillment from the pages of a book.

Novels

There are many books within a library collection that can help new readers make that transition. I mentioned Sandra Cisneros' picture book, *Hair = Pelitos* above. The text of this picture book is actually one chapter from her novel, *The House on Main Street*. In each chapter of that novel, Cisneros recalls a particular incident from her childhood in a Latino neighborhood in

Chicago. The chapters are brief, and the essential meaning of each is clear, but the writing, full of poetic images and metaphors, will challenge developing readers.

Memoirs

Memoirs, whether factual or cast in fiction as *The House on Mango Street* is, offer developing readers a comfortable introduction to longer works of literature because all of us like to hear the stories of other people's lives. Many memoirs found on public library shelves will be accessible to developing readers, particularly those preparing for GED or high school equivalency tests. Maya Angelou's *I Know Why the Caged Bird Sings,* as well as subsequent volumes of her autobiography, presents a fascinating story of one extraordinary woman's journey beyond adversity. In a collection of poems, essays, and short stories titled *Latin Deli,* Judith Ortiz-Cofer explores the conflicts she experienced moving between the island culture of her Puerto Rican parents and the American culture of her school and neighborhood in Paterson, New Jersey. In voices that are alternately feisty and quietly determined, funny and reflective, centenarian sisters Sarah and Bessie Delany recall their long and extraordinary lives, and in the process give readers a history lesson in the struggles of black Americans to achieve equality, in their popular memoir *Having Our Say: The Delany Sisters' First 100 Years.*

Collections of Newspaper Columns

Collections of newspaper columns are another good source of material for developing readers. Each column is short enough to be read and discussed in one class or as part of one writing assignment, but it also tells a whole story or states an opinion complete with supporting facts and reasoning. The columns of Bob Greene offer a case in point. In collections such as *American Beat, Cheeseburgers,* and *He Was a Midwestern Boy on His Own,* Greene introduces us to some fascinating characters such as the washroom attendant in a fancy nightclub who could sing better than many of the paid performers but only did so when the only people in the club were the piano player and other workers, or the woman who organized and promoted a convention for women named "Linda" (no "Lyndas" were allowed). The columns of Ellen Goodman, collected in such books as *Value Judgments,* address the major social issues of the day such as child care, minimum wage, working women, and the quality of education. Her focus is not public policy per se, however, but rather, how public policy affects the everyday lives of ordinary citizens.

Oral History

Oral history is another kind of literature that will appeal to new readers and has many uses within an adult literacy program. Studs Terkel is perhaps the preeminent master of the form, having compiled several oral histories around issues of social importance, including *Working,* a collection of interviews about what people do for a living and how they feel about what they do, *Hard Times,* an oral history of the Great Depression, and *Race: How Blacks and Whites Feel About the American Obsession.*

Juvenile and Young Adult Fiction

We began our discussion of literature with the picture books in the children's collection, and perhaps we should end it in the children's department as well, but this time looking at juvenile and young adult fiction. Many books in this section are what I call "crossover books," that is, books that will appeal to adults as well as teenagers. Sometimes the voice in the story is actually that of an adult looking back on his or her teenage years, as in Cynthia Rylant's *I Had Seen Castles,* in which an elderly man recalls the year he turned eighteen, fell in love, went to war, and saw his whole world change around him. Teenagers will identify with the turmoil felt by the young lovers torn between duty and desire. Older readers will also recognize the mixture of joy, sadness, and more than a tinge of regret that inevitably comes with looking back. Robert Lipsyte's classic young adult novel *The Contender* is almost thirty years old, but its powerful telling of a seventeen-year-old dropout who learns the lesson of the boxing ring–that the effort to be a contender means more than being a champion–transcends limitations of time or age of reader. Angela Johnson's *Toning the Sweep* is a contemporary novel with strong adult characters who must face the death of an elderly parent as well as the responsibility of carrying memories and culture into the next generation.

Historical fiction is a popular genre for young adults. It offers readers an engaging story as it teaches us about history by helping us imagine what it was like to live in particular times and places. Many books of historical fiction from the children's collection will also appeal to adults. One example is Paul Fleischman's *Bull Run* which takes readers into that Civil War battle in the company of sixteen different characters, eight on each side, whose lives were profoundly affected in different ways by that battle. In Eilis Dillon's *Children of Bach,* all the characters, both children and adults, are fully realized as they contend with both their mistrust of each other and their desperate need of each other in their attempt to escape the Nazis.

Reading for Information

Patrons have always come to public libraries to find information for all kinds of reasons. They come to learn who their senator is and how to get in touch with him or her. They come to find out about weather patterns when faced with a hurricane or the effects of "El Niño." They come to find out how to fix a leaky faucet or to learn the rules of soccer so they can coach their child's team. This particular aspect of library service has actually gained new prominence in this "Information Age" we live in. The way the library provides information is changing, too, as certain types of information become more easily accessible in electronic format. This change creates opportunities as well as challenges for library patrons, not to mention library staff.

Adult literacy students have always been challenged in obtaining the information they need because they lack mastery of the most basic information retrieval skill, the ability to read well. What is perhaps even more problematic, literacy students, because of their poor reading skills, missed much of the content that was presented to them through the printed word in history, social studies, science, civics, and other classes. As a result, they lack much of the background knowledge in which current information is rooted as well as the habit of referring to and applying that knowledge to the problems and situations of their everyday lives. The increasing use of ever more sophisticated technology to retrieve information has added yet another barrier for them to overcome. As a result, adult literacy students are among the most vulnerable citizens in the Information Age, surrounded by an ever-increasing flood of information, but increasingly limited in their ability to understand and apply it.

The public library can help them. Regarding the use of electronic information, most public libraries now make computers and access to information sources available to their patrons. Literacy students will need the help of their teachers or tutors, but the library's information resources actually provide them an accessible avenue to begin to learn how to use computers. The newness of the technology can be intimidating, but it can also be intriguing, especially if students are convinced that many others are just learning this technology as well.

The focus of this paper and this volume is books and reading, however, so I'll talk more specifically about books the library has to offer new and developing readers to help them find the information they need as well as learn the basic skills of information seeking that will serve them in future educational ventures as well as in everyday life.

Most literacy students are probably unaware of the fact that libraries have simple information tools such as phone books from cities across the country. Common as they are, phone books are also examples of two basic kinds of indexes that are fundamental to sophisticated electronic information retrieval systems: alphabetical indexes and subject indexes. Having students look up the name and address of a friend or relative in a distant city, or find a listing for pet stores in their neighborhood, are two simple tasks that will help them understand some of the basic principles of information retrieval. In the library, students will also find almanacs in which to look up information about weather patterns, maps to consult when planning a trip, and daily newspapers with indexes to help them find the comics, TV listings, weather maps, and other sections of interest to them.

However, literacy students often need more substantive and comprehensive information than discrete pieces of data such as the temperature in Miami for the last five days. Such information can sometimes be found electronically through periodical indexes or specific web sites, but most often it still will be found in the pages of a book.

Every public library offers books that can help adult literacy students become more skilled workers, wiser consumers, better parents, and more informed citizens. Some of these books will be in the adult section of the library, but many will come from the children's collection, which contains numerous nonfiction books appealing to adults, whether they are new readers or highly experienced readers new to the topic discussed. These books address their subject in a direct, straightforward narrative intended to convey information accurately but simply. They make extensive and appealing use of photographs, illustrations and graphic material. They are well researched and written in a style that is not condescending and never identifies children as the intended audience. These books will be written at many different reading levels. Some will be accessible to students reading on their own, others can be made accessible to students by using a variation of the language experience method known as the information reading technique. Using this technique, a teacher or tutor reads material to students a paragraph or section at a time, then discusses the material with them and asks them to explain it in their own words. The teacher then writes the students' version of the material which they then practice reading.

Let's look at a few examples. Basic information about health and disease is a topic that draws many patrons to the library. Typically, libraries offer many of the growing number of titles of consumer health books. Many of these will be accessible to developing readers, especially those working with a tutor. The children's section will also have many appropriate resources, some individual titles as well as some series titles, that explain various diseases as well as how the body works to contain disease. For example, *Sexually Transmitted Diseases* by Alan Nourse is a straightforward and informative discussion about STDs, including AIDS. *Alzheimer's Disease,* written by William A. Check, is one of several titles in the Chelsea House Publishers' series, *The Encyclopedia of Health: Medical Disorders and Their Treatment.* The same publishers also produce the series, *The Encyclopedia of Health: Psychological Disorders and Their Treatment.* Some of the topics covered in that series include suicide, depression, and eating disorders.

Students who are preparing for the GED test or hoping to continue on to community colleges need to read about topics in the areas of history, science, popular culture and the arts. Here again, the children's collection will have many resources appropriate for them. Children's Press, for example (whose books are often appropriate for adults, despite their name), produces several series in history, science, and biography that will be accessible to beginning and intermediate new readers. The biography, *Barbara Bush: First Lady of Literacy,* is a representative example. At a more advanced reading level, Chelsea House Publishers produce several series of biographies of Black Americans of Achievement, Hispanic Americans of Achievement, and Women of Achievement. Their biography, *Gordon Parks,* about the photographer, film maker, and poet, is a good example of this series which is aimed at middle and high school level and delves more deeply into the experiences and influences that shaped the lives of their many subjects.

Among writers of nonfiction for children, a few outstanding authors whose work will appeal to new readers deserve mention. James Haskins has written several books detailing specific aspects of the Civil Rights Movement, including *I Have a Dream: The Life and Words of Martin Luther King, Jr.,* and *Freedom Rides: Journeys for Justice.* Milton Meltzer is a prolific author who has written about the Great Depression in *Brother, Can You Spare a Dime?* as well as on topics as diverse as the Civil War and the lure of gold. Brent Ashabranner and Raymond Bial are two authors who combine their writing with their own exceptional photographs in their exploration of places and events. Ashabranner's book, *Still a Nation of Immigrants,* examines the changing patterns of immigration to the United States. His *Always to Remember: The Story of the Vietnam Veterans Memorial,* is a beautiful account of the planning, building, and impact of what has become Washington's most visited monument. Writer and photographer Raymond Bial's book *The Underground Railroad* is a haunting evocation of the spirits of the slaves who risked everything to reach freedom and the free men and women who sheltered and protected them on their perilous journey. For scientific information, Patricia Lauber's simple but fluid prose makes what can seem like a daunting topic both understandable and fascinating. Her *Journey to the Planets* explores our neighbors in the universe, while *Volcano: The Eruption and Healing of Mt. St. Helens* helps us understand the forces at work on our own planet Earth.

CONCLUSION

The titles mentioned here are only a sampling of the hundreds of titles available to new and developing readers. The books are on the shelves, the students are in their classrooms. All that is needed are the librarians who can bring the two together.

NOTES

1. The National Institute for Literacy. Http://novel.nifl.gov.

2. Hughes, Langston, *The Panther and the Lash.* New York: Vintage Books, 1992, p. 59.

LIST OF BOOKS DISCUSSED

Abells, Chana Byers. *The Children We Remember.* New York: Greenwillow Books, 1986.

Alcott, Louisa May. *Little Women.* New York: New American Library, 1983.

Angelou, Maya. *I Know Why the Caged Bird Sings.* New York: Random House, 1970.

Ashabranner, Brent. *Always to Remember: The Story of the Vietnam Veterans Memorial.* Photographs by Jennifer Ashabranner. New York: Dodd, Mead, & Co., 1988.

Ashabranner, Brent. *Still a Nation of Immigrants.* Photographs by Jennifer Ashabranner. New York: Dutton, 1993.

Behrens, June. *Barbara Bush: First Lady of Literacy.* Chicago: Children's Press, 1990.

Berry, Skip. *Gordon Parks.* Black Americans of Achievement series. New York: Chelsea House Publishers, 1991.

Bial, Raymond. *Underground Railroad.* Boston: Houghton Mifflin, 1995.

Bunting, Eve. *Smoky Night.* Illustrated by David Diaz. San Diego: Harcourt Brace & Co., 1994.

Bunting, Eve. *The Wall.* Illustrated by Ronald Himler. New York: Clarion Books, 1990.

Check, William A. *Alzheimer's Disease.* Series title: *The Encyclopedia of Health: Medical Disorders and Their Treatment.* New York: Chelsea House Publications, 1989.

Cisneros, Sandra. *Hair = Pelitos.* Illustrated by Terry Ybanez. New York: Knopf, 1994.

Cisneros, Sandra. *The House on Mango Street.* New York: Random House, 1989.

Clery, Margot. *Grandma Moses.* New York: Crescent Books, 1991.

Davidson, Bruce. *Subway.* New York: An Aperture Book published in association with Floyd A. Yearout, 1986.

Delany, Bessie and Sarah Delany. *Having Our Say: The Delany Sisters' First 100 Years.* With Amy Hill Hearth. New York: Kodansha International, 1993.

Dickinson, Emily. *Poems of Emily Dickinson.* Selected by Helen Plotz. New York: Thomas Y. Crowell, 1964.

Dillon, Eilis. *Children of Bach.* New York: Charles Scribner's Sons, 1992.

Feininger, Andreas. *The Mountains of the Mind: A Fantastic Journey into Reality.* New York: Viking Press, 1977.

Fleischman, Paul. *Bull Run.* New York: HarperCollins, 1993.

Frost, Robert. *You Come, Too.* New York: Holt, Rinehart, and Winston, 1959.

Goodman, Ellen. *Value Judgements.* New York: Farrar, Straus, and Giroux, 1993.

Gordon, Ruth, ed. *Peeling the Onion: An Anthology of Poems.* New York: Harper-Collins, 1992.

Gore, Art. *Images of Yesterday.* Palo Alto, CA: American West Publishing Co., 1975.

Greene, Bob. *American Beat.* New York: Atheneum, 1983.

Greene, Bob. *Cheeseburgers.* New York: Atheneum, 1986.

Greene, Bob. *He Was a Midwestern Boy on His Own.* New York: Atheneum, 1991.

Haskins, James. *The Freedom Rides.* New York: Hyperion Books for Children, 1995.

Haskins, James. *I Have a Dream: The Life and Words of Martin Luther King, Jr.* Brookfield, CT: The Millbrook Press, 1992.

Hendershot, Judith. *In Coal Country.* Illustrated by Thomas B. Allen. New York: Knopf, 1987.

Hine, Lewis. *Women at Work.* New York: Dover Publications, 1981.

Hopkins, Lee Bennett, sel. *On Our Way: Poems of Pride and Love.* Photographs by David Parks. New York: Knopf, 1974.

Hopkins, Lee Bennett, sel. *A Song in Stone: City Poems.* Photographs by Anna Held Audette. New York: Thomas Y. Crowell, 1982.

Hughes, Langston. *Don't You Turn Back.* Selected by Lee Bennett Hopkins. New York: Knopf, 1969.

Hughes, Langston. *The Dream Keeper.* Illustrated by Brian Pinckney. New York: Knopf, 1994.

Hughes, Langston. *The Panther and the Lash.* New York: Vintage Books, 1992.

Isadora, Rachel. *At the Crossroads.* New York: Greenwillow Books, 1986.

Johnson, Angela. *Toning the Sweep.* New York: Orchard Books, 1993.

Lauber, Patricia. *Journey to the Planets,* 4th ed. New York: Crown Publishers, 1993.

Lauber, Patricia. *Volcano: The Eruption and Healing of Mt. St. Helens.* New York: Bradbury Press, 1986.

Lincoln, Abraham. *The Gettysburg Address.* Illustrated by Michael McCurdy. Boston: Houghton Mifflin, 1995.

Lipsyte, Robert. *The Contender.* New York: Harper & Row, 1967.

Lyon, George Ella. *Mama Is a Miner.* Illustrations by Peter Catalanotto. New York: Orchard Books, 1994.

Lyons, Mary E. *Starting Home: The Art of Horace Pippin, Painter.* African-American Artists and Artisans series. Charles Scribner's Sons, 1993.

Medsger, Betty. *Women at Work: A Photodocumentary.* New York: Sheed and Ward, Inc., 1975.

Meltzer, Milton. *Brother, Can You Spare a Dime?* Library of American History Series. New York: Facts on File, 1991.

Morrison, Lillian, ed. *Rhythm Road: Poems to Move to.* New York: Lothrop, Lee, and Shepard Books, 1988.

Nourse, Alan E., MD. *Sexually Transmitted Diseases.* New York: Franklin Watts, 1992.

O'Keeffe, Georgia. *Georgia O'Keeffe: One Hundred Flowers.* Ed. by Nicholas Calloway. New York: Knopf, 1989.

Ortiz-Cofer, Judith. *Latin Deli.* Athens, GA: University of Georgia Press, 1993.

Pippin, Horace. *Horace Pippin.* With an Essay by Romare Bearden. Washington, DC: The Phillips Collection, 1977.

Rice, Leland. *Up Against It: Photographs of the Berlin Wall.* Albuquerque, NM: University of New Mexico Press, 1991.

Ringgold, Faith. *Tar Beach.* New York: Crown Publishers, 1991.

Rizzoli Art Series. Various titles. New York: Rizzoli International Publishers, Inc., 1992.

Rylant, Cynthia. *I Had Seen Castles.* San Diego: Harcourt Brace and Co., 1993.

Rylant, Cynthia. *Something Permanent.* Photographs by Walker Evans. San Diego: Harcourt Brace and Co., 1994.

Rylant, Cynthia. *When I Was Young in the Mountains.* Illustrated by Diane Goode. New York: E. P. Dutton, 1983.

Sandburg, Carl. *Rainbows Are Made.* Selected by Lee Bennett Hopkins. San Diego: Harcourt, Brace, Jovanovich, 1982.

Smolan, Rick and David Cohen, eds. *A Day in the Life of America.* New York: Collins Publishers, 1986.

Stein, Judith, ed. *I Tell My Heart: The Art of Horace Pippin.* Philadelphia: The Pennsylvania Academy of Fine Arts, 1993.

Stevenson, James. *When I Was Nine.* New York: Greenwillow Books, 1986.

Sullivan, Charles, ed. *Children of Promise: African-American Literature and Art for Young People.* New York: Harry N. Abrams, 1991.

Sullivan, Charles, ed. *Here Is My Kingdom: Hispanic-American Literature and Art for Young People.* New York: Harry N. Abrams, 1994.

Terkel, Studs. *Hard Times.* New York: Pantheon Books, 1970.

Terkel, Studs. *Race: How Blacks and Whites Feel About the Great American Obsession.* New York: Doubleday, 1992.

Terkel, Studs. *Working.* New York: Pantheon Books, 1974.

Watson-Guptill Publications. Various titles in conjunction with different museums.

ADDITIONAL SOURCES FOR BOOKS
FOR ADULT LITERACY STUDENTS

Ohio Literacy Resource Center. *Recommended Trade Books for Adult New Readers.* Http://archon.educ.kent.edu/Oasis/Resc/Trade/index.html
An annotated bibliography, with reading levels and teaching suggestions, of books for new readers.

Rochman, Hazel. *Against Borders: Promoting Books for a Multicultural World.* Chicago: American Library Association, 1993.

Rochman, Hazel. *Tales of Love and Terror: Booktalking the Classics, Old and New.* Chicago: American Library Association, 1987.
Both books offer extensive annotated bibliographies of books for young adults, many of which are also appropriate for adult new readers.

Weibel, Marguerite Crowley. *Choosing and Using Books with Adult New Readers.* New York: Neal-Schuman, 1996.
An annotated bibliography of over 700 books appropriate for use with adult literacy students, along with a discussion about how various types of material can be used in classrooms and tutoring sessions.

Weibel, Marguerite Crowley. *The Library as Literacy Classroom.* Chicago: American Library Association, 1992.

A discussion of the role of the library in promoting literacy and supporting a library-based curriculum for adult new readers.

Weibel, Marguerite Crowley. *Talking about Books for Adult New Readers: A Readers' Advisory Service for Librarians and Teachers.* http://bones.med.ohio-state.edu/staff/mweibel.

An online newsletter containing annotated bibliographies of books for new and developing readers. First two issues titled "Picture Books that Tell Family Stories" and "Picture Books that Discuss History and Social Issues."

Reading the Future of the Public Library

Joyce G. Saricks

SUMMARY. The goal of this article is to underscore the fact that books and reading remain absolutely central to the purpose of the library, no matter what decisions we make about technology, and that providing books remains a service patrons should expect and demand. Unfortunately, many librarians and libraries appear reluctant to acknowledge the interests of fiction readers. The author explores reasons for this phenomenon and acknowledges the growing importance of readers' advisory in the profession. She also addresses ways to promote books and reading, justifications for supporting reading and the concomitant technology that helps us serve patrons and their reading interests better, and validation of the personal pleasure found in what we read and in the service we provide to other readers. *[Article copies available for a fee from The Haworth Document Delivery Service: 1-800-342-9678. E-mail address: <getinfo@haworthpressinc.com> Website: <http://www.haworthpressinc.com>]*

KEYWORDS. Fiction, popular reading, readers' advisory, book groups, electronic communication

Those of us who promote the importance of books in libraries, especially at this time when the profession seems too often to prefer technology to books, are always on the lookout for validation, empirical and statistical. This summer I found both in a single event.

My library is currently involved in a building project that will ultimately almost double our space. Several libraries in our area have built new build-

Joyce G. Saricks is Literature and Audio Services Coordinator, Downers Grove Public Library, 1050 Curtiss, Downers Grove, IL 60515.

[Haworth co-indexing entry note]: "Reading the Future of the Public Library." Saricks, Joyce G. Co-published simultaneously in *The Acquisitions Librarian* (The Haworth Information Press, an imprint of The Haworth Press, Inc.) No. 25, 2001, pp. 113-121; and: *Readers, Reading and Librarians* (ed: Bill Katz) The Haworth Information Press, an imprint of The Haworth Press, Inc., 2001, pp. 113-121. Single or multiple copies of this article are available for a fee from The Haworth Document Delivery Service [1-800-342-9678, 9:00 a.m. - 5:00 p.m. (EST). E-mail address: getinfo@haworthpressinc.com].

ings or remodelled, and they warned us that our circulation and number of visits by users would decrease during the construction. Perhaps that has happened, but more than a year into the building project, we still have not seen a significant drop in overall visits and/or circulation. More interesting, as we prepared for a three-week closing to move into the completed addition, readers reacted dramatically to the fact that *their* library was going to be closed. Even though the checkout period for materials was extended to six weeks to cover the time we were closed, books and librarians would not be immediately available at their library for three whole weeks! (This will seem even more dramatic if you understand that there are at least four other public libraries within a 15-minute drive of my library. Reciprocal borrowing is allowed and reference queries are answered regardless of residence.) Panic is one way to describe the reaction.

We announced the closing three weeks in advance, and I was on desk that first evening. Early on, a fiction reader, one of our regulars, came to me for reading suggestions. Instead of the three to four books she usually requested, she wanted ten. We found her an interesting range of books, and on her way to the circulation desk to check out her hoard, she asked me to pull 20 more titles she would enjoy; she would be in next morning to pick them up. I realized then that we were going to be busy, and all of our resources–mental (for finding enough books for readers) and physical (simply having enough books)–would be stretched. I was right. In those three weeks before our closing, we circulated about 1,400 books just from three book displays near our desk. That means that about 55 books a day that we *selected* for the displays were then checked out by frantic readers. Every day we also personally assisted more than 30 readers in finding titles. By mid-week of the first week, we were beginning to share our patrons' panic. All copies of books by most of our most popular authors had already disappeared from the shelves, including the extra paperbacks we had ordered in anticipation of the demand. (What do you do when there are *no* books by Mary Higgins Clark or Nora Roberts or John Grisham? An exciting challenge indeed!) About 1,000 fiction titles were checked out every day, plus about 110 books on tape, an increase of 50% over the average June fiction circulation. This period presented a real test of the staff's readers' advisory skills!

While the circulation figures are certainly interesting and give evidence of a strong reading community that desperately fears being caught with no books, even more interesting was the reaction of individual readers. "How will I survive during these three weeks?" patrons continually asked us. If there had been any doubt before, it now became really clear to all of us, both readers and staff, just how important to the community the library is, with its access to books and conversation about books and reading. I do not believe my community is an anomaly.

If this is the situation in my library, and thousands of others across the country, how did we get ensnared by this ridiculous dilemma: Books or Computers? Now that surely is a lose/lose proposition if I have ever heard one! This is not, of course, the first time this choice has been posed and the end of the book, forced out by technology, has been forecasted. I am not foolish enough to believe that the format of books might not change. But stories will live on and libraries will continue to be their primary cost-free purveyors. That must remain one of our major roles, no matter what.

All of us can bring forward statistical evidence from our own libraries that supports the importance of fiction, and thus of reading for pleasure. It is encouraging to see that the results of the Harris Poll of leisure activity, released this summer, indicated that 30% of the 1000+ adults polled listed reading as their number one pastime.[1] Television, second by only 3% on the first leisure poll in 1995, now trails by 9%. Equally satisfying are the Gallup Poll findings that showed 66% of adults are library users.[2] But the bottom line for me, and no doubt for all of us, is how the experience of our own libraries tallies with such results.

Polls and personal testimony verify that many readers see reading, books, and libraries as important–and connected. Common knowledge among librarians is that fiction accounts for at least half of all adult book circulation. If that is the case, why are so many librarians reluctant to help readers with fiction questions? Perhaps my outlook is skewed because I have been lucky enough to work in a library that values books and fiction readers; that sees fiction questions as important and provides staff to help fiction readers; that recognizes that most of its adult circulation is related to fiction; and that assigns high priority to these readers and their questions. Not every library feels that way, but more and more do, as is evidenced by the dramatic rise in attendance of fiction-related programs at state and national library conferences, the growing number of librarians subscribing to Fiction_L (a valuable readers' advisory listserv), and the general increase in interest in expanding readers' advisory skills among library staff around the country.

Conversations with librarians have isolated five basic reasons why their libraries do not provide readers' advisory. The first is that readers' advisory queries, questions related to the fiction collection and reading interests, are often seen as impossible questions, questions for which there are no correct or straightforward answers. How can you answer the question "What's a good book?" from any standard reference source? Of course, you cannot. Answering this type of fiction question involves a much more intimate and often time-consuming interview than many staff want to undertake or have time to consider. Those of us who encounter this question daily have developed strategies that allow us to probe reader interests and use both our own reading knowledge and tools (book and electronic) to provide a range of answers. This is an intellectual exercise of a different nature than that routinely undertaken by reference librarians. One aspect that definitely makes readers' advisory interviews different is that there *are* no correct answers to queries relating to readers' interests, and no perfect sources to consult. Luckily the increased interest in and practice of readers' advisory has meant a startling increase in the number of tools available, and often simply consulting one of these reference sources will help put us on the right track, even if it does not answer our immediate question. Still, none of these is the *perfect* source. A lot of what we do in readers' advisory is based on impressions, both of what we think a patron wants and what we think might work. It is intuitive, not precise. There are tools, and there are techniques, but the fact remains that this conversation is a more intimate, personal interaction than a straight reference interview and to do it well we need both practice and nerve.

The second issue for many staff is a lack of training to provide this kind of specialized service. Although it is now increasingly taught in library schools, for years no one learned about readers' advisory in library school, or even had professors who acknowledged that there was more to working with patrons, even in public libraries, than finding answers to factual questions. In the past 15 years there has been a real change in the profession's commitment to training in this growing field. The Public Library Association, especially, has been a leader, with Cluster Workshops, preconferences, and myriad programs at PLA conferences devoted to Readers' Advisory. ALA's RUSA has also formed a readers' advisory committee, which has sponsored successful programs (with around 500 attendees each) at the last three annual conferences and published an annotated guide to readers' advisory resources. Both *Booklist* and *Library Journal* acknowledge the importance of readers advisory in articles, and in *Booklist,* especially, there is a clear commitment from the editor and reviewers to highlight information useful to readers' advisors in its reviews. That training is unavailable is becoming less and less an excuse for failure to provide service, as organizations on national, state and local levels are providing more and more opportunities.

As suggested above, there is also a rumor floating around the library world that fiction is not really important. Certainly not as important as non-fiction. That constitutes the third reason many librarians are reluctant to provide service to fiction readers. There is a feeling among some librarians that fiction is just that frivolous extra libraries think they need to buy. Our circulation figures tell us otherwise. And in this day of easy Internet access in many homes, libraries must reconsider this bias against fiction. More and more of our patrons who were accustomed to asking for information at the library are now surfing the Web–at home and at our libraries. With access to factual information readily available through other channels, fiction collections may be the salvation of public libraries in the 21st century.

Published research into the importance of fiction reading in the lives of adults is increasing, and it complements parallel research on the importance of fiction and fairy tales for children. In his excellent article, "Valuing Fiction,"[3] Duncan Smith addresses this, and he writes in some detail about reading fiction as a creative act and how fiction affects the lives of adult readers. There seems to be a general increase in the number of books that expound the pleasures and importance of reading. Lynne Sharon Schwartz's *Ruined by Reading,*[4] Sven Birkerts' *The Gutenberg Elegies,*[5] and Daniel Pennac's *Better than Life*[6] are among those recently published. Genre research affirms the importance of patterned reading, which satisfies a deep-seated need in adults, similar to that in children who are satisfied by rereading the same story time and time again. More and more, we are discovering that students need not only information on drunk driving, they also need books that either reflect or help them escape the difficult issues they face in their everyday lives. Businessmen need not only stock quotes or information on building sun decks, they need novels to challenge or inspire them or simply to take them away. All of us need books, fiction and/or non-fiction, to help us escape when our world becomes too much.

The Benton Report, featured in the June/July *American Libraries,* confirms this. Its recommendations, especially those that tell us to put *high touch* before *high tech* and to root technology in books and reading, uphold the basic tenets of readers' advisory.[7]

The fourth reason staff give for not helping readers with fiction is that people do not ask for help. We have thoroughly misguided our patrons in systematically training them to believe that anything to do with fiction and leisure reading is not a legitimate question. How many times, even at libraries that offer assistance, do we hear "I don't want to bother you, but I'm going on vacation tomorrow, and I just need something to read." Even after we have helped readers on a regular basis, or they have seen us helping others, the idea that this "really is a frivolous question that I shouldn't bother you with" is deeply ingrained. We may not be able to train patrons to operate our computerized card catalogs successfully, but, alas, we certainly have done a fine job of training them which questions not to ask.

Finally, the biggest deterrent to helping readers with fiction questions, in almost every library, is that there really is not enough time to answer all the questions to the extent we would like to. We never have enough staff on the desk; we never have enough off-desk time to recover and prepare. Unfortunately, it seems always to be the fiction questions that are not answered. I have never yet heard a librarian say they are too busy, and they can no longer answer business or health questions. Yet we seem perfectly comfortable not helping fiction readers, probably because their questions are less straightforward and we are not always prepared to deal with such queries.

In many libraries readers are comfortable asking for help with reading interests. In all libraries, however, there are steps we can take to advertise our willingness to talk about books and help readers make additional selections. Right now the most important and visible library program that promotes reading is the book discussion group. Librarians everywhere, but especially readers' advisory librarians, owe Oprah Winfrey a huge debt of gratitude for promoting reading and book discussion groups. Not that we have not run book discussion groups, very successful ones, for years, but all of us have had readers tell us that Oprah has started them reading again–or for the first time. We are also serving more leaders of book discussion groups, helping them find discussable titles as well as information about their chosen authors and titles in books and magazines and increasingly on the Web.

Author programs, too, are growing in popularity at libraries to promote the link with reading. We readers enjoy hearing authors talk about their works and the creative process, whether they are our favorite authors or new ones we have never read before. And authors usually appreciate the introduction to the library world and readers there.

Reading clubs for adults have also surged in popularity in the last few years. Many of us schedule adult summer reading clubs that run the same dates as those for children at our libraries, and we can encourage the kids to sign their parents up at the same time. Other libraries have extended the concept throughout the year with additional, often seasonal, clubs. Such programming does not require a lot of effort or money, and we have been surprised at the great popularity of reading clubs with adult readers, who seem to read as much for pure satisfaction as to win the prizes.

We also rely heavily on passive readers' advisory promotion techniques. Signs are the most obvious of these, but they are often problematical. Individual librarians may have little say about the signs that direct readers to their collections. Certainly there should be very visible signs that direct patrons, but what and where they are posted are often decisions made by Library Boards and administrators. When we opened in our new addition, the most frequently asked question was, "Where are the Mysteries?" We now have a very large, though temporary, sign directing readers to this popular collection and plans to make collections very visible when we get our permanent signs.

If we want readers to feel comfortable asking for assistance with fiction, it is useful to post signs that advertise this service. Possible suggestions include "Ask here for a good book," or "Not sure what to read, ask here," or as Duncan Smith suggests, a pin that says, "Tell me about a book."[8] Think what a response such a pin might elicit! At our desk, since its creation in 1983, we have posted "Rosenberg's First Law of Reading: Never Apologize for Your Reading Tastes."[9] For us this sets the tone we want to convey and has, in fact, been the start of more than one conversation about books.

Displays are another excellent way to attract readers and to underline that we value reading and books. We have always been careful about the type of displays we mount. We *select* books, rather than filling the displays random-ly. We have never had a display of books with yellow covers, or books from the bottom shelf, or books that have not circulated. These displays only work if there are quality yellow books, or good books from the bottom shelves, or forgotten favorites that never circulate. Readers trust our judgment and ex-pect the books on display to be worth their time. They expect books to be *chosen,* not just any book off the shelves.

Our most popular display is the "Good Books You May Have Missed" truck, a display of 21 titles, known to be "good," and reflecting a range of popular genres and titles. We keep the truck near our desk and fill it continu-ously. Many patrons have told us it is the first or last place they stop when they come to the library for books and that they always find something there. Other libraries have similar displays that cover a range of titles and genres that staff have suggested.

Although they require more time and expertise, annotated booklists and bookmarks are also valuable promotional tools. When we do such an anno-tated list, we always display it with books on the booklist and other similar titles. However, we also have a display unit in which we simply place book-lists and bookmarks created by the department over the years. Our clerk changes the display every week, and patrons love to browse there for reading suggestions as well.

We regularly promote books and reading simply by talking about books among staff at the desk as well as with readers. Whether with friends, fellow staff, or patrons, there is nothing like talking about books to make you want to talk *more* about books. And to *read* more books for that matter. We all have friends with whom we talk frequently, and no conversation is complete until we have discussed what we are reading. There is simply nothing like the joy of sharing a good book. In a library where staff talk about books, patrons will see it is acceptable behavior to talk about books and to ask for reading suggestions as well. This is a technique that snowballs. Browsers overhear us talking about a book with a patron, and when we leave that area, they take the book themselves. Or they feel safe enough to talk with other patrons, usually complete strangers, about books they have enjoyed. The only adverse reper-cussion I have noticed is that patrons and staff members tell me about more wonderful books than I will ever be able to read!

In fact, there is a secret that those of us who work with books and adult readers know, a secret we do not always share with other library staff: work-ing with fiction, talking about books with staff and other readers, is fun. While information may be interesting and challenging, not to mention fun (no one loves a good trivia source as much as I do), reading and sharing books provide a particular pleasure and satisfaction sometimes absent in our work. More and more we need to realize that readers' advisory is not only a service we provide for our patrons, but reading and sharing books is something we should do for ourselves as well. When I do workshops on readers' advisory techniques, I stress this point. I encourage participants to keep a list of every book they read–just a simple notation of author and title in a notebook. Over the years, I have had extensive feedback on the technique and have yet to encounter anyone who has tried it for at least a year and not found it successful. We are always amazed about how much we can remember about books we have read, simply by reviewing the list. Personally, I cannot always remember plots or characters, but I can usually retrieve the particular satisfaction that book gave me, and that sense is what I try to share with other readers. We need to be reminded that it is all right to talk about books, about titles that give pleasure as well as those that raise questions and issues of importance. As readers, all of us have books that have touched us in some way, and whether they are fiction or non-fiction, we can relate to the feeling of satisfaction that patrons tell us they find in really good books. We can be sympathetic to the plea that "I haven't found *anything* good to read lately. Can you help?" We should know, too, that this is as legitimate a question as any reference query we receive. Many librarians simply need to be given permission to share their own pleasure in books and help readers find similar pleasure.

Staff talking about books and helping readers with leisure reading interests help change the atmosphere at our public libraries. Readers overhear us talking about books with other readers, or personally talk with us about their reading interests, and then feel more comfortable asking other questions. A willingness to talk about books, often a more personal conversation, indicates that we can be trusted with other questions as well. When we address patrons' reading interests, we change the way readers perceive the library and its staff. We make our service seem more personal, less anonymous, and we, as library staff, become more approachable and accessible, and thus, better public service staff overall.

It is crucial that the library profession not set up an artificial dichotomy between books and technology. We need to provide both printed and electronic sources for our patrons, to the fullest extent we can. Those of us who love books are not trying to win a battle against technology. We take advantage of that technology in serving patrons with reading interests. However, we do not want information needs to force reading and literature out of our public libraries. And, to survive as libraries and individuals, we do not want the importance of information to overwhelm the satisfactions that derive from reading a good book, whether a classic or best seller or pure escape. In the best of all worlds–and libraries–books and technology will continue to supplement each other.

NOTES

1. "Novels Get the Nod in Leisure Survey," *Chicago Sun Times,* July, 19, 1998, p. 39.

2. *American Libraries,* August, 1998, p. 6.

3. Smith, Duncan, "Valuing Fiction," *Booklist,* March 1, 1998, pp. 1094-95.

4. Schwartz, Lynne Sharon. *Ruined by Reading: A Life in Books.* Boston: Beacon, 1996.

5. Birkerts, Sven. *The Gutenberg Elegies: The Fate of Reading in an Electronic Age.* Boston: Faber, 1994.

6. Pennac, Daniel. *Better than Life.* Toronto: Coach House, 1994.

7. Bales, Susan Nall, "Technology and Tradition: The Future's in the Balance," *American Libraries,* June/July, 1998, pp. 82-86.

8. Smith, p. 1095.

9. Rosenberg, Betty. *Genreflecting: A Guide to Reading Interests in Genre Fiction.* Littleton, CO: Libraries Unlimited, 1982.

Reaching Library Patrons
with Special Services and Materials

Kathleen O. Mayo

SUMMARY. This article covers the services, reading materials, and delivery formats offered by the Lee County (FL) Library System to assist children and adults using its Special Services programs. Bookmobile, Books-by-Mail, Family Literacy, and Talking Books programs reach patrons who have difficulty using a library, yet still want something good to read or view. Staff are attuned to the needs of their patrons for reader's advisory assistance and materials in special formats. Whether it's a descriptive video for a woman with low vision, graphic novels for a reluctant teen reader, or a bilingual picture dictionary for someone learning English, they are all routine requests for Special Services staff. *[Article copies available for a fee from The Haworth Document Delivery Service: 1-800-342-9678. E-mail address: <getinfo@haworthpressinc.com> Website: <http://www.haworthpressinc.com>]*

KEYWORDS. Lee County (FL) Library System, Bookmobile, Books-by-Mail, readers' advisory

---

Kathleen O. Mayo is Head of Special Services, Lee County Library System, 2050 Lee Street, Fort Myers, FL 33901.

The entire Special Services staff contributed to this article: Ann Bradley, Karin McLeish-Delgado, and Chris Nafziger from the Talking Books Library; Literacy Coordinator Donna Rosenheck; Judy Eaton and Nick Rolfe, from the Bookmobile; Dave Wilkinson from Books-by-Mail; and Pat Barrett, who is shared with both Books-by-Mail and the Bookmobile. Although they work at three different locations, they are familiar with each program and often fill in at other sites when there are staff vacancies.

[Haworth co-indexing entry note]: "Reaching Library Patrons with Special Services and Materials." Mayo, Kathleen O. Co-published simultaneously in *The Acquisitions Librarian* (The Haworth Information Press, an imprint of The Haworth Press, Inc.) No. 25, 2001, pp. 123-130; and: *Readers, Reading and Librarians* (ed: Bill Katz) The Haworth Information Press, an imprint of The Haworth Press, Inc., 2001, pp. 123-130. Single or multiple copies of this article are available for a fee from The Haworth Document Delivery Service [1-800-342-9678, 9:00 a.m. - 5:00 p.m. (EST). E-mail address: getinfo@haworthpressinc.com].

The Lee County Library System serves 400,000+ people living on south-west Florida's Gulf coast. A vital part of that operation is the Special Services section that reaches children and adults who have difficulty visiting the system's 11 libraries. Special Services includes the Bookmobile, Books-by-Mail, Family Literacy, and Talking Books, and the additional outreach that they offer through deposit collections and assistive technology. While these people have widely different ages, disabilities, and living conditions, they all want the same thing: something good to read or view.

This article covers Special Services patrons, their reading needs, and the ways that staff try to connect them with library services and materials. This is a group effort that involves more than the nine Special Services staff members. To make outreach efforts successful, they work with the library system's two collection development librarians, the technical services team, and the automation support staff.

BOOKS-BY-MAIL

Books-by-Mail serves over 500 people who are unable to use a library due to temporary or permanent medical and physical disabilities and their care givers. Although primarily elders, patrons include children who are reached through the school system's Homebound and Hospitalized program. The adults are highly motivated readers who miss their regular trips to the library. Many must conserve their limited energy for shopping or doctor visits.

Because they can no longer browse the stacks, staff encourage them to check reviews in newspapers and magazines, offer them customized lists from NoveList and other sources, and send them a quarterly newsletter with annotated listings of recent titles. The newsletter is available in both large print and audio formats. Like most readers their age, they have definite preferences for certain genres and authors.

The program's application features an extensive list of fiction and non-fiction categories which patrons can check to indicate their reading interests. After an initial phone conversation to meet the patron and learn more about their reading, staff enter a reader profile in the patron's record. This is valu-able information for serving those patrons who want help with selecting materials. The Dynix Homebound module keeps a record of all titles that a person has checked out. In addition, patrons rank the books that they return from "1" to "10" and staff enter that information in their record to use when making future selections.

Staff select about half of the titles that they mail out. While most patrons want materials from certain genres and authors, staff are often successful in introducing them to new areas of reading. This is a necessary step when someone has read all the British historical romances with a time travel element or the complete works of Tom Clancy.

Audiocassette books are the most circulated items, followed closely by large print titles. Books-by-Mail fills requests from its own core collection of large print and McNaughton bestsellers. In addition, staff rely heavily on the resources of the regional library where it is located and also place holds on any item in the library system's collection. Staff process a few interlibrary loans each month, but fill most requests locally.

Before the program started in 1993, patrons had to rely on friends and relatives to select their materials. Books-by-Mail gives them back a sense of independence and privacy in library use. Plus, patrons can get as many books as they want as often as they like. This is an advantage for avid readers who might read a book every day.

Books-by-Mail staff also operate Senior Outreach, a deposit collection service with large print titles for persons in residential and day-care facilities. Over 30 facilities participate in this service, checking out 50-100 titles every two to three months. Facility staff encourage their most active readers to participate in Books-by-Mail. In addition, facilities may borrow BiFolkal programming kits to use in their monthly activities. These popular reminiscence kits cover a host of subjects of high interest to elders.

BOOKMOBILE SERVICE

The Lee County Bookmobile operates from the same regional library as Books-by-Mail; the two programs share a staff member and cooperate on many activities. The Bookmobile makes 26 regular stops every two weeks to reach children and adults living in low-income neighborhoods. The majority of their patrons are children who they see after school and in the early evening.

The Bookmobile reaches people from some very different environments: from the RV camp where poor families live in tents and trailers to some large housing projects with mainly African-American children and rural neighborhoods with the children of Spanish-speaking farm workers. They also serve the juvenile residents of a halfway house and a drug addiction program and children at several after-school and day-care programs.

Seventy-five percent of the collection's materials are for children. The youngest ones browse through the board books, picture books, and beginning readers while those in school are often looking for more specific subjects and authors. The insatiable demand for the *Goosebumps* series seems to be waning, but there are always requests for series books. The most sought after non-fiction books are on sports (individual and team biographies), animals (especially big books with lots of photos), drawing, crafts, poetry, cars, jokes, magic, hair styles, martial arts, and military vehicles.

Publishers should note: there is a market for books about young musicians and TV/movie stars. Older children want anything available on rap artists and usually have to find it in magazines like *Fresh* and *Black Beat*. The Bookmobile's collection of books on famous black Americans is not sufficient for kids who want to read about people their own age who they see on TV.

The Bookmobile circulates magazines. Aside from the popular African-American titles, they also see a big demand for sports, racing cars, and highly illustrated magazines like *People*. Their Hispanic patrons seek out *Vanidades* and *Latino* and the Spanish editions of *People* and *Cosmopolitan*. They subscribe to multiple copies of 26 titles and supplement them with Post Office donations of "undeliverable as addressed" items. The staff say they could use four times that many.

Since most of the children are reading below their grade level, staff see a real need for more short chapter books with illustrations. High interest/low reading level titles like the *Bank Street* and *Bailey School Kids* series are very popular. These books have attractive covers, larger print, and enough white space to be inviting to the reluctant reader. Graphic novels are another format that is attractive for these readers. Their colorful illustrations in comic book-style format make them a staple for children and teens.

While school-related requests are in the minority, they do get some students looking for help with homework projects. Since the Bookmobile visits stops every two weeks, that means patrons need to leave with something that day. When the non-fiction collection does not help, staff check the two sets of circulating encyclopedias for information.

While adults are a definite minority, staff are always trying to increase their numbers–especially among parents and grandparents of the young readers. The adult collection includes McNaughton bestsellers, paperback fiction, and the most popular non-fiction areas (cookbooks, poetry, baby care, travel guides, and GED test books). There are also lots of large print titles that they supplement from the Books-by-Mail collection.

The Hispanic children generally speak English once they reach elementary school. They like bilingual books that they can share with other family members. The youngest children enjoy the Spanish editions of the Spot, Clifford, and Arthur books that their parents read to them. Staff have expanded the Spanish offerings for adults as well as holdings on Latin American countries and cultures and ESL texts. They are always looking for more biographies of popular Hispanic personalities like Selena.

Since the Bookmobile holds 3,000 to 3,500 books, they can only fill requests for the most popular titles. Staff encourage patrons to place holds for the books they cannot find and deliver them on their next visit. The first place these patrons check when they come on is the holds shelf where they look to find their name on the pink request slips attached to book spines. Patrons also call the Bookmobile office to request that a book be delivered to their stop.

Bookmobile staff provide deposit collections for adults and juveniles in local correctional facilities. These readers want paperback copies of popular fiction from authors such as King, Koontz, and Goines as well as westerns, poetry, sports biographies, dictionaries, macho action adventures, and mysteries. Juveniles tend to favor science fiction, sports, and love poetry.

FAMILY LITERACY

Among its many activities, the Family Literacy program provides a collection of materials for adult new readers and their tutors at each library and the Bookmobile. These materials, called the READY collection, are used by many groups and individuals: adults working independently to improve their reading and math skills, home schoolers, students and tutors in various literacy programs around the county, and speakers of other languages who are learning English. Many literacy patrons are unable to describe their own needs and have difficulty in using the library. These collections help them locate some of the materials that can help.

At each library, there are READY materials in free-standing, plexiglass shelving units that are both visible and attractive. A staff member at each location is responsible for sharing new materials with staff, requesting replacement items, keeping the collection in good shape, and passing on requests to the Literacy Coordinator. The Literacy Coordinator submits orders for new and replacement items.

The student collection includes materials at all reading levels, including books for people who have no reading skills at all. The focus has been on materials to help improve math and reading skills. Staff purchase from many publishers and curriculums including both the Laubach (New Readers Press) and Literacy Volunteers of America (LVA) programs. There are curriculum series for adults, GED-based items, literature for adult basic education students, and textbooks. While most of the materials are in paperback format, there are also many book/audiocassette combinations and videos.

The English for speakers of other languages (ESOL) materials are used especially by new immigrants, some who are not literate in their native language. The bilingual *Oxford Picture Dictionaries* are an important part of this collection and libraries have them in a dozen languages. The book/audiocassette combinations are especially useful for ESOL students. Staff have recently added the *Crossroads Café* video series to each of the READY collections, along with its printed resource materials. This popular series uses a situation comedy format with "word play" commercials to provide 26 half-hour lessons in language development. Unlike some classroom materials, it can be used effectively in a non-instructional setting.

Tutors can find a range of materials to help them improve their skills. There are books on tutoring techniques and practices, the teacher's editions of various curriculum materials, information on learning disabilities, and reproducible work sheets and lessons.

Providing the READY collection is the library system's way of supporting the literacy efforts of all programs in the community. Staff actively solicit suggestions for new materials from tutors and students and notify local literacy providers about their purchases. Recommended lists from other literacy programs are an important source of selection information as well as conference exhibits and reviews in literacy publications.

TALKING BOOKS LIBRARY

The Talking Books Library reaches over 1,300 adults and children with print disabilities. These patrons have visual or physical disabilities that prevent them from holding books or reading standard print. Although the majority are people in their 70s and 80s, staff serve individuals of all ages. Like the Books-by-Mail program, Talking Books staff see few of their patrons and know most of them through phone calls. They represent a cross-section of the population: a few are well known celebrities, but most resemble a grandparent or co-worker.

Talking books are especially successful for avid readers who want to continue reading books and magazines in spite of their disability. Some patrons can still use large print books but most find them too difficult to read for any extended periods. Although far from high tech, the four-sided talking book cassettes present an obstacle for many people. Staff spend a lot of time in guiding new patrons through the steps of operating a cassette player.

The Talking Books service offers a range of fiction and non-fiction titles in audiocassette format. The National Library Service (NLS) produces about 3,000 titles a year for the program. The library keeps at least one copy of every title produced in the last two years and borrows older titles from the extensive collection at the network's regional library in Daytona Beach. NLS produces books in many languages but few of Lee County's patrons want anything besides English. Staff are starting an outreach program to introduce talking books to eligible Hispanic readers.

Patrons receive *Talking Book Topics,* a bi-monthly publication with annotated listings of the latest recorded books. They also can receive an assortment of subject bibliographies on topics like entertainers, careers, and love stories. Staff ask readers to keep a request list of at least 50 titles so that there will always be new books available to send out when one is returned. When patrons have no one to help with selection, staff often sign them up for "auto select." This option allows the computer to select titles based on an extensive profile of a patron's reading interests. Many readers like this arrangement and feel that they get a more interesting selection of books than when they select themselves.

What do Talking Books patrons read? There are few surprises here. These readers have the same interests as others of similar age and experiences. Some stick to narrow selections of genres and authors while a smaller number like to experiment with new interests. The patron who wants only westerns without Indians narrated by men who sound like John Wayne is extreme, but there are some patrons who test the library's resources with their rigid demands. Women read more than men. They tend to want fiction, especially romances, and enjoy biographies of the stars. One woman insisted that staff send only biographies of her famous friends and acquaintances.

Readers are particular about narrators, often preferring men or women to read certain genres and wanting to exclude narrators with specific traits like British accents or dramatic flair. It is not unusual for a patron to request anything produced by a favorite narrator. Other common exclusions are sex, violence, or strong language. Staff often explain that most of today's novels have some of these elements. Some readers resort to fast forwarding over the rough spots–a process not unlike skimming the printed page.

Since all talking books are unabridged, some titles can be quite lengthy. The library has a few patrons who have trouble reading books that are longer than one or two tapes. Often staff refer patrons who are looking for shorter titles to Books-by-Mail where they can access the library's extensive collection of abridged audiocassettes. Many readers use both services to get the assortment of titles that they want.

In addition to audio materials, Talking Books circulates descriptive videos. These are feature films with voice-over narrations that describe the visual elements of a production: the clothing, setting, and action on the screen. Persons who are blind or have low vision often miss out on the full experience of watching a movie, even when a sighted friend or spouse is trying to describe it. Descriptive video allows people to follow even the most complicated action film by adding well-written narration between the dialogue segments. These are popular with many patrons who missed the full impact of an Indiana Jones movie or had trouble understanding the comic elements of a popular film. The library also owns a number of PBS documentary series in this format.

Talking Books staff are responsible for the library system's assistive technology. These devices increase, maintain, improve, or replace the functional capabilities of individuals with disabilities. Assistive technology makes life easier in working, playing, communicating, and living independently. The library system's devices are available for use in its libraries and for short-term loan to persons who wish to try out this technology in their homes. The primary audience is Lee County's large number of retirees who are trying to remain independent through their later years. Talking Books staff demonstrate and circulate over 120 devices such as talking calculators, book stands, lighted magnifiers, personal listening devices, reachers, and TTYs. The library is a satellite site for the state's network of assistive technology centers.

Although Special Services patrons have interests that are similar to their friends and neighbors, they are unable to use libraries in a traditional way. These programs provide them with a range of accessible library services that offer the resources they want in a usable format.

AUTOMATION

Automation plays an important role in delivering special services. It gives staff the tools to be effective in their jobs and frees them to provide the personal interaction that patrons need. For starters, all staff have direct access to the networked resources of the library system, including the Internet. In addition, these services use some specialized technology applications. Books-by-Mail uses the Dynix Homebound Module to prepare packing lists for orders and to keep reader histories and requests. The library is replacing the Bookmobile's hand-held, computerized data collectors with technology that will put it on-line with the Dynix system. Talking Books will soon have a new automation system to expand the capabilities of that service.

Flow:
The Benefits of Pleasure Reading and Tapping Readers' Interests

Cathleen A. Towey

SUMMARY. Flow is examined, an optimum psychological state that is induced by pleasure reading more then any other reported activity. To reach flow a persons' skill must meet the challenge, there must be clear goals, concentration, control, a loss of time and a temporary loss of self. The type of texts that most often create flow are fiction which is self-selected and on an appropriate skill level for the reader. The author discusses how public librarians can develop active and passive readers' advisory services in libraries to assist adults in selecting high interest books to maximize reading experiences. *[Article copies available for a fee from The Haworth Document Delivery Service: 1-800-342-9678. E-mail address: <getinfo@haworthpressinc.com> Website: <http://www.haworthpressinc.com>]*

KEYWORDS. Popular reading, psychology of reading, fiction readers' advisory

People of all ages come to public libraries to find good stories. In recent surveys, 80% of the patrons who visited their public libraries did so specifically to get a book.[1] A study in *Public Libraries* (Jan./Feb. 1997) showed that 49.9% of the annual circulation in 11 city libraries' circulation was fiction.[2]

Cathleen A. Towey is Director of Adult Services, Port Washington Public Library, One Library Drive, Port Washington, NY 11050.

[Haworth co-indexing entry note]: "Flow: The Benefits of Pleasure Reading and Tapping Readers' Interests." Towey, Cathleen A. Co-published simultaneously in *The Acquisitions Librarian* (The Haworth Information Press, an imprint of The Haworth Press, Inc.) No. 25, 2001, pp. 131-140; and: *Readers, Reading and Librarians* (ed: Bill Katz) The Haworth Information Press, an imprint of The Haworth Press, Inc., 2001, pp. 131-140. Single or multiple copies of this article are available for a fee from The Haworth Document Delivery Service [1-800-342-9678, 9:00 a.m. - 5:00 p.m. (EST). E-mail address: getinfo@haworthpressinc.com].

After the role of providing programs for children, the next most important service that patrons choose for public libraries is purchasing new books and other printed materials.[3]

Finding fiction and nonfiction that reads like narrative are crucial reasons why patrons use public libraries. Yet, library school graduates who go into public library work almost always do so with no course work on adult fiction (or other popular material like videos and audios). Library school courses heavily reflect the importance of fact and information and the tools and skills required to store and access information, but virtually ignore narrative for adults, relegating discussions of fiction to courses for children and young adults. Is there any value in reading for pleasure? What types of materials provide optimum reader satisfaction? If fiction is important, how does a librarian best approach adult fiction and readers' advisory work in a public library setting?

PLEASURE READING AND FLOW

There is a surprising dearth of research on reading for pleasure. Although there seems to be a basic assumption among educated people that pleasure reading is more beneficial than, say, television viewing, do studies prove this true?

In *The Journal of Adolescent & Adult Literacy* (October 1995), research shows that older adults who read for pleasure are rarely lonely.[4] The reason for this may be explained by the concept of "flow." Flow is an optimal psychological state that individuals reach when they are so engrossed in an activity that nothing else matters. Reading for pleasure is the most frequently reported flow activity. In flow, individuals find great satisfaction in an activity regardless of their external circumstances. Mihaly Csikszentmihalyi, author of *Flow: The Psychology of Optimal Experience,* states:

> At the core of the flow experience is enjoyment. For an activity to be truly enjoyable it must have clear goals, permit immediate feedback, require effortless involvement and have a clear chance of completion. A truly enjoyable experience leads to an altered sense of time duration, a sense of control over one's own action, and the emergence of a stronger sense of self.[5]

Flow activities are solitary, self-directed and contribute to a sense of control and well-being. The benefits of reading for pleasure are particularly significant for older people, who may be limited in their circumstances by isolation from friends or family due to death or relocation, poor health or economics. When an elderly homebound woman was asked how she felt about being alone, she pointed to her books and said, "I'm not alone. I have the whole world right here with me."[6]

Flow activities require skill, an investment in mental energy, concentration and a challenge. Flow occurs when the challenge of the task and the skill of the participant are equal. Skills needed for narrative reading include concentration, literacy, an understanding of the rules of written language, the ability to transform words into images, empathy toward characters, and the ability to follow a story line. In its broadest sense, fiction reading demands a manipulation of symbolic information into an understanding of a story. These skills demand mental exertion and create the challenge, the unraveling of a narrative.[7] The absorbed state a reader reaches with an engrossing narrative can be so intense that it can be likened to a trance, thus the expression, "lost in a book."

When a reader reaches a flow state while reading, it is most frequently with a text that has been self-selected. Assigned texts generally do not induce flow unless there was a previous interest in the subject by the reader. Seventy percent of the texts which provided flow were self-selected materials.[8] The one type of assigned text that was mentioned as a flow experience was history texts, "because of the interesting stories."[9] Self-selecting materials does not guarantee that a reader will reach a flow state but it is clear that previous interest in a selection is significant in predicting the success of the reading experience.

In the McQuillan study of the conditions of flow during reading, subjects indicated that the texts that produced flow were most often those on topics or authors in which they had a prior interest (80%); those that readers believed gave them some personal or intellectual benefit (63%); and those on topics where they had some prior knowledge, or where they acquired new information or refreshed some "forgotten" information (59%).[10]

Fiction was named by 69% of the study participants as the type of material that allowed them to reach a flow experience. Pleasure reading is by far the most common type of flow reading. The level of materials that most frequently induced flow were those that were not too difficult for the reader. Texts that are easier for the reader were able to hold their attention successfully; materials that were too challenging and out of the reader's comfort level proved distracting. Readers themselves were the best selectors of their appropriate reading level materials.[11]

The necessity of skill level and challenge being equal may support the value of series reading for adults and children. Because of their familiarity, series books minimize the risks of reading. In self-selecting a series book, interest is established by the reader. Readers are already familiar with the author and the type of stories they write, comfortable with the format and somewhat predictable plot, the range of vocabulary and writing style. Still, each series book, though comfortably familiar and accessible, brings the challenge of finding out what is going to happen this time. Flow is created by the novelty (challenge) of this unique story told in a comfortable reading environment (equaling skill).

A lack of challenge may also result in loss of interest in the writing of a particular author. When an author's work becomes too predictable, the challenge of reading one of his or her books no longer exists. When the challenge is gone, a reader will seek out a new author to regain the full use of abilities required to reach a flow state.

A recent survey of preferences for solitary activities in *American Demographics* (July 1998) showed that for women, only cooking was a more frequent solitary leisure activity than reading books.[12] When they are alone, men spend slightly more time watching TV than reading. Although much leisure time in America is spent in front of the television set, television viewing is not considered a flow activity. The simplistic and repetitive nature of much television programming requires little thought, concentration or challenge. People report low levels of skill, concentration, clear thinking and choice while viewing television.[13]

PASSIVE READERS' ADVISORY

We have established that self-selection is essential in readers reaching a flow state, the optimal state of pleasure and satisfaction during an activity. We've also established the fact that fiction works best in creating flow. How can this information translate into practical applications in a public library environment?

The importance of self-selection is key in developing services to fiction readers. Through Readers' Advisory Services, libraries can passively and actively promote fiction to readers. Passive readers' advisory is the act of grouping, displaying or highlighting books to make them accessible to readers seeking to self-select titles. In the Port Washington Public Library, the majority of the reading patrons first go directly to the new fiction section to choose their own books. Grouping all the new fiction in one place is an effective form of passive readers' advisory. Other examples of passive readers' advisory, such as our "crime/suspense" bookcase, work well here in Port Washington, allowing patrons to self-select within a specific genre. Staff preselects titles in this area, which move so quickly off the shelf that we have difficulty keeping up with demand. This same passive service works well in the genre specific mystery and romance stacks and the genre spine labels we use for items that belong in these sections.

This year, our staff added a book shelf on the counter next to the charge desk as a new form of passive readers' advisory. The placement of this bookcase has been a tremendous success. Just as people waiting at the super-market browse and buy the magazines displayed at the counter, so, too, do our patrons select titles while waiting to charge out books. The small clear plastic unit allows books to face forward and provides an optimum visual display of approximately 15 carefully selected books. The counter display has been particularly useful for promoting titles that patrons have forgotten they wanted, usually recent, very popular books such as *Angela's Ashes, Midnight in the Garden of Good and Evil,* and movie tie-ins like *The Horse Whisperer* or *The Ice Storm.* Patrons already have an interest in these titles. Staff remind them of their interest by putting books out in an obvious place.

The staff also added a literary bulletin board right next to the new fiction section to promote information about books. The bulletin board is used to post book lists initiated by staff or culled from the media, short articles about authors, publishers or literary news and in-house advertisements about book-centered programs being sponsored at the library. Recently posted was the much-discussed 100 best books chosen for the Modern Library. The staff has also developed a bookmark that says "The Staff Suggests" which sticks up above the spine of books they particularly recommend in the new fiction and nonfiction area. We use these bookmarks to highlight strong sleeper titles that we want our readers to be aware of. This enables staff to suggest an individu-al title to a patron, and the user to self-select without the pressure of a librarian standing by. Some library patrons prefer to be left alone in their selection process, enjoying the solitary and serendipitous pursuit of brows-ing. With preselected displays available, staff is making unspoken sugges-tions by what they put out on the shelf. The patron's own interests then take over the selection process.

Passive forms of readers' advisory not only help patrons get to books they may like more quickly, but also establish the library staff as experts in sug-gesting books. For some patrons, grouping and displaying preselected books is a sufficient readers' advisory service. For others, personal one-on-one interaction with a staff person is effective. As Joyce G. Saricks points out in *Readers' Advisory Service in the Public Library,* these staff-patrons interac-tions are ideally "conversations" about books where the staff person sug-gests, not recommends, titles.[14]

Preparing to Suggest

Before a conversation takes place, the librarians' role in the service has to begin by thinking and talking about books on a regular basis. Initially, indi-vidual staff should evaluate their own personal reading patterns and prefer-ences. This will help them understand the type of book they personally enjoy, and engender more sensitivity to patrons' preferences. In the Port Washing-ton Library, a monthly book discussion group has been initiated which helps staff think about, discuss and keep records of what they are reading. Each staff person maintains a journal recording of what she has been reading. During the meetings staff members describe books that they have recently enjoyed. Each person tries to link her choices to other books with similar appeal in order to strengthen skills in connecting a book a patron enjoyed to similar titles they might like. Staff meetings have improved participants' ability to talk to patrons about books and have spun off into more book-based conversations between the staff and with patrons.

The discussion group is large enough that reading interests embrace a number of genres, so participants learn about new books in genres they normally might not read for pleasure. As a result of the group, all of the participants have read outside of their typical preferences, generally at the persistent prodding of a fellow staff member!

Readers' advisory is challenging work. In 1995, 7,605 works of fiction were published.[15] Even if a librarian reads two books of fiction per week, that comes to only 156 books read each year (this doesn't even consider the number of excellent narrative-style nonfiction that serves well in readers' advisory work). Even if they are regular book and review readers, librarians still have to deal with the challenge of connecting a unique reader with a distinctive personal history and interests to a book that they might enjoy.

A good readers' advisor has to have an appreciation of the value of reading for pleasure and a broad understanding of adult fiction. They should read widely, both books and reviews, and retain titles, authors, and an understanding of the unique appeal of specific books, adding new titles regularly to their repertoire as books are published. They should be familiar with readers' advisory tools on-line and in book format. An active readers' advisor has to be an excellent listener when working with a patron, asking questions about reading preferences, thinking quickly and carefully about what the patron is sharing about his or her reading tastes, then suggesting similar titles for the reader, often with other patrons standing at the desk waiting for help.

Patrons consider librarians to be experts on books and that we are knowledgeable about what is good to read. However, because the public believes that we are experts, when staff suggests a title patrons may feel that he or she should take home the book. Patrons need to be given the freedom to reject a title if it doesn't suit their interests. It is essential that when actively interacting with the public, librarians are sensitive and diplomatic and don't judge a patron's reading tastes. Readers' advisory work is an art, not a science, and there is tremendous subjectivity with reading choices. One person's trash is another one's treasure.

ACTIVE READERS' ADVISORY

One of the benefits of readers' advisory services is that they provide an opportunity for the staff to promote books that the public might not find otherwise. Really good works of fiction are rare and ought to be promoted to the public. Staff should be advocates for exceptional fiction. Readers appreciate it when librarians share their discovery of a book that is remarkably well written, original, engrossing, has strong characterization, plot or a distinctive setting.

The Port Washington Library purchases multiple copies of titles that the staff has found to be exceptional and so strong that they satisfy the reading interests of a broad sector of our patrons. A current staff favorite is *Midwives* by Chris Bohjalian. We have purchased extra copies of this book in hardcover and paperbacks to place in our displays and to handsell to patrons when they ask for a really good book. As stated by Thomas Leitch in *Kirkus Review*, May 15, 1998, "One of the primary functions of reviewing . . . is . . . the recommendation of some books as more worthy of readers' time and attention than others."[16] As librarians, we know which books are particularly worth the time, and we should put them in a place where readers can readily access them.

An active readers' advisory interview can be initiated by the patron or the staff person. A patron may approach a desk and ask for "a good book," perhaps for an upcoming vacation or just because they've run out of self-generated ideas for what they want to read next. A patron may be wandering the fiction stacks and be approached by a librarian and asked if they'd like some suggestions. In Sarick's book, the authors suggest "tell me about a book you really enjoyed," as the best query to make of the patron.[17] Careful listening for why the patron liked a book is essentially the next step in the interview.

As a way to start, most pleasure readers can be divided broadly into those who like strong characterization or those who prefer plot-driven books. A good example of a character-driven text is one of my favorite books of 1998, *Starting Out in the Evening* by Brian Morton. This book is written with strong and subtle character development and a palpable New York City setting but nothing earth-shattering happens in the story; there are no murders, kidnappings, or international intrigue. In the narrative, there is a new friendship and family members who are fond of one another. The crisis of the book is an illness. The story is primarily about relationships and most of the action in the narrative is within each character. This type of character-driven story is appealing to the readers who are interested in a subtle, slower paced, thoughtful read. Women are usually more interested in character-driven fiction than men.

Compare this to a fast-paced, action-oriented story like James Lee Burke's latest, *Sunset Limited*. The characters and the setting are quickly drawn and many of the characters are familiar from Burke's previous books. The pace of the story is rapid and readers are swept up immediately into a plot where many things are happening and there is plenty of action. Subtle character development is not essential to readers who prefer his type of narrative. Most important, there have to be lots of events leading to a strong denouement. Men often prefer this kind of story, but some women like them, too.

The first thing to listen for after asking the critical readers' advisory question, "tell me about a book you liked," are comments about character and pace. If a patron says, "it grabbed me right away" or "there was lots of action," your reader is probably a plot person. If they say something like, "well, there's this nice guy who is a disappointment to his parents," they probably prefer character books.

Once a librarian commits to the importance of promoting fiction and begins to practice the skills needed to be a readers' advisor, they will become increasingly aware of patron patterns in reading preferences. The more actively a professional is involved in the process, the more successful they will become in suggesting titles.

THE FUTURE OF FICTION IN PUBLIC LIBRARIES

Through circulation figures and surveys, public library patrons communicate their interest in and passion for fiction. Although more study needs to be done in this area, what research is available indicates that there are psychological benefits in reading for pleasure. Within the profession, there is a strong interest in readers' advisory work. This is indicated by high levels of attendance at recent Readers' Advisory programs sponsored at annual A.L.A. conferences. At graduate library schools of library and information science, understanding and studying fiction and ways to promote reading for pleasure for adults are generally ignored.

Some bias against services to readers may be a result of the element of pleasure in leisure reading. Our puritanical heritage values work (information) as more important than play (reading for pleasure). Has fiction been downplayed in libraries because of a belief that our role as a place for recreation is more frivolous than our role as a place for education or information? Are readers' advisory and fiction taught in library schools to children's and young adult librarians because pleasure reading supports children's education and is, therefore, valuable? Our adult patrons show us what they believe is valuable by their patterns of library use.

Public libraries should actively work on their roles as a place not only where books are stored, but where staff knows about individual books and are anxious to share their knowledge with the public. Independent bookstore staffs have always been skilled in promoting individual titles and understanding readers' preferences. Librarians can learn from independents the skills of how to promote books to the reading public. This personal touch, not the size of the stock or the discounted prices, draws customers to these stores. Libraries, too, can promote the personal service of connecting books with readers in a not-for-profit environment.

As Internet use increases, patrons who own computers will be able to access information at home and may come to the library less for reference services. Public libraries will need to develop and improve services to ensure that patrons continue to visit and support their public libraries. Promoting pleasure reading and readers' advisory services to patrons who crave narrative may be a key service for public libraries in the new millennium.

NOTES

1. Francine Fialkoff. "Readers' Advisory," *Library Journal* (March 15, 1997), 48.

2. Hazel M. Davis and Ellen Altman. *Public Libraries 36* (January/February, 1997), 42.

3. *Buildings, Books and Bytes: Libraries and Communities in the Digital Age* (Washington DC: The Benton Foundation, 1996), 27.

4. Donna Rane-Szostak and Kaye Ann Heath. "Pleasure Reading, Other Activities, and Loneliness in Later Life," *Journal of Adolescent & Adult Literacy* 39:2 (October, 1995), 100.

5. Ibid. 101.

6. Ibid. 100.

7. Mihaly Csikszentmihalyi. *Flow: The Psychology of Optimal Experience* (New York: Harper & Row, 1990), 50.

8. Jeff McQuillan and Gisela Conde. "The Conditions of Flow in Reading: Two Studies in Optimal Experience," *Reading Psychology 17* (April-June, 1996), 119.

9. Ibid. 121.

10. Ibid. 121.

11. Ibid. 128.

12. Editors of Roper Reports. "Solitary Pursuits," *American Demographics* (July, 1998), 34.

13. Csikszentmihalyi, 30.

14. Joyce Saricks and Nancy Brown. *Readers' Advisory Service in the Public Library,* 2nd ed. (Chicago: American Library Association, 1997), 59.

15. *Bowker Annual* (New Jersey: R.R. Bowker, 1998), 522.

16. Thomas Leitch. "What Is Criticism For?" (Part One), *Kirkus Review* (May 15, 1998), 671.

17. Saricks, 70.

BIBLIOGRAPHY

Buildings, Books and Bytes: Libraries and Communities in the Digital Age. Washington DC: Benton Foundation, 1996.

Csikszentmihalyi, Mihaly. *Flow: The Psychology of Optimal Experience.* New York: Harper & Row, 1990.

Fialkoff, Francine. "Reader's Advisory," *Library Journal,* March 15, 1997, p. 48.

Mayes, Walter M. "The Art of Handselling," *Publishers Weekly,* April 14, 1997, pp. 27-29.

McQuillan, Jeff; Conde, Gisela. "The Conditions of Flow in Reading: Two Studies of Optimal Experience," *Reading Psychology,* April-June, 1996, pp. 109-135.

Nell, Victor. *Lost in a Book: The Psychology of Reading for Pleasure.* New Haven: Yale University Press, 1988.

Rane-Szostak, Donna; Heath, Kaye Ann. "Pleasure Reading, Other Activities, and Loneliness in Later Life," *Journal of Adolescent & Adult Literacy,* October, 1995, pp. 100-108.

Ross, Catherine. "Reading the Covers Off Nancy Drew: What Readers Say About Series Books," *Emergency Librarian,* May/June, 1997, pp. 19-23.

Saricks, Joyce G.; Brown, Nancy. *Readers' Advisory Service in the Public Library.* Second edition. Chicago: American Library Association, 1997.

Shearer, Kenneth D., ed. *Guiding the Reader to the Next Book.* New York: Neal Schuman Publishers, Inc., 1996.

Wiegand, Wayne A. "MisReading LIS Education," *Library Journal,* June 15, 1997.

Cues from Conversations:
An Overview of Research
in Children's Response to Literature

Pauletta Brown Bracy

SUMMARY. A descriptive discussion of fifteen research studies in children's response to literature is introduced as insightful information to assist librarians involved in readers' advisory work and reading guidance with children and young adults. Implications of the findings for practice suggest ways that librarians can enhance services in this area. *[Article copies available for a fee from The Haworth Document Delivery Service: 1-800-342-9678. E-mail address: <getinfo@haworthpressinc.com> Website: <http://www.haworthpressinc.com>]*

KEYWORDS. Children's reading, readers' advisory, young adult reading

Pauletta Brown Bracy is Associate Professor, School of Library and Information Sciences, North Carolina Central University, POB 19586, Durham, NC 27707.

[Haworth co-indexing entry note]: "Cues from Conversations: An Overview of Research in Children's Response to Literature." Bracy, Pauletta Brown. Co-published simultaneously in *The Acquisitions Librarian* (The Haworth Information Press, an imprint of The Haworth Press, Inc.) No. 25, 2001, pp. 141-160; and: *Readers, Reading and Librarians* (ed: Bill Katz) The Haworth Information Press, an imprint of The Haworth Press, Inc., 2001, pp. 141-160. Single or multiple copies of this article are available for a fee from The Haworth Document Delivery Service [1-800-342-9678, 9:00 a.m. - 5:00 p.m. (EST). E-mail address: getinfo@haworthpressinc.com].

The readers' advisory transaction is defined as an exchange of information between two people with the purpose of one person suggesting text for the other's later reading (Shearer, 1996). That recommendation is expected to meet a recreational, emotional, psychological or educational need. Most often in children's and young adult services in public libraries and school library media centers, readers' advisory is called reading guidance and requires some familiarity with children's and young adult literature to in part ensure a successful transaction. The library profession has documented and investigated reader's advisory work. An approach in this exploration, which has not received much attention, is response to literature. To gain insight on how children respond to literature could enlighten our profession on how younger patrons articulate their reading experiences. Understanding their expressions could, in turn, assist librarians in facilitating the readers' advisory transaction. Thus, this speculation guided the following descriptive review of research related to children's response to literature.

The fifteen studies address a variety of subjects including developmental levels; contextual environments; literary elements; and ethnic and cultural perspectives. Though mostly set in the classroom, the ethnological and case studies have discernible implications that are presented in the concluding discussion.

The two most prominent and influential theories on this subject are offered by Rosenblatt (1982) and Applebee (1978). Rosenblatt contended that the literary text is a symbolic prelude to a transaction that occurred once the reader and text interacted. The reader bringing experience to this interaction thus places an emphasis on the reader instead of the text. She also defined two kinds of reading: *aesthetic* in which the child includes the personal, the qualitative, kinesthetic, sensuous resonances of the words; and *efferent* in which the child must learn to focus on extracting public meaning from the text. Applebee proposed a developmental scheme in which clarified experiences across age levels are described. A more specific area of interest was how children develop concept of story. Several researchers have advanced research agendas by further exploring the seminal work of these two theorists.

Rosenblatt's transactional theory of literature provided the conceptual framework for a study which analyzed events of students reading and discussing literature with one another and a teacher in a classroom setting. Anzul conducted research in a small K-6 school with two sections at each grade level (1993). As librarian in the school, she directed a literature discussion enrichment program, which met weekly. Throughout a two-year period, fifteen students participated in the program.

To approach the transactional theory, it was necessary to change the behavior of the students. More accustomed to traditional type classroom interactions, students were encouraged to speak directly with one another. Next, they had to become aware of their responses to literature, and finally, to reflect critically on those responses. In moving toward the aesthetic stance, several strategies were devised. First, time for reading either silently or by the researcher from the work of literature featured in the discussions was allowed in class. Another strategy was to include an opportunity for students to write, and sometimes draw. Not all students spoke as fluently as they wrote, and some did not wish to share their personal experiences with a group. Students were urged to be aware of what they were experiencing as they read. Attention was directed back toward the text during the discussions to see what evoked particular responses or what could support a reader's interpretation or predictions. Rereading of texts and future returns to texts were also suggested. The accumulation of literary experiences over time, and resultant growth, was evident as students began to refer spontaneously to books previously read and compare one book with another.

Evidence of aesthetic reading was most discernible in the act of reading whenever time was given for silent reading. A position of relaxation often accompanied the absorption in a story and strong verbal expressions of feeling confirmed involvement in a literary experience. During class discussions, students became more articulate in their explorations of responses in the group. The desire to share responses became a hallmark in the class following creation of trust and openness. Making connections between literature and life situations became increasingly common. As the study progressed, the students were spontaneously achieving higher levels of thinking. In a final phase of exploration, Anzul examined the response to literature within an emotional context. Observations revealed that the most fertile discussions evolved from emotional tensions. Among their characteristics were unwonted fluency, an excitement fueled over ideas being discussed, joy and a sense of play that accompany the proliferation of building ideas, or sudden moments of quiet and withdrawal.

Some positive outcomes were noted. As children learned to take more responsibility for their own discussions, they became more adept at marshalling reasons to explain their interpretations. As membership in the groups became more open, children not considered top readers saw themselves as capable of participating in this activity and they were eventually moved to a higher placement in the classroom. Finally, the value of transactional theory as a framework in which to design educational programs and the power of the experiential nature of aesthetic reading were fully realized.

Holland, Hungerford, and Ernst have noted that the study of children's response to literature is a relatively young area of research and pedagogy, indicating that until 1979 most often the foci were on adolescents and adults (Holland et al., 1993). Hickman's milestone study examined developmental aspects of children's response and thus substantiated the need for further investigation. Her research was pioneering for a number of reasons. She presented children's literature as legitimate literary work and discovered that children respond to literature in their own unique ways. In her ethnographic study, she defined three developmental levels in childhood with characteristic responses distinct to each. She asserted the importance of Rosenblatt's transactional theory for researchers investigating children's response and recognized the importance of the teacher in creating contexts for response among children.

Hickman sought to determine children's response to literature as expressed in classrooms and also ascertain developmental levels within social-instructional contexts (1981). Three multi-age classes designated as grades K-1, 2-3, and 4-5 with a total enrollment of ninety students aged 5-11 years comprised the population. Conducted over a four-month period, the primary means of data collection was observation.

Varied verbal and nonverbal responses were labeled "response events" and categorized accordingly:

Listening behaviors
    Body stances; laughter and applause; exclamation, joining in refrains

Contact with books
    Browsing; showing intensive attention; keeping books at hand

Acting on the impulse to share
    Reading together; sharing discoveries

Oral responses
    Retelling, storytelling; discussion statements; free comments

Actions and drama
    Echoing the action; demonstrating meaning; dramatic play; child-initiated drama; teacher-initiated drama

Making things
    Pictures and related artwork; three-dimensional art and construction; miscellaneous products–games, displays, collections, cookery, etc.

Writing
    Restating and summarizing; writing about literature; using literary models deliberately; using unrecognized models and sources.

In a comparison among age groups, some modes of response were distinctly characteristic. K-1 students were most likely to use their bodies to respond. Children in the 2-3 group were concerned with accomplishing and demonstrating reading skills. In the 4-5 class, the predominant response event was intensive attention to books. Only at this level were children observed to be so engrossed in stories that they were oblivious to their surroundings. Generally, the children's responses reflected their level of thinking and language development. Older children also showed greater facility with language in abstracting a theme statement from a simple story.

Another pattern in comparing age-related responses was what Hickman identified as an erratic progression toward conscious manipulation of modes and strategies for responding. The K-1 group answered questions by retelling a story. The strategy continued among fourth and fifth graders but more summarization than straight retelling was evident. The directive, "Tell me something about the story," was interpreted as a request for a summary.

Probing the variable of manipulative context, Hickman concluded that various responses were permitted, facilitated, or generated by the climate of the school and classroom. Within the environment, a high regard for children's literature was evident and the primary means of reading instruction were wide reading of trade books. Teachers and students shared a positive perception of literature; books were central to the total school experience.

From the same study in a report published later, Hickman focused on the occurrence of spontaneous response, variation in solicited responses, and the implications of nonresponses as related to the classroom teacher's role (Hickman, 1983).

Revisiting the study, the children's experiences with two books of the many read in the original study were examined. Throughout the study, she observed that the books that generated the most talk and varied responses were those that the teacher had made a point of sharing with the group. Several teacher behaviors assumed by the children included practicing the techniques of sharing picture books; reading aloud to nonexistent audiences in the story corner; older children adopting question and answer strategies; and using the teacher's intonation as well as vocabulary. She concluded that teachers influenced both the quantitative and qualitative aspects of the response expressed by children. The role of the teacher proved to be a powerful determinant in children's expressions of response to literature.

Understanding literature as revealed through picture books was the interest of another researcher. Sipe gathered data over a period of seven months in a study in which he observed and engaged first and second graders as they listened to picture storybooks (1998). He was concerned with children's talk before, during, and after the storybook read-alouds to determine what constituted literary understanding for the children and how the teacher scaffolded this understanding. Observational field notes and audiotapes were transcribed for in-depth analysis.

Several conclusions were drawn. First, it is important to let young children talk during storybook reading by the teacher. By allowing children to talk during read-alouds, teachers can assist children in constructing meaning; and, they can also observe how children assist each other in this activity. In the study, two-thirds of the discussion took place during the reading, while one-third took place afterward. Second, discussion about illustration and illustrational style results in a great deal of meaning making by the children, which can be analyzed semeiotically. Sipe suggests that teachers and others look at the ways in which children interpret the illustrations in terms of the text, and the text in terms of the illustrations. Close examination of illustrations is a rich source of understanding, which must be acknowledged and embraced by teachers first. Third, the making of intertextual connections acts as a crucial conceptual pivot, allowing the children to respond by analysis, to take on the role of characters, and to position themselves above the dynamics of the narrative. Teachers can point out connections to other books and praise and probe those made by the children. One of the simplest ways to ensure understanding of this concept is to have children read multiple variants of a single tale. Fourth, some children may have a cluster of typical responses that constitute their signature. With exposure to many books, children may develop individual styles of response quite early. Those who work with children can watch for and encourage children's development of particular interests, realizing that the diversity in response can enrich the social construction in the classroom. Fifth, different texts vary by genre, and openness to differing interpretations may evoke quite different responses. It may be most powerful for children's developing literary understanding if they are exposed to a variety of literary genres, styles, and forms. Children's responses should not be subjected to any type of developmental scale or sequence to clarify literary understanding. Sixth, the teacher is most significant in the construction of meaning for the children as the one most involved in extending or refining a child's response. The key to the teacher's role seemed to be the ability to perceive the rich potential inherent in each child's response and capitalize on it. Last, the insights and perspectives provided by literary criticism of many different types provide new ways of understanding young children's responses during storybook read-alouds, and thus new ways of viewing literary understanding. For example, the researcher recognized "performance response" as an expression of the reader's or listener's aesthetic creativity.

Reading comprehension and response to literature as complementary processes shaped the research design of a study of developmental factors of children's response to realistic fiction and fantasy. Cullinan, Harwood, and Galda (1983) conducted a naturalistic investigation involving eighteen fourth, sixth and eighth grade students and a title of fantasy and one of realistic fiction. After reading books of choice, children were interviewed individually and convened in same-sex groups to discuss the books. The main question was to have them tell about the story. They were also asked what they liked about the story, what made it good or not so good, whether the book or symbol had any special meanings, and whether the book reminded any of them of any other book they had ever read. Protocols for both *stated* (obtained through interviews and in groups) and *revealed* (obtained through observations during discussions) concepts of story were determined and compared for each reader. Comprehension was assessed in six areas.

In *Form*, basis for verifying comprehension was the classification of recall data offered by Applebee (1978). Those categories were Retelling; Synopsis; Analysis; Generalization. Fourth grade readers when recalling the books used synopsis with some retelling. The sixth graders progressed on the developmental scale, one-half of them using synopsis and one-half using summaries. Eighth grade readers began where the sixth grade readers left off, with most of the eighth graders giving summaries, which ended in analysis. It was clear from story recall of all students that comprehension is not just related to understanding of the plot but is also reflected in the form in which a reader retells the work.

In a second area, *Content* of the reader's textual comprehension was determined. Responses were grouped according to literal, interpretive, and evaluative categories. For the realistic fiction, fourth grade readers comprehended at a literal level. Sixth graders also comprehended at a literal level and occasionally at an interpretive level. Eighth graders comprehended the realistic fiction at all levels. Fantasy posed problems for the fourth graders who did not comprehend at even a literal level; the complex plot confused them. They complained of lots of big words in long sentences. All sixth graders comprehended the story at a literal level and some at an interpretive level. They understood the complex ending and symbolic usage. The eighth grader readers comprehended the story at both a literal and interpretive level and were able to make evaluations as to meanings in their own lives.

Metaphorically, fourth graders saw no special meanings in the stories. Sixth graders were tentative, and eighth graders saw numerous possible meanings to the title. *Symbolically,* fourth graders did not remember symbolism and sixth graders saw some symbolism. Eighth graders clearly recognized symbolic meaning and were able to generalize from the story to their own lives and with philosophical perspective.

In *Thematic* comprehension, a question about the most important part of the book was posed. For realistic fiction, fourth graders commented on the theme. Sixth graders identified the same theme but also cited other thematic elements. Eighth graders went further, probing the theme and describing a character's growth in the story. For fantasy, plot was the most important part for the fourth graders. Sixth graders repeated the theme and supplemented discussion with other extended themes. Eighth grade readers also spoke of theme but in more in-depth description. The researchers concluded that by the fourth grade all students have the idea that books are thematic and can try to articulate that theme. The differences across grade levels are apparent in a development of sophistication of those articulated themes.

A final area related to comprehension was *Effects of Evaluation and Expectation on Comprehension*. Fourth graders expected their books to be funny, about true matters, and have happy endings. They enjoyed family stories. As a group they were plot readers and wanted continual action. Sixth graders were aware of what they liked and did not like in a book, but were unable to exactly express what made them like or dislike a book. Eighth grade readers expressed strong and varied preferences in the books. They also expressed how they read and what they expected in literature. For fourth graders, evaluation was based on two points: their ability to comprehend the story and whether they liked the events of the plot. Sixth graders based their evaluations on genre preference. Books found to be complicated were judged mediocre. All eighth grade students reported liking both books and openness to new literary experiences. Their evaluations included discussion of literary techniques such as pacing and imagery. Because student expectations became criteria for evaluation, the researchers resolved that story expectation and preference is an important factor in assessing comprehension.

In conclusion, data confirmed that there are clear developmental levels in children's comprehension of literature. Reader response provides a way to look at the multidimensional nature of comprehension rather than looking at a single aspect of the reader's interpretation of a text.

The distinctions Rosenblatt made between efferent reading and aesthetic reading became the bases of an exploration by Eeds and Well (1989) who wanted to learn what happened when children and adults talked about books they had all read. From this research emerged the approach of "grand conversations" which are primarily child-centered discussions in which participants share personal stories inspired by their reading. Undergraduate reading students who facilitated discussion and maintained journals of their experiences led fifteen study groups of fifth grade students. The emphasized role with the children was to construct meaning rather than to act as all-knowing interpreters of the text. The researchers acted as participant-observers and took extensive field notes.

An in-depth analysis of typescripts of the discussion sessions led researchers to label types of utterances defined as remarks or groups of remarks, which could be reduced to an essence. Utterances were grouped into five categories: *Conversation Maintenance* (comments which began, maintained, and occasionally stopped conversations); *Involvement* (comments which indicated that the text had inspired a personal association); *Literal Comprehension* (literal retellings, references to descriptions and reiterated facts); *Inference* (comments which seemed to have required interpretation, knowledge or implicit meaning or evidence that predictions were being made); and *Evaluation* (four types: *Glo-*

bal–no explanation given; *Categoric*–how the text worked; *Analytic*–reference to a literary element; *Generalization*–analysis of the author's intended message).

Commonalties among the utterances in the kinds of talk in which the children and their leaders engaged were delineated in four characteristic categories. First, each group spent time *constructing simple meaning* where the teacher and students lived the action and then shared their impressions and ideas and problems or difficulties they encountered in constructing meaning. Understanding at simple reading levels appeared to be guided by particular personal histories and experiences brought to the text by the individual readers. Examples of meaning construction ranged from the sharing of disjointed responses to particular aspects of the reading for the day to actual resolution of an agreed-upon meaning where there had been lack of understanding. In all of the groups, the teachers and children worked together to determine meaning.

A second major category of talk was *personal involvement*. Defined as the recounting of personal stories inspired by the reading or discussion, researchers observed that being able to talk about the text in oblique and personal ways seemed to help students develop the personal significance the text had for them. In discussions, students moved from making of meaning to sharing of personal stories.

Actively hypothesizing, interpreting and verifying was labeled *inquiry*. Responses in this category of talk suggested that students were questioning what they were reading in a conscious effort to uncover meaning. In all groups, students were predicting the plot and characters' motivations.

A fourth major category of talk was *critique*. This included talk which addressed the issue of what was liked and why. Although not always articulated, the group members had strong ideas about what they thought was appropriate and what delighted or disappointed them. There were many responses and questions, which indicated that the group participants were valuing and evaluating the text. In all the studies, the children alluded to the elements of literature. They may not have known a particular label for what they were discussing, but the discussions about development of literary elements emerged naturally in the group discussions.

The researchers had observed that children and teachers built meaning by working together. Teachers regularly admitted that they had not thought of a particular interpretation offered by a child. Children within the groups became collaborative rather than competitive. Although all of the groups engaged in all of the behaviors at varying rates, the researchers did not perceive all of the studies to be successful. In one less than successful case, the teacher behavior focused on maintaining the conversation and missed many opportunities for picking up on what the children offered through their comments.

Asserting that three areas of research–reader response, teachers as readers, and the role of discussion in creating meaning–could benefit literacy practice by providing insight into the nature of children's and adults' responses to literature, Lehman and Scharer (1995) designed a research action project which sought to explore similarities and differences between the two response groups. A second purpose was to determine the role of discussion in shaping adults' perceptions about books and their understanding of children's responses.

One hundred twenty-nine adults enrolled in children's literature classes who responded in writing to a book, were encouraged to record their thoughts and feelings during reading and note portions of the book they wished to discuss with their peers during class. They also collected verbal and/or written responses in the forms of conversation, pictures and journals from at least one child in grades 3-8 as the child read or listened to the story. Both sets of responses were shared in large group discussions.

Analysis of the data, which included questionnaire-based reflections, revealed two broad sources of response. The first, reader-based responses, related to personal feelings, values, and preferences, and connections made by the reader to experiences or other reading. Text-based responses constituting the second category were more analytical and/or interpretive in relation to the literary elements and literary structure of the text and the author's style. The categories are delineated below:

Reader-Based
Focus; Identification/feelings; Experience/background; Evaluation

Text-Based
Symbolism; Language; Imagery; Characterization; Plot; Foreshadowing/suspense; Themes; Settings; Point of view; Tone; Writer's craft.

Finally, coding categories were defined to describe differences and similarities in the responses of both groups.

Initial responses by both children and adults were more reader-based than text-based. In reader-based responses, considering focus, adults believed that children tended to take the book at "face value" and read for enjoyment. In contrast, the adults emphasized the literary elements. Children *identified* more with the child characters, sometimes with the characters most near in age to themselves; adults identified with all the characters regardless of age. Children had more limited past experience and knowledge upon which to draw in relating to the book. While adults compared the book to their own lives, they also stated their enjoyment of books that do not reflect their personal experiences. The approach to *evaluation* also provided a contrast. Most children enjoyed the book overall and boys were less enthusiastic than girls. Responses from children revealed personal preferences compared to adults who based the evaluation more on literary criteria.

Only the most salient comparisons of the text-based responses were reported. Most of the children's responses related to the *characters*, particularly their behavior and emotional well-being. Similarly, adults focused on reasons for the character's actions, but also noted how the characters were revealed, e.g., a character's strength; a character perceived as lively and imaginative. A few children were unsure about the ending, expecting a twist in the *plot* and adults noted how the plot tied everything together. Children stated that the *suspense* kept them interested in the story as they discovered clues throughout their reading. Likewise, adults noted foreshadowing. In comments about *theme*, children had little to share. Adults revealed more insight and compared the book with titles of similar themes. Both groups reported that the story "flowed" thus complimenting the *author's craft*.

The second question of this research on the role of discussion in shaping perceptions revealed three insights. First, class discussions were important for adult readers' responses to the book in eliciting more text-based responses. Second, the nature of discussion influenced adults' insights. Third, discussion was important to adults' understanding of children's responses in: recognizing comparisons of both groups' responses; understanding how children at different age levels respond differently; and realizing that individual children respond differently based on unique prior experiences.

The researchers recommend that teachers engage in book discussions with other adults as well as with children. Discussing children's responses with other adults can foster better understanding. Teachers should consider the potential of meaningful discussions, which encourage participants to express thoughts and feelings. As facilitators, teachers can also gain insights from children, which can bring refreshing and broadened perspectives to discussions.

Recognizing aspects of children's response which are neither developmental nor personal, but are instead social, led to the concept of "community of readers" (Hepler and Hickman, 1982). Its most important function is to provide a model set of reader behaviors, which tell children how readers act.

Hepler (1981) described elementary classrooms as social settings, termed "communities of readers" where children established their own information networks. In this dynamic, the children help each other become readers and they are encouraged to talk about their reading in ways that support each other. In a ten-month observation in a combined classroom of fifth and sixth graders in which reading was taught with trade books, she described distinguishing behaviors. Children talked about their reading, using each other to develop their reading abilities. They taught each other how to talk about books, how to pick out important plot elements, how to categorize meanings for themselves. They practiced comprehension skills. In small groups, children had a chance to react to a book in the company of similarly focused readers. As the teacher provided the setting, the children talked their way through the books.

Guice conducted a study to provide a holistic view of readers' responses to literature by considering the routine acts of reading and writing across a language arts period as responses to books (1995). She also sought to gain insight into communities of readers by describing them from the readers' perspective.

Twenty-one children in a sixth grade language arts class were subjects in the study. Data collection was conducted in three phases: analysis of field notes; children's writing, audiotapes of class discussions and information interviews and the coding of data in context files along with interviewing children to explore emerging themes; and finally, validating the analysis through a return classroom visit.

Several characteristics that supported children's responses to books were identified. The children were strongly encouraged to read and write about books; the teacher had high expectations for the children; the teacher loved children's literature and had a varied classroom library; and she planned integrated reading and writing activities from a response-oriented perspective. However, there were instructional factors which appeared to limit the children's responses to books. Students were encouraged to follow all steps of the writing process in linear fashion each time they wrote. Except when holding peer conferences, the children were not allowed to talk among themselves and were often reprimanded for talking. Talk for the sake of selecting topics for writing, for discussing books and authors, for sharing texts, and for sharing process was not condoned.

Despite the rules concerning talking, the children talked constantly and enjoyed events such as reading books in common that promoted a feeling of togetherness and community. Classroom situations were categorized in four contexts: silent reading (brief discussions of characters, plot, shared text passages and opinions about books; discussion about reading progress); book selection (shared titles, interests, opinions, book talks; discussed text length); writing (editing suggestions, role playing, sharing drafts and professionally published texts); and aesthetic activity (shared various artistic products, e.g., artwork). At any given time, during a typical period, children chose how and when they would complete response-based assignments. Hence, all four contexts could occur simultaneously. Thus, contexts were interactional frames transcending blocks of time, rules and assignments. Common across all four contexts were the children's spontaneous, purposeful and supportive responses to books. The results of the study confirmed that the students were highly involved in construction of text meaning across the four contexts. Oral responses were strikingly similar to those reported in previous studies of supportive classrooms as a context for responding to books. The children's context-specific responses to and beyond the texts were spontaneous, natural and supportive and reflected the purposeful nature of children's talk about books. Talk among the children helped to shape both their individual responses and the responses of the community of readers.

The failure of previous empirical research of children's preferences for picture books provided impetus for a pilot study on the reactions of first and second grade children to the genre. In a natural setting, Kiefer (1983) assumed the role of participant-observer in the classroom, recording background data and events by means of descriptive notes, anecdotal records and tape recordings. Daily logs of all behaviors of the children and the teacher were maintained. Written work and photographs of child-centered products were collected as well.

Data were organized in three general categories: variations among children, changes over time, and the context in which responses occurred. Children had many opportunities to choose books through a classroom collection of 400 to 500 books and weekly visits to the school library. They generally experienced books in group reading, partner reading and/or sustained silent reading and exhibited a wide variety of behaviors.

When children talked about books, they used specialized vocabulary such as *technique, media, collage* and described books with creative metaphors or words reflective of their own experiences. When at a loss for words to express abstract qualities of art, children would point to pictures to explain their meaning. For the children, books also engendered detailed discussions with the teacher and their peers. When asked to look at a new book and describe how they look at books, they stated that they looked at the books "carefully," paying particular attention to detail. The majority of children indicated that they look at all of the pictures first and then begin to read. Several behaviors were recorded. The children repeated readings of books usually after one reading. New books were often connected with previously read books. Contact with picture books was reflected in stories later told or written. In three instances, children dramatized the picture books. Response was expressed artistically in murals and individual renderings.

It was noted that children's responses could change over a period of time on an individual basis from a rejection of a book to an enthusiastic response, which influences others' interest in the book.

Context also figured prominently in this study. Characteristically, the classroom was filled with a variety of genres and artistic styles. Children were encouraged to talk about books and share with each other. The teacher who encouraged children to look at picture books believed that she was developing areas of understanding and enhancing critical thinking skills.

The significance of this study is the confirmation of the wide range of behaviors which children exhibit in responding to picture books. Moreover, Kiefer suggests that researchers may gain insights regarding oral language and reading behaviors connected to picture books.

Furthering the investigation about picture books, Day held and read picture books to sixty elementary school children. This was examined as part of a study in which she wanted to determine what schemata children actually brought to the act of reading picture books (1996). She read three recently published books to children in third and fourth grade classrooms at one-week intervals. After listening to the stories, the students met in groups to respond and discuss the pictures. The children were asked what they noticed about the pictures and the stories. Conversations were recorded, transcribed and coded.

Doonan's two categories of *denotation,* responses in which children name pictures as objects and *exemplification* in which responses interpret pictures to function as art objects, served as a starting point for coding the responses. Three other categories were designated: references to artistic techniques; allusions to other literature; and created dialogue for the characters in the pictures. Of the 686 responses analyzed, 41 percent defined the category of denotation; 43 percent, the category of exemplification; 10 percent, artistic technique; and 3 percent each for categories of allusion and construction of dialogue.

Based on the data, Day concluded that the style employed by the author/ artist clearly influences the child's ability to understand and interpret the story. As experience will build schemata to assist understanding of unfamiliar styles, teachers are encouraged to explore styles of art and writing that are challenging to young readers. Children are able to understand that artists and authors use various styles as a means of expressing their ideas to tell stories and such understanding can expand the reader's or viewer's knowledge beyond basic comprehension.

Considering factors that interact to influence reading and response to literature, Galda examined how the interaction between a reader factor–age as reflected by grade–and a text factor–genre–affects evaluative responses (Galda, 1990). Expanding the work of Applebee's data about age differences in evaluation of literature, she explored the movement from the categoric responses of nine year olds (fourth grade) to the analytic responses characteristic of thirteen year olds (ninth graders) by examining responses to novel-length texts of two genres within the context of small group discussions. The following questions were addressed: How do the evaluative responses of fourth through ninth grade children change across time; and how do these responses vary according to genre?

The longitudinal study involved thirty-five children in grades four, six, and eight. Two texts by contemporary authors of books for children of fantasy and realistic fiction were selected for each year of the four-year study. One informal observation per classroom was made to observe the materials and general practices followed by each teacher when reading and discussing literature. Students were then interviewed about their literature curriculum and personal reading histories and concepts of story. Following interviews, subjects were placed in same-sex discussion groups of three and asked to read the texts themselves. The researcher or assistant using open-ended questions led discussions and provided non-directive prompts. All interviews and discussions were audiotaped and transcribed, and coded for evaluative responses according to Applebee's hierarchy. For purposes of this study, three levels comprised the scheme: *categoric* evaluation in which responses are linked to categories with clear attributes; *analytic* evaluation which reflects a concern for mechanics, structure, images, symbols, and ordering the work into categories based on concrete attributes; and *generalization* with emphasis on the work "as the statement of a point of view" (Applebee, 1978).

Analysis revealed that fourth grade readers with a lack of literary vocabulary were unable to generalize when asked to define story. The fifth graders had acquired some vocabulary and were beginning to formulate general definitions of story. Beginning with the sixth graders, the ability continued to develop and with the eighth/ninth grade subjects, the ability to provide abstract and general definitions using literary lexicon was evident. Preferences varied across the grade levels as well. Fourth graders wanted contemporary stories, which were "funny," "exciting," and "interesting." In the fifth grade, the preferences were more eclectic, but similar preferences of the fourth grade group were expressed. In the sixth grade, preferences were split according to gender: the girls were interested in romance novels and the boys were intrigued with science fiction and fantasy. Other comments included desire for adventure, excitement and "fast pace," books that would absorb them and provide escape from the real world. They mentioned identification with the characters, and relationships and escape. In the seventh grade, preference for romance continued among the girls, and boys maintained interest in science fiction and fantasy. There was continued preference in becoming involved with characters and plot. Genre preferences were more specific for eighth grade students who liked historical fiction of the 30s and 40s, and identification with characters was absolutely paramount. The younger readers produced more categoric responses, and the older readers produced more analytic responses with generalization appearing infrequently beginning in the sixth grade.

Tracking the types of responses and examining contextual aspects, the research noted that the movement from heavily categoric responses in the fourth and fifth grades to more analytic responses in the sixth and seventh grades documented the growth of the students as readers of literature.

In terms of reader factors, the types of evaluation changed with age. To clarify this phenomenon, Galda reviewed initial interviews and discussion data. Sixth and seventh grade girls who preferred romance and stated a dislike for science fiction and fantasy consistently responded with categoric evaluation to the fantasy texts, for example: "It's not my type of book . . . " In contrast, the boys who enjoyed science fiction responded analytically.

Regarding definitions of story, the subjects' definitions also revealed differences. While the youngest readers were categoric in their preferences and definitions, the older readers spoke of approaching a variety of literature with an open mind. Interest in characters rather than plot also increased with grade. The evaluations of the younger readers, whether positive or negative, were categoric and linked to their stated preferences. Positive evaluative comments included "adventurous," "exciting," and "interesting" while negative evaluations included "boring" and "a girls' book."

Text factors focused on genre, which played an important part in the response process. Data revealed a difference at the sixth grade level. When reading the more difficult genre of fantasy, the readers relied on their well-developed strategies for categoric responses whereas, when they discussed the easier realistic novels, they practiced their developing analytic strategies. This same pattern was evident in the seventh grade data as well. The majority of readers responded with categoric evaluations to the fantasy novels and analytic evaluations to the realistic novels.

Another developmental study focused on the literary element of theme. Defining theme as "an abstraction that can link stories and ideas in general terms without including specific elements of plot," Lehr's purpose was to characterize the nature of a child's sense of theme in narratives as it develops across three grade levels and also to determine the role of literature in that development (1988).

Sixty kindergarten, second and fourth grade students were chosen for the study. The *Revised Huck Literature Inventory* was administered to assess the children's exposure to children's literature. Children were assigned to groups, and a group of picture books reflecting high quality of text and illustrations and appropriate to the children's cognitive development were selected. The group consisted of three books in each of the genres of realistic fiction and folktales, and within each genre, two books, which shared a common theme, were matched with one that did not. Undergraduate children's literature students were asked to identify the books with shared themes and write about that theme.

The books were read aloud and children were then asked to draw pictures about the stories that they thought had the same theme. Interviews were conducted with each child and contained questions that encouraged the children to consider the stories from the author's perspectives, to compare stories to former book experiences, and to make personal evaluations. Interview transcripts were analyzed for children's ability to generate thematic statements for the books read to them. Their statements were rated for text-congruency and level of abstraction. Each thematic statement was scored on a devised thematic scale.

All of the children attempted to match two books that they perceived as having the same theme. Children at all grade levels were more likely to identify realistic books with shared themes than folktales. Second and fourth graders made the same selections as adults more often than kindergarten children did. Only one child, in second grade, was unable to give any kind of thematic response.

The level of abstraction and ability to summarize revealed some variation in abilities. Some children were unsuccessful in their attempts to link two books with a thematic statement. Some were able to identify concrete similarities between the two stories related by theme, but were unable to abstract and verbalize the theme. Many children offered statements concretely tied to the plot. Most children in all three age groups were able to summarize stories. A number of children, especially at kindergarten age, gave plot summaries rather than theme statements.

Statements that were not congruent with the texts occurred most often with folktales. Compared to realistic fiction, they were more complex, longer, had more events to remember and included more character interactions. Thus, children may have had difficulty with recall or comprehension. Another explanation offered was that realistic fiction is closer to the child's experience whereas themes in folktales are abstract concepts and delivered in unfamiliar settings. Fourth grade children were less likely to include information incongruent with the text than were kindergarten and second grade children.

In comparison to adult responses, the majority of the children's thematic statements differed from any of those offered by adults. The differences were more distinct with kindergarten children than with fourth grade children. The kindergarten children's concerns were more literally connected to the stories than the adult concerns and were stated with absolute values, indicating that they had formed their own perspectives of the stories based on their existing knowledge about how the world functions. Of importance is the notion that although most children's responses were not congruent with adult choices, most were congruent with the text, which suggests that young children process meaning in literature with perspectives that differ from those of adults. Moralistic tones pervaded children's responses, which were stated in absolute terms, with no offered alternatives or choices for characters. Most often, they were stated as admonitions and they were verbalized as those similar to adult warnings typically given to children and were most apparent with folktales.

Children at all three grade levels talked at length about characters and their internal motivations. Discourses revealed obvious linkages to their personal lives. Second and fourth grade children identified with characters and expected them to change whereas kindergarten children did not want to change actions of characters or restructure events. In cases of restructuring, the children's endings to the stories were much more satisfying and predictable.

Cultural and ethnic factors in readers' advisory work and reader response have been documented. Bracy discovered the introduction of variables in those transactions involving children's literature (1996). In a review of reader response literature, Cullinan identified research on culturally diverse populations and literature as an area in need of further investigation (1993). Three studies, which focused in this area, are briefly described.

Smith substantiated the need to connect the literature to reader (1995). She was interested in how three African American students would respond to texts selected by the teacher; the kinds of texts the students self-selected; and how the students would respond to the texts that had themes and illustrations that most closely mirrored their own life experiences and culture. Two of the students were vocal, particularly during shared readings. Often, they participated in the cultural habit of call-and-response behavior. Each of the students most frequently self selected literature and patterned their writing after experiences, events, and texts that culturally mirrored them. The students responded to the texts within a common frame of reference–"their people's story."

Sims (1983) reported on an extensive interview with a ten-year-old African American girl who responded to books about Afro-Americans. In summary, the reader responded positively to experiences which related to her own; distinctly Afro-American cultural experiences; Afro-American female characters with whom she could identify; characters who were strong, active, clever; humorous situations; lyrical language; and aesthetically pleasing illustrations. She responded unfavorably to books she considered boring with easily predictable plots or unrealistic characters; and to events in which black characters are denied human dignity or treated unjustly.

The power of the parental voice was evident in a study of Puerto Rican middle school students' responses to literature (Egan-Robertson, 1993). She discovered the presence of family voices in children's analyses and interpretations of culturally reflective books as the readers constructed meaning of texts. Like the children in the case studies previously cited, Puerto Rican students drew on their collective cultural memories and frames of reference acquired from their own experiences, thus bringing their cultural experiences to the reading process.

This rich body of research has some significant implications for those who actively engage children in their reading pursuits and provides guidance as we assist the children. Adults can influence what children read. It is important to realize our impact when we make recommendations. The sanction of a book by an adult whether librarian or teacher validates the book for the child. During transactions, personal endorsements present opportunities to identify books that meet special needs–an introduction to a new author or genre; a more literately challenging book. Literary understanding can be enriched through picture books; hence knowledge of this genre is imperative especially for recommendations to be shared with young children. Children do have some sophisticated appreciation for artistic style as a means of telling a story. Development preferences for genre and understanding literary elements do exist. Knowledge about them is important, but should be approached with caution. Generalizations about individual children should not be made but that data can be used as guidelines. Children can discuss literature in meaningful ways and appear to flourish in group discussions. Librarians can involve children in these kinds of discussions and learn from group dynamics how children respond to each other. It has been confirmed that they do seek advice from their peers. Children also bring personal experiences to their reading. Gentle, intrusive probing can enlighten the advisor about familiarity sought through reading. There is a value in discussing children's literature with adults. Such discussions can advance adult understanding of children's response to literature. And finally, knowledge of, respect for and sensitivity to cultural and ethnic backgrounds can ensure appropriate matches for all children who look for themselves in the books we share with them.

Inherent in these suggestions is motivation to read which can serve as a framework for readers' advisory services. A survey (1994) of third and fifth grade students in a year-long study to ascertain what motivates them to read revealed several factors that influence their behavior: their classroom libraries are book-rich; they receive books as gifts; they choose their own books; they have some prior experience; they read series books; and they talk about books with others. This understanding of what motivates the children to read underscores the findings of the research on response to literature and reiterates our professional responsibility in serving the children's needs in reading guidance.

REFERENCES

Anzul, M. (1993). Exploring literature with children within a transactional framework. In K.E. Holland, R.A. Hungerford, & S.B. Ernst (Eds.), *Journeying: Children responding to literature* (pp. 187-203). Portsmouth, NH: Heinemann.

Applebee, A.N. (1978). *The child's concept of story.* Chicago: University of Chicago.

Bracy, P.B. (1996). The nature of the readers' advisory transaction in children's and young adult reading. In K.D. Shearer (Ed.), *Guiding the reader to the next book* (pp. 21-43). New York: Neal-Schuman.

Cullinan, B.E. (1993). Commentary on research: Response to literature. In K.E. Holland, R.A. Hungerford, & S.B. Ernst (Eds.), *Journeying: Children responding to literature* (pp. 317-322). Portsmouth, NH: Heinemann.

Cullinan, B.E., Harwood, K.T., & Galda, L. (1983). The reader and the story: Comprehension and response. *Journal of Research and Development in Education, 16* (3), 30-38.

Day, K.S. (1996). The challenge of style in reading picture books. *Children's Literature in Education, 27* (3), 153-166.

Eeds, M., & Wells, D. (1989). Grand conversations: An exploration of meaning construction in literature study groups. *Research in the Teaching of English, 23* (1), 4-29.

Egan-Robertson, A. (1993). Puerto Rican students respond to children's books with Puerto Rican themes. In K.E. Holland, R.A. Hungerford, & S.B. Ernst (Eds.), *Journeying: Children responding to literature* (pp. 204-218). Portsmouth, NH: Heinemann.

Galda, L. (1990). A longitudinal study of the spectator stance as a function of age and genre. *Research in the Teaching of English, 24* (3), 261-278.

Guice, S.L. (1995). Creating communities of readers: A study of children's information networks as multiple contexts for responding to texts. *Journal of Reading Behavior, 27* (3), 379-397.

Hepler, S. (1991). Talking our way to literacy in the classroom community. *The New Advocate, 4* (3), 179-191.

Hepler, S.I., & Hickman, J. (1982). "The book was okay. I love you": Social aspects of response to literature. *Theory into Practice, 21* (4), 278-283.

Hickman, J. (1981). A new perspective on response to literature: Research in an elementary school setting. *Research in the Teaching of English, 15* (4), 343-354.

Hickman, J. (1983). Everything considered: Response to literature in an elementary school setting. *Journal of Research and Development in Education, 16* (3), 8-13.

Holland, K.E., Hungerford, R.A., & Ernst, S.B. Introduction: Mapping the journey. In K.E. Holland, R.A. Hungerford, & S.B. Ernst (Eds.), *Journeying: Children responding to literature* (pp. 1-5). Portsmouth, NH: Heinemann.

Keifer, B. (1983). The responses of children in a combination first/second grade classroom to picture books in a variety of artistic styles. *Journal of Research and Development in Education, 16* (3), 14-20.

Koskinen, P.S., Palmer, B.M., & Codling, R.M. (1994). In their own words: What elementary students have to say about motivation to read. *Reading Teacher, 48* (2), 176-178.

Lehman, B.A., & Scharer, P.L. (1995-1996). Teachers' perspectives on response comparisons when children and adults read children's literature. *Reading Research and Instruction, 35* (2), 142-152.

Lehr, S. (1988). The child's developing sense of theme as a response to literature. *Reading Research Quarterly, 23* (3), 337-357.

Rosenblatt, L.M. (1982). The literary transaction: Evocation and response. *Theory into Practice 21* (4), 268-277.

Shearer, K.D. (1996). The nature of the readers' advisory transaction in adult reading. In K.D. Shearer (Ed.), *Guiding the reader to the next book* (pp. 1-20). New York: Neal-Schuman.

Sims, R. (1983). Strong black girls: A ten-year-old responds to fiction about Afro-Americans. *Journal of Research and Development in Education, 16* (3), 21-28.

Sipe, L.R. (1998). First- and second-grade literary critics: Understanding children's rich responses to literature. In T.E. Raphel & K. Au (Eds.), *Literature-based instruction: Reshaping the curriculum* (pp. 39-69). Norwood, MA: Christopher-Gordon.

Smith, E.B. (1995). Anchored in our literature: Students responding to African-American literature. *Language Arts, 72* (8), 571-574.

"The Heart's Field":
Landscapes of Children's Literature

Anne Lundin

SUMMARY. "The heart's field" is Eudora Welty's image for the meaning of place in fiction. Anne Lundin muses on the storied landscape of literature, particularly the geography of her favorite books of childhood. The essay invites the reader to reflect on the places of childhood and their connection to our own stories as well as fiction. Landscape is viewed as always dual: the one outside the self, the other within. Places are linked intertextually as the product of identity, ideology, narrative tradition, and the imagination. Children's books are the site of adult re-creation of an earlier geography. Some of the works discussed include folktales, *Alice in Wonderland, The Wizard of Oz,* The Laura Ingalls Wilder series, Beatrix Potter's Hill Top and Lake Country, *Wind in the Willows, The Secret Garden,* and *Charlotte's Web.* In an age when many despair the fate of the book or library, the power of place remains as the text of a book enters the text of a life. *[Article copies available for a fee from The Haworth Document Delivery Service: 1-800-342-9678. E-mail address: <getinfo@haworthpressinc.com> Website: <http://www.haworthpressinc.com>]*

KEYWORDS. Eudora Welty, fiction, children's reading, future of the book

The image of "the heart's field" is from Eudora Welty, who writes in her essay "Place in Fiction" that "Location is the proving ground of 'what

---

Anne Lundin is Assistant Professor, School of Library and Information Studies, The University of Wisconsin-Madison.

[Haworth co-indexing entry note]: "'The Heart's Field': Landscapes of Children's Literature." Lundin, Anne. Co-published simultaneously in *The Acquisitions Librarian* (The Haworth Information Press, an imprint of The Haworth Press, Inc.) No. 25, 2001, pp. 161-176; and: *Readers, Reading and Librarians* (ed: Bill Katz) The Haworth Information Press, an imprint of The Haworth Press, Inc., 2001, pp. 161-176. Single or multiple copies of this article are available for a fee from The Haworth Document Delivery Service [1-800-342-9678, 9:00 a.m. - 5:00 p.m. (EST). E-mail address: getinfo@haworthpressinc.com].

happened? who's here? who's coming'–that is the heart's field" (118). Fiction depends on place for the simple truth that feelings are bound up in the land, in homeland, that most contested real estate. Environments imprint themselves on our physicality and spirit, and we respond in war and peace, young and old.

I am struck by the meanings of places I have known, houses where I have lived, locales that continue to form my own sense of inner and outer reality. The vacant lot on the corner of Castleman Street in Pittsburgh where I romped at will with the street kids on our pirate isle, the earth under our nails. The summer place at Lake Chautauqua, New York, which was my own Victoriana preserve and my first experience of perfect freedom. My grandparent's stucco house strewn with ivy in the idyllic village of Mendham, New Jersey, which was where I always wanted to live, and which I try to re-create in a symbolic way every place I live. The speckled islands off the coast of Penebscot Bay, Maine, which recall for me a line from the poet Yeats who said that for each of us there is an image that if we were but to know it, it could direct our lives. The Cornish coast where I have walked, its Northern reaches of black headlands and stormy sea reminiscent of Maine, the softer Southern edges whose cliffs are steep meadows speckled in heather and golden gorse. Is it piney woods or piney islands in the sea, or perhaps, in the words of the wandering Odysseus, "the honey lights of home"? Landscapes are personal for they answer the basic questions–who we are, where we came from, and where we are going. Landscapes are also cultural myths of sense-making that exist at a deep, unconscious layer.

Think of the places of your childhood. The paths you walked in the woods and found remnants of bird nests. An old swimming hole that smelled like leaves. A pier where you caught fish with your brother, or the dock where you sat in the summer–on one of those limitless blue afternoons–to have your picture taken in the new tank suit. The July night camping out in a pup tent and gazing at the vista of an endless sky of stars. Or open, rolling fields of wildflowers now crowded with new developments, euphemistically called "Devonshire" or "Canterbury Hills." The pastoral idyll just in the far horizon of memory, twenty, thirty, or more years back.

The landscape contains our stories, and we find a passionate attachment to the places of childhood, real and imagined, what Eleanor Cameron calls "the country of the mind." Readers take pilgrimages to fabled birthplaces and literary homes of favorite authors, hoping to capture in Stratford or Hilltop Farm an aura or shadow of the author's muse. Writers often return to their own vanished worlds, looking for remains or re-creations. We recall Thomas Hardy's Wessex or William Faulkner's Yoknapatawpha County, Mississippi, which he called his "own postage stamp of native soil," now forever part of the American myth of the New South. To writer Virginia Woolf, the coastal landscape of Cornwall became the setting for her novel, *To the Lighthouse*.

Twain's riverboat days on what he described as "the great Mississippi, the magnificent Mississippi, rolling its mile-wide tide along"–became not only his preferred narrative settings but also his name, his pseudonym the old river term, a lead-man's call, meaning safe water. Or Kenneth Grahame's revered Thames country, Cookham Dene in Berkshire. Hans Christian Andersen's Denmark, where his fairy tales evoke the meadows and canals and waysides of his own land. Heidi's Alps. Lucy Boston's manor house at Hemingford Grey whose gabled, towering walls became transformed timelessly. Frances Hodgson Burnett's garden. Maurice Sendak's dreamscape, Robinson Crusoe's vision. Russell Hoban's notion of territory. Eric Carle's creaturely skyscape. Ezra Jack Keats's Brooklyn with its snowy days and billboard art.

Literature itself is a kind of atlas, an imaginative map of the universe, a guide book. Culturally, we read the landscape, romance our remembrances at holidays, and even attempt to make our technology familial with words like "home pages" and "visiting sites." I think the attraction of landscape is its rhythms–an ebb and flow that, as Margaret Drabble writes, "represents at once the changing and the unchanging" (8). In Annie Dillard's *Pilgrim at Tinker Creek,* she sees the yearning for landscape to be just this: "to explore neighborhood, view the landscape, and discover at least *where* it is that we have been so startlingly set down, if we can't learn why" (12).

You may wonder how I am using the term 'landscape." It is just as uncertain and elusive a term as "text" or "literature," or, surely, "children's literature." Like Proteus, it can take a number of shapes, making its central features and continuity difficult to recognize. The concept of landscape is a bit of a mystery drawn from various sources, a complex, multilayered palimpsest of geography, history, and myth. There is a sense of extension and depth, spatial and temporal. The word originated at the end of the sixteenth century from "landschaft," which meant a way to organize space and a place for habitation. The word "scenery" is even more recent, dating from the late eighteenth century. "Topography" means the writing of a place. The words we used to describe locale are continually interpreted, as writers, painters, historians, archaeologists, and geologists have demonstrated. To poet and naturalist writer Annie Dillard, the essence of landscape is "the texture of intricacy," in which the texture allows for "a beauty inexhaustible in its complexity" (142). The landscape historian, J. B. Jackson, who was perhaps the first, in the early 1950s, to use the phrase "to read a landscape," defines it as "a concrete, three-dimensional, shared reality" (5). The emphasis, for me, is the phrase "shared reality," a conjoined existence in a topsy-turvy universe. Our landscapes are, as Barry Lopez reminds us, always dual: the one outside the self, the other within. The external landscape is the one we see–the topology of the land as well as its natural inhabitants, the weather, seasons, and evolution all about. The second landscape is interior–a projection within a person of a part of the exterior landscape–in Welty's words, "the heart's field." Our patterns of thought are influenced by the patterns of nature in the particular place we inhabit. The poet William Stafford writes that "all events and experiences are local, somewhere. And all human enhancements of events and experiences–all the arts–are regional in the sense that they derive from immediate relation to felt life" (92).

Geographers suggest that this "human enhancement" of place is cultural, a network of patterns and templates through which we make sense of our experience. Landscape is socially constructed, a concept predicated on the values and ideals of its own time. We envision natural and domesticated structures in terms of cultural values relating to our very model of society itself. Historian J. B. Jackson speculates that the typical farm scene–with its barn, shed, outbuildings, and nearby town–is symbolic of a parent surrounded by offspring (Meinig, 228). The British geographer Denis Cosgrove sees the idea of landscape not only as "a way of seeing" but as a profoundly ideological concept that reveals the way classes portray themselves and their world through an imagined relationship with nature. Some have begun to refer to the "biography" of a landscape or use the metaphor of the landscape as a text, as a book. Anthropologist Clifford Geertz has long advocated looking at culture as text. To him, culture is something that is "read" as one might read written material. The use of the term "to read a landscape" reinforces the connections between landscape and literature.

Associated with the concept "text" is intertextuality, the textual context of a literary work. Originating in literary criticism, the term has stirred interest among historians, anthropologists, and cultural geographers. I teach my children's literature course in terms of intertextuality: the way texts draw upon other texts, that themselves are based on yet different texts, and so on. Umberto Eco perhaps best describes it in his extraordinary novel, *The Name of the Rose,* when Brother William suggests the conversations that take place in a medieval library, where "books speak of other books," and the narrator Also recognizes the library as "the place of a long, centuries-old murmuring, an imperceptible dialogue between one parchment and another, a living thing, a receptacle of powers not to be ruled by a human mind, a treasure of secrets emanated by many minds, surviving the death of those who had produced them or had been their conveyors" (286).

I want to suggest that books not only speak of other books as a common landscape, but of other places, lived, remembered, read, re-created. We see these places through our earliest vision of them, shaped by our minds which are continually sketching, illustrating, filling in the gaps. J. R. R. Tolkien suggests this power when he writes,

> If a story says "he climbed a hill and saw a river in the valley below,"
> the illustrator may catch, or nearly catch, his own vision of such a
> scene, but every hearer of the words will have his own picture, and it

will be made out of all the hills and rivers and dales he has ever seen but specially out of The Hill, The River, The Valley which were for him the first embodiment of the word. (80)

Landscape, then, may be the construction of stories that we tell ourselves about ourselves, which arise from frameworks of national identity, ideology, narrative tradition, and the imagination.

Landscapes remembered from childhood are continually re-made in literature as well as in our lives. This is essentially Romanticism: the idea that childhood is the foundation of later human experience. The poet reaches back into childhood spent in a particular landscape in a quest for the wholeness of the self. William Blake evokes the magical purity of childhood perception, where children live without labeling or dividing the world into abstract categories and thus feel a natural kinship with all that they behold. William Wordsworth writes in *Ode: Intimations of Immortality*: "So was it when my life began./ So it is now I am a man./ So be it when I grow old./ Or let me die!" "So was, So is, So be–past, present, and future." These are not always sanguine possibilities. John Clare suffered from the loss of the familiars in his own beloved Northamptonshire countryside, where his family had farmed for generations, now in the eighteenth century transforming common open fields into private holdings. Clare poignant-ly speaks of every exile when he writes, "I've left mine own old home of homes/Green fields and every pleasant place." The Romantics straddle these kind of contraries of place, this uprooted land. In Blakean terms, we carry the vision of Innocence forward into the years of Experience.

Our first landscapes remain a prism through which actual landscapes are and will be viewed. Piaget's developmental studies confirm the creativity of children in making intentional worlds that help to confront meaninglessness and chaos. Edith Cobb's *The Ecology of the Imagination in Childhood* is a classic study of a child's innate connection with the natural world. Imagina-tion is the ecological field that connects outer and inner worlds. This ani-mated, dynamic, and interactive universe is captured in the words of Walt Whitman's "Leaves of Grass":

There was a child went forth everyday
And the first object he looked upon, he became,
And that object became part of him for the day or a certain part
of the day,
Or for many years or stretching cycles of years.
The early lilacs became part of this child,
And grass and white and red morning glories, and white and
red clover, and the song of the phoebe-bird,
And the Third-month lambs and the sow's pink-faint litter, and
the mare's foal and the cow's calf.

And not only a light and airy Spring appealed, but also "the noisy brood of the barnyard" and "the mire by the roadside." This is the geography the child wishes to explore–that of life itself, its spacious country of hills and vales and the spaces between.

Children's books are the site of adult re-creation of an earlier geography. The locales of many children's books are the enshrouded landscapes of childhood, re-made, re-visioned. The backward glance is borne by the surety that what "I was" is part of what "I am." Such nostalgia thrives in moments of transition, in which the gaps and slippages quicken a longing for continuity. Novelist and historian Gillian Avery writes a brief remembrance of being eight years old and including in her birthday card for her mother, along with her usual threepenny bunch of violets, a most unusual two lines from a favorite childhood hymn, "Time, like an ever-rolling stream, bears all its sons away" (words written by Isaac Watts, noted Puritan hymnist and juvenile poet) which suggests, to me, that these thoughts are not confined to jaded adults. The author as traveler holds memories of the past while, paradoxically, knows the past is gone. The tension is centrifugal–outgoing, away–as well as centripetal, indwelling, homebound. Such utopian as well as nostalgic tension makes children's books a site for the confluence of time and place, which Virginia Hamilton calls "hopescape." Books are tethered to physical places in which we are where we lived, and we are what we have read. A story maps roads traveled and less traveled, and landscape reveals, in every sense of the word, a "point of view."

I would like to explore this broad topography through a glance at just a few of the children's books, mostly from the Victorian and Edwardian period, whose landscapes strike me, shape me, intertextually. I surveyed a vast panorama of titles in which the locales or wilderness, rural and urban, are evocative, indeed essential, in the co-mingled genres of folklore, fiction, and memoir. I winnowed down the sites to but a few titles with brief commentary, just a sampling to stir the imagination about the place of place in our lives and in the books we read, write, and share with children–in William Blake's words "the Echoing Green." So many of the titles openly proclaim *place:* the Emerald City of Oz, a garden, a land where wild things are (not just the wild things), a house on the prairies, a river chattering stories, as well as the other designations that come to mind suggesting a willowed wonderland, the Wild Woods, or even Neverland. My concern is with the ideas of space, or place, that ground these works intertextually in the mapping of a literary landscape of childhood.

I begin with the fairy tale, whose wilderness haunts our dreams, our psyche, our shadow selves, in Jungian terms, or, in Joseph Campbell's mythic words, "the primer of the picture-language of the soul." Joyce Thomas, in an early article in *Children's Literature in Education* and reprinted in the latest edition of the anthology *Only Connect*, considers the setting of stories we take for granted as the grounding of other narrative fiction. In her piece, "Woods and Castles, Towers and Huts," Thomas discusses the heightened significance of setting in providing the atmosphere for a tale's action and theme, which is often a dialectic between matter and magic, internal and tangible. The forest is a threshold to the supernatural, a separate peace between humanity and nature, an enchanted place where words cast spells, children once lost become found, and identities of worldly power are blurred. This is the perilous faerie realm. The castle, a bastion of material mass, is impervious to the animations within, while, at the same time, creating its own exotic enchantment. The tower, as a small part of the whole, is akin to the attic in its associations (I am reminded here of Gilbert and Gubar's Victorian study, *The Madwoman in the Attic*). The tower, like a trunk, suggests treasures waiting to be found; the tower, as a symbolic construct of vertical space, rises rather unnaturally in the landscape as focus and locus. The hut, however, stands alone, a different kind of life, more akin to nature than not. Thomas suggests that these points are much more than occupied space but teach about the uses of setting, the importance of place. She writes, "We flutter away from one landscape to another, changing locales like disoriented migratory fowl, yet whenever, wherever, we temporarily settle, we reconstruct our personal nests, delimiting a tiny patch of earth or woods for our own castle, tower, hut" (128). Who is not such a homesteader? For particularity, in a tale like Cinderella, we have the cemetery, the garden, the hearth, the palace–all resonant of nestlike settings that confine and liberate. This is the wisdom of folklore, the message taken to heart by writers as diverse as Lewis Carroll, Kenneth Grahame, Rudyard Kipling, L. Frank Baum, Beatrix Potter, J. M. Barrie, and so many other architects of children's native land and Neverland.

In fiction, these well-worn threads and bits of straw are transformed, spun into gold. While the role of landscape in fiction is larger than the square-foot of any writing, I wish to explore a few such places, ways of seeing. Several texts come to mind related to faerie: Lewis Carroll's *Alice in Wonderland* and its American kin, L. Frank Baum's *The Wizard of Oz*. Both reflect a surrealistic setting that fits. Carroll's original title–"Alice Among the Elves"–suggests his own recognition of that connection: that a small child is sent out into a magical world. Alice's world, as in so much folklore, is a place to visit but not to live. While she is there, she wonders if she will ever experience a natural life again, which to her means an ordered and civilized world. Clearly, she feels distant from the setting of the garden, which is an artificial one at that. The story begins with a riverbank setting, a pastoral picnic, but one where the protagonist tires of such reverie, is put off by books without pictures or conversations, and wanders off, in a true folkloric way, on to adventure, away from home. As Carroll describes in his introductory verse:

> The dream-child moving through a land
> Of wonders wild and new,
> In friendly chat with bird or beast,
> And half believe it true.

This dream child wanders, however, without a map, without guidance or formula. What is left is the sheer grit of a heroine determined to make sense without social, spatial, temporal, or moral structure. While folkloric backgrounds are often as threatening, Alice's adventures are unique in her control of the environment, in the sense of entrance and exit. The real setting she faces is anthropomorphic, what has been described as "a post-Darwinian tent." John Fowles's suggestion in *The French Lieutenant's Woman* that *Dr. Jekyll and Mr. Hyde* is a psychological guidebook to Victorian literature seems to apply here to Alice's quest to understand "self" and the "other."

L. Frank Baum's *The Wizard of Oz* is meant to be an American Alice, with less excess. As Baum writes in his Introduction, this story will be "a modernized fairy tale, in which the wonderment and joy are retained and the heartaches and nightmares are left out." Whether this intention is realized is problematic. But the landscape is clearly the most distinctive aspect of the story. Readers clamor for stories about Oz, not about Dorothy as such. And the yellow brick road to the Emerald City is just as real as any map and destination. And this destination is just as elusive as Alice's garden, both quests, but Dorothy and her friends are in search of the Wizard and the American Dream. This dream, as Mary McCarthy notes in *The Stones of Florence,* is not the typical quest for treasure, which seemed close enough to most American readers, but, rather, for courage, knowledge, heart, adventure, or, simply, home.

Home is the abiding landscape in the tale, and this is no pastoral. Kansas is described as:

> a great grey prairie on every side. Not a tree nor a house broke the broad sweep of flat country that reached the edge of the sky in all directions. The sun had baked the plowed land into a gray mass, with little cracks running through it. Even the grass was not green, for the sun had burned the tops of the long blades until they were the same gray color as to be seen everywhere. Once the house had been painted, but the sun blistered the paint and the rains washed it away, and now the house was as dull and gray as everything else. (10)

From this poor dirt farm, Dorothy moves to a land of milk and honey, a world ripe with fruit, flowers, birds, and streams, what is described as "the Garden of the World set in the midst of the Great American Desert" (Attebury, 281). One critic has described Oz as "a kind of secular paradise . . . an Eden before the fall, and that this, in turn, is a mirror of the American dream as an unspoiled land of opportunity" (Bracewell, 18). America writ at large becomes the landscape of Oz, a life promising more than a fairy tale because here no magical solutions are required, just an endless plain of possibilities.

Other books that struggle with the representation of the prairies–as fantasy and reality–are the Laura Ingalls Wilder series, Pam Conrad's *Prairie Songs,* and Patricia MacLachlan's *Sarah, Plain and Tall.* "The Little House" series begins with the suggestion of fairy tale: "Once upon a time, sixty years ago, a little girl lived in the Big Woods of Wisconsin, in a little gray house made of logs," and the series closes with her entering a little gray house on the prairie, which she describes as "so wide and sweet and clear." In *Prairie Songs,* the story begins with a different image:

> The prairie was like a giant plate, stretching all the way to the sky at the edges. And we were like two tiny peas left over from dinner, Lester and me. We couldn't even see the soddy from out there–just nothing, nothing in a big circle all around us.

Sarah, Plain and Tall turns on the conflict between two symbolic and very real landscapes: the prairie and the sea. The prairie is described when Sarah arrives, as "green grass fields that bloomed with Indian paintbrush, red and orange, and blue-eyed grass"; and Maine as "rock cliffs that rise up at the edge of the sea . . . hills covered with pine and spruce trees, green with needles." The crucible in this novel is the choice between terrains. This short novel for young readers powerfully conveys the correlation of landscape to mindscape.

Transported from the vast plains to the more intimate English countryside, Beatrix Potter's tiny compass portrays the farmlands, gardens, and villages of Westmorland remembered from childhood's slow accrual of summers. Potter's picture books are rooted in the Lake Country, which she frequented with her family on holiday and where she finally settled as a sheep farmer and preservationist. Many of the tales are set in her home of Hill Top, a picturesque beamed cottage built around 1690 along with a 212-acre working farm, situated near Winderemere in the Lake District, or in the stunning landscapes of the region. Potter set her stories in actual locales, which she sketched with meticulous detail. The beautiful lakes and hills near Hill Top are seen in the tales of *Mrs. Tiggy-Winkle, Jemima Puddle-Duck, Squirrel Nutkin, Mr. Tod* and others. The interior of the farmhouse is depicted in *Samuel Whiskers,* and the garden is evident in *Tom Kitten.* The nearby village of Sawrey is the setting of *The Pie and the Patty Pan* and *Ginger and Pickles.* The street scenes in *The Tailor of Gloucester* are Gloucester. Always a serious student of the natural world, Potter's expeditions with her brother through the forests and fields of Scottish highlands prompted her interest in natural history studies, where nothing in or on the ground escaped her attention. Peter Rabbit and his sisters "lived with their Mother in a sand-bank, underneath the root of a very big fir-tree." This humble sandbank is one of the most famous addresses in children's literature, and her beloved Lake District, a perfect splotch of a hamlet with its whitewashed shops, slate-roofed shops, winding lanes hemmed in by towering stone walls, and rolling green hills, attracts over 80,000 visitors a year, many of them from the opposite side of the globe. And many more enter this geography through her small books, big words, and accomplished watercolors. Potter's picture books present a delicate balance–in critic Fred Inglis's words–between "a colonized, accomplished horticulture and agriculture, and the stable but mysterious Nature which lies untamed beyond the garden wall" (109). Many classic children's books continue this dialectic.

Kenneth Grahame's *Wind in the Willows* is about home as well, an autobiography of feelings toward nature: river, field, and moor. Grahame re-creates here the landscapes Grahame remembered from his years with his maternal grandmother in Cookham Dene, a village near the Thames in Berkshire, where he later in life returned to live while writing this novel. The Cornish town of Fowey is also interwoven, a place of retreat with friends like Arthur Quiller-Couch and Edward Atkinson, a place that he describes in the book as "the little grey sea town that clings along one side of the harbour." Grahame's seasons: the passing of summer in the willow herb, comfrey, and meadowsweet. The winter where Mole "was glad that he liked the country undecorated, hard, and stripped of its finery. He had got down to the bare bones of it, and they were fine and strong and simple" (47). The swallows explain their migration and their return home: "The call of lush meadow grass, wet orchards, warm, insect-haunted ponds, of browsing cattle, of haymaking, and all the farm buildings clustering around the House of the Perfect Eaves" (170). The animal creatures, so familiar to the fable and fairy tale. The woods in the winter, the long days of summer, picnic feasts on the river, "messing about in boats," afternoon tea, dulce domum–all these images are potent pastoral dreams. As biographer Peter Green writes, this is a book that stops the clock, that presents old England, the nostalgic rolling hills and enchanted riverbank of Kate Greenaway and Randolph Caldecott. As in Wordsworth's "Prelude" or in Mark Twain's Mississippi, the river dominates as narrative and shapes our relationship to the phenomenological world. The river in *The Wind in the Willows* is described as a "sleek, sensuous, full-bodied animal" and as a storyteller. The opening chapter's paean to the river resounds in the Rat's ninth chapter dream of the sea: "what seas lay beyond, green, leaping, and crested! What sun-bathed coasts . . . What quiet harbours, thronged with gallant shipping bound for purple islands of wine and spice, islands set long in langurous waters" (171). This is also a text that is often examined for its signification of classes and social roles with respect to external nature: the civilized and the wild, the gendered world of male cama-raderie, the Old England and the New.

Another book of contested landscape is *The Secret Garden,* my most favored childhood text. No book has ever stirred such a feeling for the land as lived, with all of its rich metaphorical texture. With my deep affinity for this book, I lose the critical eye, wanting to preserve the place as stable, as it was and remains for me. To others, the layers of colonial India, English gentility, and country Yorkshire disrupt the ground of their reading. Here is my walled vision, my reading. Mary Lennox comes to Misselthwaite Manor, her uncle's Yorkshire home in the moors, "where nothing grows on but heather and gorse, and nothing lives in but wild ponies and sheep." She learns to play in this new landscape: to run, to skip rope, to plant seeds, to make things come alive from the ground, "daffodils and snowdrops and lilies and iris working their way out of the dark." The fertile ground for this play is the secret garden. With the help of Dickon and the robin, a spade, seeds, and a bit of earth, the garden comes to life as she does. As this once pale creature blos-soms, she reaches out to share her green patch of life. Here is a garden enchanted, one based on a lived experience as well as imagined. Burnett relates how she was inspired by the neighborhood in Manchester, where she lived as a young girl before moving to America, and where she wondered what was behind a locked fence of an abandoned house and by using her imagination turned the soil into a flowering garden of roses, violets, and hyacinths. Burnett spoke of her experience in Manchester as being an exile and found the thickets, woods, and mountains of Tennessee to be her home. But it was the abandoned garden of her childhood that was her formative landscape experience of the pastoral. At the end of her life, Burnett wrote an essay on the experience of gardening, where she says: "As long as one has a garden one has a future; and as long as one has a future one is alive" (30).

In approaching such a representation of nature in children's books of the late Victorian and Edwardian period, it is important to consider both a real as well as a mythical element. Raymond Williams argues in *The Country and the City* that despite the tendency of each generation to cite the mythical lost Golden Age in the previous generation, there are those who "lived" that history, and to whom any change was very real. *The Secret Garden,* like *The Wind in the Willows,* derives much of its strength from the Romantic tradi-tion's representation of childhood and nature. Both works, however, are far from idyllic in the worlds they represent. In *The Secret Garden,* Mary travels across the moors to her new home, in a bleak midwinter that captures her emotional state:

On and on they drove through the darkness, and though the rain stopped, the wind rushed by and made strange sounds. The road went up and down, and several times the carriage passed over a little bridge beneath which water rushed very fast with a great deal of noise. Mary felt as if the drive would never come to an end, and that the wide, bleak moor was a vast expanse of black ocean through which she was passing on a strip of dry land. (21)

Mary's experience with the land–part domestic, part wild–is a movement to interior space as well as social order. Burnett, I believe, is suggesting the transformative power of the imagination–as part and parcel of Nature–to effect changes in the external as well as internal worlds. This is the belief that Fred Inglis holds for children's books: that they can somehow be a force of "radical innocence." In this story, I sense the redemptive power of nature, of a deep love for the world that can come from its earth, of the communion we share in searching for what is on the other side of the wall, for what is the magic beneath the surface. This book was my beginning, my adventure into a world still revealing its mysteries, and where what was lost is found.

Another book that holds this promise for me is E. B. White's *Charlotte's Web*. Talk about lost causes–trying to keep a pig from the slaughterhouse, from being the holiday feast. This is a story about the sweetness of life, tempered by the nearness of death, and set in a quintessential American landscape: a New England farm. In a letter to a fifth grade student in Larchmont, New York, White writes:

It is true that I have a farm. My barn is big and old, and I have ten sheep, eighteen hens, a goose, a gander, a bull calf, a rat, a chipmunk, and many spiders. In the woods near the barn are red squirrels, crows, thrushes, owls, porcupines, woodchucks, foxes, rabbits, and deer. In the pasture pond are frogs, polliwogs, and salamanders. Sometimes a Great Blue Heron comes to the pond and catches frogs. At the shore of the sea are sandpipers, gulls, plovers, and kingfishers. In the mud at low tide are clams. Seven seals live on nearby rocks and in the sea, and they swim close to my boat when I row. Barn swallows nest in the barn, and I have a skunk that lives under the garage. I didn't like spiders at first, but then I began watching one of them, and soon saw what a wonderful creature she was and what a skillful weaver. I named her Charlotte, and now I like spiders along with everything else in nature. (*Letters*, 367)

That speaks eloquently to me about the power of this book–and other such landscapes–to engender such liking. While there are many levels to this book, which could be called a treatise on parenting, friendship and writing, there is always the barn. As I can't do justice to White's words, this is my favorite passage from the book and in all of its oppositions suggests a kind of Utopia where I could reside:

> It was the best place to be, thought Wilbur, this warm delicious cellar, with the garrulous geese, the changing seasons, the heat of the sun, the passage of swallows, the nearness of rats, the sameness of sheep, the love of spiders, the smell of manure, and the glory of everything. (183)

E. B. White's sense of melancholy sentiment fits my own sensibility perhaps better than other books. Frances Hodgson Burnett believes a bit more in Magic than I, and while that book may have been the touchstone of my childhood, White's barnyard world is more who I am now, as I contemplate the place of friends and writers in my life, as I make a litany of the things I really like.

I wish to close these ruminations with a few conclusions, of my own and others. I am reminded of Fay Weldon's description, in *Letters to Alice on first reading Jane Austen,* of fiction as "A City of Invention." Writing letters to a niece who objects to reading Jane Austen and other obsolescent texts, Weldon draws a stunning image:

> Let me give you, let me share with you, the City of Invention. For what novelists do (I have decided, for the purposes of your conversion) is to build Houses of the Imagination, and where houses cluster together there is a city. And what a city this one is, Alice! It is the nearest we poor mortals can get to the Celestial City: it glitters and glances with life, and gossip, and color, and fantasy: it is brilliant, it is illuminated, by day by the sun of enthusiasm and by night by the moon of inspiration. It has its towers and pinnacles, its commanding heights and its swooning depths: it has public buildings and worthy ancient monuments, which some find boring and others magnificent. It has its central districts and its suburbs, some salubrious, some seedy, some safe, some frightening, Those who founded it, who built it, house by house, are the novelists, the writers, the poets. And it is to this city that the readers come, to admire, to learn, to marvel and explore. (15-16)

Later, in the same book, she writes,

> Truly, Alice, books are wonderful things: to sit alone in a room and laugh and cry, because you are reading, and still be safe when you close the book; and having finished it, discover you are changed, yet unchanged! To be able to visit the City of Invention at will, depart at will–that is all, really, education is about, should be about. (77-78)

What persists, changed, unchanging, is landscape, which exists on several levels: imaginative and real, in a Nature that is omnipresent in city as well as country.

In the broadest sense, all landscapes are symbolic. As historian J. B. Jackson writes, every "landscape is a reflection of the society which first brought it into being and continues to inhabit it," and ultimately landscapes represent a striving to represent a spiritual goal: they are "expressions of a persistent desire to make the earth over in the image of some heaven" (Meinig, 228-229).

A peaceable kingdom exists for me in these childhood and children's narratives, which recall and re-make origins, where as T. S. Eliot writes, "home is where one starts from." Locales are important to the text of the book and the text of our lives from the density and tactile "feel" of specificity. Writers, whether grounded in the countryside or in the city, resemble the mythical figure of Antaeus, the giant whose strength came from having at least one foot on a specific patch of ground. Good writing, to me, is the ability to imagine fully the place one knows, and my knowledge of the world is surely fuller, richer. Such narratives shape a child's sense of identity, one that is both private and public, a spatial sense of being "home" in the world.

And in this age when many despair the fate of the book or predict the need of the library as an institution, perhaps a vision of landscape is needed. Libraries in all of their sensory pleasures, their history, their architecture, embody a sense of place, more than possible in any virtual libraries, more than in any virtual space. As Lewis Thomas writes in *The Lives of a Cell: Notes of a Biology Watcher:*

> Although we are by all odds the most social animals–more interdependent, more attached to one another, more inseparable in our behavior than bees–we do not often feel our conjoined intelligence. Perhaps, however, we are linked in circuits for the storage, processing, and retrieval of information, since this appears to be the most basic and universal of all human enterprises. It may be our biological function to build a certain kind of Hill. (14)

And so we do, we build certain hills, certain places in the external world that are mediated through subjective human experience. Libraries are a landscape, a shared reality, a body of literature, an intertextual way of seeing the world. The recent anthology, *Reading Rooms,* and a host of new bestseller titles on the pleasures of reading in hallowed places (and precarious times), stake a claim for an idea: that landscape is a complex cultural construction shaping what we read, where we read, and why. The "when" is the unique contribution of children's literature, the timing of books being read and an imagination being grown with such simultaneity–and formative powers.

I am left with a sense of how the world inside a book changes the world outside the book, how the text of a book enters the text of a life. And this is where I fold the map, close the guidebook. Annie Dillard begins her book, *American Childhood,* at a point where I end. She writes,

> When everything else has gone from my brain–the President's name, the state capitals, the neighborhood where I lived, and then my own name and what it was on earth I sought, and then at length the faces of my friends, and finally the faces of my family–when all this has dissolved, what will be left, I believe is topology: the dreaming memory of land as it lay this way and that. (3)

I believe that this dreamy land is the landscape of childhood and a storied literature, lying this way and that, in the thorny paradise about.

WORKS CITED

Attebury, B. "Oz." In *The Wizard of Oz,* ed. by M. P. Hearn. New York: Schocken Books, 1983.

Avery, Gillian. *The Echoing Green: Memoirs of Victorian Youth.* New York: Viking Press, 1974.

Baum, L. Frank. *The Wizard of Oz.* Chicago: Rand McNally, 1900.

Bracewell, Michael. "The Never Ending Story." *The Times Magazine* (January 29, 1994, 18-19).

Burnett, Frances Hodgson. *In the Garden.* Boston: The Medici Society of America, 1925.

_____ . *The Secret Garden.* New York: J. B. Lippincott, 1962.

Cameron, Eleanor. *The Green and Burning Tree: On the Writing and Enjoyment of Children's Books.* Boston: Atlantic-Little, 1969.

Cobb, Edith. *The Ecology of the Imagination in Childhood.* New York: Columbia University Press, 1977.

Conrad, Pam. *Prairie Songs.* New York: Harper & Row, 1985.

Cosgrove, Denis E. *Social Formation and Symbolic Landscape.* London: Croom Helm, 1984.

Dillard, Annie. *An American Childhood.* New York: Harper & Row, 1987.

_____ . *Pilgrim at Tinker's Creek.* New York: Harper's Magazine Press, 1974.

Drabble, Margaret. *A Writer's Britain: Landscapes in Literature.* London: Thames and Hudson, 1979.

Geertz, Clifford. *The Interpretation of Cultures.* New York: Basic Books, 1973.

Gilbert, Sandra and Susan Gubar. *The Madwoman in the Attic: The Woman Writer and the Nineteenth-Century Literary Imagination.* New Haven: Yale University Press, 1979.

Grahame, Kenneth. *The Wind in the Willows.* New York: Charles Scribner's Sons, 1954.

Green, Peter. *Kenneth Grahame: A Biography.* New York: World, 1959.

Guth, Dorothy Lobrano, ed. *Letters of E. B. White.* New York: Harper & Row, 1976.

Inglis, Fred. *The Promise of Happiness: Value and Meaning in Children's Fiction.* London: Cambridge University Press, 1981.

Jackson, J. B. *Discovering the Vernacular in Landscape.* New Haven: Yale University Press, 1984.

Lopez, Barry. *Crossing Open Ground.* New York: Charles Scribner's Sons, 1978.

MacLachlan, Patricia. *Sarah, Plain and Tall.* New York: Harper & Row, 1985.

McCarthy, Mary. *Stones of Florence.* New York: Harcourt, Brace, 1959.

Meinig, D. "Reading the Landscape: An Appreciation of W. G. Hoskins and J. B. Jackson." In *The Interpretation of Ordinary Landscapes: Geographical Essays,* ed. by D. W. Meinig. New York: Oxford University Press, 1979.

Thomas, Joyce. "Woods and Castles, Towers and Huts: Aspects of Setting in the Fairy Tale." In *Only Connect: Readings on Children's Literature,* 3rd ed. Edited by Sheila Egoff, Gordon Stubbs, Ralph Ashley, and Wendy Sutton. New York: Oxford University Press, 1996.

Thomas, Lewis. *Lives of a Cell: Notes of a Biology Watcher.* New York: Viking, 1974.

Tolkien, J. R. R. *Tree and Leaf.* Boston: Houghton Mifflin, 1965.

Toth, Susan Allen and John Coughlan. *Reading Rooms.* New York: Washington Square Press, 1991.

Weldon, Fay. *Letters to Alice on First Reading Jane Austen.* New York: Carroll & Graf, 1991.

Welty, Eudora. *The Eye of the Story: Selected Essays and Reviews.* New York: Vintage, 1979.

White, E. B. *Charlotte's Web.* New York: Harper & Row, 1952.

Wilder, Laura Ingalls. *Little House in the Big Woods.* New York: Harper & Row, 1932.

Williams, Raymond. *The Country and the City.* London: Chatto & Windus, 1973.

LIBRARIANS IN FICTION

From Cosmo and Alec
to the Tallest Man in the World:
Some Fictional Librarians
and Their Patrons

Grant Burns

SUMMARY. The author discusses a number of librarians and their relationships with readers in various works of fiction, from George Mac-Donald's 1865 *Alec Forbes of Howglen* to Elizabeth McCracken's 1996 *The Giant's House*. Although fictional librarians can prove vehicles for professional stereotyping, their best characteristics, including a nurturing attitude toward their patrons and a desire to help them explore new worlds, serve as a good standard for librarians even in the digital age. Even fictional librarians who fall short of meeting professional ideals nevertheless perform good and useful services for their clientele. *[Article copies available for a fee from The Haworth Document Delivery Service: 1-800-342-9678. E-mail address: <getinfo@haworthpressinc.com> Website: <http://www.haworthpressinc.com>]*

Grant Burns is Assistant Director, Frances Willson Thompson Library, University of Michigan-Flint, Flint, MI 48502.

[Haworth co-indexing entry note]: "From Cosmo and Alec to the Tallest Man in the World: Some Fictional Librarians and Their Patrons." Burns, Grant. Co-published simultaneously in *The Acquisitions Librarian* (The Haworth Information Press, an imprint of The Haworth Press, Inc.) No. 25, 2001, pp. 177-187; and: *Readers, Reading and Librarians* (ed: Bill Katz) The Haworth Information Press, an imprint of The Haworth Press, Inc., 2001, pp. 177-187. Single or multiple copies of this article are available for a fee from The Haworth Document Delivery Service [1-800-342-9678, 9:00 a.m. - 5:00 p.m. (EST). E-mail address: getinfo@haworthpressinc.com].

Editor's Note: The author is too modest. This article is a shadow of what is to be found in his marvelous, fascinating and rewarding book: *Librarians in Fiction; A Critical Bibliography* (Jefferson, NC: McFarland, 1998, 191 pp., paper, $25). Here are the good and the bad, the intellectuals and the foolish as found in over 370 novels. Each entry has a witty, descriptive and evaluative entry by Mr. Burns. Highly, but highly recommended for librarians and would-be librarians as well as for any reader.

KEYWORDS. Fictional librarians, fiction, librarian stereotypes

In the innocence and ignorance of my youth, it did not occur to me that librarians, as keepers of the books, served any special purpose other than to maintain decorum in the library. At the age of nine, when I spent entire summer afternoons rummaging around my small-town public library, "maintaining decorum" was not, to be sure, a phrase that entered my head. "Keeping everyone quiet" was more like it.

As a rule, the only library staff person in sight (who was probably not a librarian, but what did I know?), who observed my utterly unsystematic investigations of the stacks from the loan desk, suffered little difficulty in maintaining that decorum, or even in keeping everyone quiet. As I look back on those distant, hazy afternoons, when I moseyed from the juvenile section to the sports section, to the adult fiction, the science fiction and the science books, with no plan in mind, with no discernible logical link from one area of inquiry to another, its seems to me now that I spent a great many of those afternoons as my town library's solitary patron. The librarian(?) on duty must have found it tediously easy to enforce a peaceful atmosphere: The only noise I made came from the building's old floor boards creaking under my sneakers.

My memory of being the lone patron on those hot summer afternoons in the stale air of the old Carnegie library must be wrong. At any rate, my company there could not have exceeded more than a handful of fellow readers at any time, and the majority did not linger long in the unairconditioned stuffiness. They came, they found their books, and they left. I stayed.

Why, then, did the "librarian" never once ask me if I would like some help finding something that would suit me? Why did she not intervene in her loyal patron's curiously aimless forays in the stacks to see if she might help him establish something like a focused attack, or at the very least, fix him up with an armload of likely books that would keep him occupied and happy?

To be sure, I found happiness in my very aimlessness, and might have resented any intrusion of authority in my eccentric bibliographic explorations. But possibly not. A little discreet reader's advice might have proved just the medicine I needed. I received no reading guidance in my public

library, or in my school library, either. The result was many years of chaoti-
cally-selected reading, and an amazing discovery: One of my first professors
in library school suggested that I might enjoy working as a reader's adviser.
That such an office existed in libraries astonished me. Imagine being paid to
make suggestions to people about what books they might like to read! I saw
myself seated at a desk in some great reading room, a sign hanging from the
ceiling above my head: "Reader's Adviser." How could anyone call such an
occupation "work"?

For a good many years, now, I have spent a sizeable portion of most
workdays at a desk with a sign hanging over my head. The sign says "Reference & Info." Apparently the sign maker ran out of space, thus the forced
attenuation of "Information" to "Info." As any experienced reference &
info librarian knows, providing either one or the other is, generally, a bit of
work. I have always found the "info" part especially challenging.

Once in a while, fording the daily river of typical not-quite-to-the-point
questions that surface in an undergraduate library ("Where are the magazines?" "Where are the history books?" "Do you have the Internet here?"),
we reference & info librarians do get to play Reader's Adviser, if only briefly.
Once in a while, a patron wants to talk books and reading, not because of an
assignment ("I need to get three articles on the last British election, and I
don't care where they're from"), but because this blessed patron knows that
the joys of books and reading are among the few distinctions between human
beings and animals that the former can point to without embarrassment.

Recently a young man engaged me at the reference desk in a conversation
about his personal library. He mentioned that his father had been a postal
worker, and gave me enough other clues that I felt safe in suggesting a novel,
Charles Bukowski's *Post Office*. (For my money, it is one of the funniest
books ever written, but not everyone's idea of a "good read.")

"I think you'd enjoy it," I told my patron.

My patron sounded enthusiastic.

"Yeah," he said. "I'll give it to my dad and he can read it!"

The consequences may not prove equally serious, but reading books suggested to another can be like taking a roommate's prescription drug.

"Um, yes," I said. "But I think you might want to read it first."

Most librarians in fiction spend as little time as real-life librarians in
leisurely reader's advice. Like their three-dimensional counterparts, fictional

librarians find themselves occupied with the more humdrum chores involved in running their libraries, whether that means locating the misplaced wrench that opens the main doors, seeing that the voice mail is set up properly, explaining to a would-be philanthropist cleaning out his basement why the library does not really need a complete thirty-year run of the *Farm Journal,* or trying to put back in working order a computer workstation that some local genius has rendered comatose. In fact, the foregoing tasks are much more various than those of the majority of fictional librarians. Judging by much fiction with library settings, the librarian's daily chores consist almost exclusively of cataloging books and charging them out to borrowers. Many, if not most, authors seem to be unaware that librarians may be up to other business.

Exceptions to the rule exist in library fiction, exceptions in which alert authors show librarians doing what many of them like to do most: telling others what they might like to read, and helping them discover paths to the knowledge and ideas that they seek. Among the most flattering portraits of fictional librarians acting in this role are those in Floyd Dell's *Moon-Calf,* and Rose Wilder Lane's *He Was a Man.*

Moon-Calf, a novel with pronounced autobiographical overtones, traces the life of Felix Fay, a small-town American boy with aspirations to a literary life. Dell, who became editor of the Socialist journal *The Masses,* was a prominent literary figure in both Chicago and New York City. He received encouragement in his writing from librarian Marilla Freeman. An early visitor to his public library, Fay finds his reading habits encouraged by the librarian, "a strict but kindly old lady" who supplies him a diet of popular boys' fiction. Her intentions are good even if her reading guidance falls short of the mark: Felix, a lad of rapidly evolving tastes, already hungers for more mature work, including that of Victor Hugo.

The great influence on Felix proves to be Helen Raymond, chief librarian in the town of Port Royal. There Felix works hard on his poetry, with Helen as his inspiration and tutor. Only a few years older than Felix, Helen nevertheless becomes an object of almost divine worship for the young poet: "Something in her light step, her serene glance, personified for him the spirit of literature; she *was* its spirit, made visible in radiant cool flesh." Helen finds in Felix someone who shares her own enthusiasm about books, reading and writing. The two meet often in her office to discuss literature and life; Helen reads Felix's poems critically. "I want to *help* him," she decides.

Between the lines of the high-minded relationship of Felix and Helen, one detects a hot current of frustrated desire that has more to do with hormones than with poesy. When Helen leaves town to continue her career in another city, Felix considers her responsible for his joining "a wonderful world of friendship with poets and novelists and beautiful women." Although the reader feels some disappointment in the stifled romantic link between the two, Felix will always think of Helen "as the spirit, half familiar and half divine" that helped give birth to his literary life.

Many writers have received assistance from librarians. Jack London turned for guidance to Oakland, California librarian Ina Coolbrith (1841-1928). Coolbrith, who in 1919 became poet laureate of California, receives passing homage in London's novel, *The Valley of the Moon* in the form of Mrs. Mortimer. Mortimer, a former head of a public library, offers on-the-road couple Billy and Saxon Roberts refuge on her San Jose-area farm. There she impresses them with her resourceful business manner. In *He Was a Man*, a novel of a writer's rise to fame, Rose Wilder Lane's hero Gordon Blake bears considerable resemblance to Jack London. Here it is librarian Mr. Stein who puts the young man's career in motion. Stein recognizes Blake's literary talent, however raw it is when they meet, and encourages him to submit articles for the newspapers. He helps Blake smooth the rough edges of his prose for a "family" audience–and even introduces him to his future wife. As many readers probably know, incidentally, Lane was *Little House on the Prairie* author Laura Ingalls Wilder's daughter.

Clyde Brion Davis's *The Anointed* is a thematic sibling of *The Moon-Calf*, with London-esque overtones. Rough-hewn sailor Harry Patterson yearns to improve his spiritual life and "to navigate" his mind. Fortunately for his ambitions, he meets the lovely Marie Snyder, a young librarian with the San Francisco Public Library. Love comes for Harry at first sight. "I've never seen a woman that could compare with Marie for goodness, and smartness, too," exults Harry.

Marie returns Harry's interest, and, in spite of the crude intellectual material he presents, helps him set sail on a self-directed reading program that leads Harry away from his dead-end job as a deck hand. If Marie's choice of authors, such as George Eliot, seems a little unlikely for a neophyte would-be litterateur, Harry is apparently too smitten and too grateful to notice.

The works above advertise in common one of the most frequently-noted traits of fictional librarians, their nurturing nature. This nature appears often in librarians' relationships with young readers and students. In the largely forgotten Depression novel, *The Sun Sets in the West*, Myron Brinig's Montana mining town librarian, Gertrude Field, is "a slender, virginal spinster of forty. . . . When Miss Field entered the library, the world was obliterated, and she, herself, became a character in a book." Miss Field observes the omnivorous reading habits of David Sandor, son of a local storekeeper. She encourages his reading, and, when he is older, sometimes discusses books and reading with him through the night, at her house. As in the *Moon-Calf*, a powerful undertow of Eros pulls at the librarian and her young literary protege in *The Sun Sets in the West*. Miss Field's readerly all-nighters with David predictably arouse suspicion among the townsfolk. Although she maintains a blameless approach to the young man, the town fathers seize upon the appearance of illicitness in their relationship as a convenient excuse to sack Miss Field and close the library, which they see as a needless drain on the town budget. For one who has devoted her life to literature and the encouragement of young readers, these moves are devastating. They leave Miss Field "trapped in a town that, without rows of bookshelves, had become the ugliest, most God-forsaken in the world."

No one would confuse the delicate Gertrude Field with Elizabeth Cloud, John Hersey's pugnacious librarian in *The Child Buyer.* Cloud prides herself on helping bright, curious children in the town of Pequot satisfy their reading interests. A state senate committee on a witch hunt brings Cloud to testify one day; when one of the lawmakers begins ranting about how public libraries busy themselves "dealing out sex and sadism," Cloud stands firm. "If you come down to the Town Free Library in Pequot with the intent of pulling out books and making a bonfire of them, sir, I'll be there to welcome you–with a fourteen gauge shotgun." One imagines the hardy Elizabeth Cloud, weapon in hand, standing at the library door against the assault of censorious legislators, while in the background one glimpses her young readers perusing the usual suspects on the Morals Squad's bad-book list: *The Adventures of Huckleberry Finn, Catcher in the Rye, To Kill a Mockingbird,* and other perennial favorites of the censors.

Elizabeth Cloud would be glad to share office space with Miss Mergan, August Derleth's town librarian in *The Shield of the Valiant,* a volume in his *Sac Prairie Saga.* Miss Mergan, who has fought the good librarian's fight in Sac Prairie for many years, has kept the library open to books of all kinds, "regardless of those who were against this or that on various trumped-up grounds of bigotry and ignorance." Miss Mergan takes special pains to provide good service to adolescents and children. She treats the young gently, and helps them with their books in a caring, personal way.

Fictional librarians often influence children and young people, and nearly as often succumb to the influences of their young library charges. Sometimes the circumstances of the relationship between librarian and young patron go far beyond anything that occurs in the typical library. In *The Proof,* French writer Agota Kristof's intense, harrowing novel of life in a country enduring war and revolution, town librarian Clara becomes the lover of Lucas, a young man whose family has been wiped out in the fighting. Lucas initially approaches Clara in the hope that she will be able to furnish him something interesting to read. Clara, a 35-year-old widow whose husband the authorities executed for treason, and who suspects that Lucas is a spy, slowly accepts Lucas's aid and comfort, until she trusts him enough to read to him banned books that she has saved from the library and hidden in her cellar.

One of the most effectively-drawn librarians in recent fiction plays the heroine in Elizabeth McCracken's *The Giant's House*. Narrator, reference librarian and public library director in Brewsterville, Cape Cod, Peggy Cort is an adept professional whose private life lacks fulfillment. She finds the fulfillment, to an extent, in her relationship with James Sweatt. She meets him in 1950, when James, about to enter adolescence, is already taller than most men. Peggy not only looks after James's intellectual development, but, especially following the death of his mother, does what she can to guard the health and welfare of the boy who becomes the world's tallest man. In addition to its portrayal of the touching relationship between Peggy and James, *The Giant's House* offers highly perceptive insights on how a good reference librarian goes about the job. McCracken, a librarian herself, may well be as good at that profession as she is at writing.

An early, sentimental, and yet very enjoyable librarian-reader pairing is that of Alec Forbes and Cosmo Cupples in George MacDonald's 19th-century tale, *Alec Forbes of Howglen*. Alec, a student in a Scottish college, turns to college librarian Cupples for guidance and support. The frequently-tipsy but kindly and multi-talented Cupples helps Alec study for exams, advises him on human relations, and takes the young man on as a student assistant in the library. The relationship between Alec and Cupples is emotional, sometimes tumultuous, and even violent. The liquor that both consume in large quantities has something to do with the extremes in their friendship. Readers generous enough to take the novel's sentimental measures with an indulgent shrug will enjoy the story of Alec and Cosmo Cupples; the only real caveat: MacDonald's use throughout of heavy dialect in the dialogue will pose a challenge for most visitors to the story.

If George MacDonald's novel presents the scholarly librarian in the most traditional environment imaginable, Japanese author Haruki Murakami's *Hard-Boiled Wonderland and the End of the World* places the librarian in the most bizarre. A melange of fantasy, science fiction and surrealism, this novel features "The Library" in a village at the "End of Time." There the attractive Librarian (yes, it's capitalized) accepts what one might call the novel's Janus-brained narrator as the sole "Dreamreader" eligible to use the library. The Librarian's function is "to watch over the old dreams and to help the Dreamreader." Help him she does, from demonstrating dreamreading techniques to providing a cool towel for his tired eyes, and warm milk to drink.

Murakami's narrator also resorts to a young reference librarian in Tokyo for assistance with unicorns. Although skeptical of his sanity, she hand delivers to his apartment her library's unicorn references, and reads passages aloud to him. Later in the novel the narrator takes the Tokyo librarian out for dinner; she eats with the gusto of a wild animal. As for The Librarian who introduced him to dreamreading, he finally "reads out" her mind. Why not? In the end, the narrator says, "I know she waits for me in the Library."

"Or whatever," as the Tokyo librarian notes after a night of unicorn reading, ravenous eating, and not-so-successful lovemaking.

Moving back from the edge several steps, we can retreat to the comforting confines of the small-town library. (Memories of the old hometown library seem to haunt a good many authors of fiction.) Ray Bradbury, who has carved out a good section of small-town turf in his work, returns to familiar territory in his story "Exchange," a tale of a librarian with four decades on the job as a small-town librarian. Miss Adams has been a conscientious librarian, but after all these years the job has become "too much." Miss Adams finds some of her former vigor restored thanks to a visit from a long-ago patron. One evening at closing, she admits a man in military uniform. She recognizes him as a favorite patron when he was a boy; she still has the stamped book cards from the books he borrowed as a youngster. He tells her how important she was to him when she gave him, as a child, the privilege of using the library's adult section.

Nikki Giovanni's story, "The Library" approaches childhood library use from a fantastic angle. This piece describes a young black girl's discovery of her African heritage in the local "Colored Only" Carnegie library. There the black librarian leads the girl to a secret vault, the Black Museum, home of the written record of African-American history and future history. The librarian metamorphoses before the girl's eyes into an exotically dressed African woman.

Most serious fiction concerning librarians focuses less on their work with the public than on their personal and private struggles. Individual characters sometimes set the nettles of these struggles aside, and find relief in their library work. Sometimes that work comes with its own nettles, with which fictional librarians deal in their own ways. Few public service librarians but the saintly will fail to chuckle at Kingsley Amis's librarian John Lewis when, in the novel *That Uncertain Feeling,* Lewis dismisses patrons with an ironic quip. As he dishes out romance novels to borrowers, his answer to his favorite question—"Is it a good book?"—combines a fine blend of gentle condescension and outright contempt: "You'll like it," he says.

Lower on the evolutionary ladder of that good old public-service attitude resides Ethel Long, Chicago public librarian in Sherwood Anderson's *Beyond Desire.* Ethel, materially ambitious, pretty much loathes her patrons. She spends her work-life "handing out dirty soiled books to dirty soiled people day after day . . . having to be cheerful about it and act as though you liked it. . . . Such tired weary faces most of the working people had." And they're not getting any sympathetic assistance from librarian Ethel, either. They're probably lucky that she doesn't swat them, or demand that they go home and bathe.

At the very bottom of the reader's adviser heap sits the sourest librarian in fiction, Sir Hugh Walpole's Miss Milton, town librarian of Polchester in the novel *The Cathedral.* Fictional librarians too often, alas, embody stereotypically negative traits. They may prove ornery, humorless, fussy, neurotic, authoritarian, unlovable, or, in that most dreary and common of descriptions, "spinsterish." No other fictional librarian equals the depravity of the altogether contemptible Miss Milton. A ghastly, incompetent librarian, she has somehow clung to her post for two decades. She literally sits on new novels to save them for patrons in her good graces (which are few), while lying to others about which books are out. A snob who hates children, she knits "endless stockings" while on duty as she peers at the world through her "little red-rimmed eyes." Miss Milton's dreadful performance finally costs her job, but she takes cruel vengeance on the novel's tragic hero, Archdeacon Brandon, whom she blames for her own disgrace.

The world of fictional librarians is by no means largely populated with Miss Miltons, or even pale shadows of that unsavory character. Most of those who fall short of meeting a professional ideal mean well, and perform useful work, and sometimes do noble work for their patrons. Most readers will recall librarian Carol Kennicott, who came to Gopher Prairie, Minnesota, in Sinclair Lewis's *Main Street,* aiming to bring high (or at least higher) culture to the American outback. Carol is more typically "a librarian" if we must identify typicality, than the evil Miss Milton.

Elizabeth Yates, who won the Newbery Medal for her 1950 book *Amos Fortune, Free Man,* presents in *Nearby,* her novel of a New England village, another example of what one might see as the archetypal well-meaning fictional librarian. Village librarian Miss Patch is interested in providing her small-town fellow citizens "the best" in literature, as well as seeking to help protect her clientele's morals. If these ambitions, doubtless shared by numerous Miss Patches, are neither imaginative nor inspirational, they spring from good intentions and their fruits, although of pastel colors and muted flavors, helped maintain the town of Nearby and communities like it, and helped give their citizens some confidence in their world, in what they knew, and how the future would be, for many decades. "In the eyes of the town fathers she was a good librarian," was Miss Patch. "Culture was safe in her hands, though not dynamic."

True, Miss Patch's views are circumscribed, but she is a product of her time and place. If she refuses to buy Thomas Hardy's great novel *Jude the Obscure* for the library, on moral grounds, she nevertheless lobbies effectively for an increase in the library's acquisitions budget, and welcomes the rare opportunity to discuss ideas with someone whose knowledge is adequate to challenge her own. It should not risk too much to say that the values and manners of Miss Patch come reasonably close to echoing those not only of most small-town librarians at most times in the past, but those of most other professionals, including teachers, doctors and lawyers.

The sedate public library where I spent so many afternoons as a boy, a library where our local equivalent of Miss Patch may well have observed a peculiar, solitary child lurking for hours in the stacks, and who let him have his way there, is fast fading from present reality, and with it the moral certainties and the "typical" librarian who appears in so many works of fiction. The library world is some distance from realizing the vision of Haruki Murakami, but the old world is rapidly changing to one in which what once were "library schools" are now "schools of information," in which librarians who once practiced to become good story hour readers now learn hypertext protocols, and in which even small-town libraries often make the whole of human endeavor–the good, the bad, and the deranged–available to their patrons through the World Wide Web. Today's champions of "family values" may convince themselves that a "book of virtues" and librarians who proffer it can somehow help restore those solid, small-town middle-class ethics that presumably characterized the past. Their convictions are most likely illusory; the world has changed too much and too fast, and neither change nor time can be stuffed back into yesterday's containers.

My little fantasy back in library school about the life of the "Reader's Adviser" bore little resemblance to the way public service librarians actually interact with their patrons. Opportunities for sustained exchanges about reading, authors and literature at large simply do not, as a rule, fit into the business of the day. In *The Giant's House,* Elizabeth McCracken has Peggy Cort speak of the shallowness of the librarian's connections with her clientele: "Despite my clumsiness with the outside world, I was the perfect public servant: deferential, dogged, oblivious to insults. Friendly but not overly familiar. It was one of the reasons I loved being a librarian: I got to conduct dozens of relationships simultaneously and successfully. I conformed myself always to the needs of the patrons (they certainly did not care about mine), told them they were right, called them Mr. and Mrs. and Miss when they did not bother to learn my smallest initial. Do you wonder why we're called public *servants?*" (p. 54).

At its best, the reality of the librarian's life is better than that. Most transactions are superficial, but the development of long-term relationships between librarians and patrons is not unknown. Even the superficial transactions can be touched with grace; one must seize passing moments that allow a fleeting connection with the patron as a human being, not merely as a customer. If one can establish by word, tone of voice and manner in a few minutes or less a sense of common humanity, one that helps provide a basis for the patron's trust in the librarian's counsel, that is as much as the librarian can reasonably hope to achieve.

One hopes that however the technology advances, or however the emphasis in librarianship shifts from "Keeper of the Books" to "Reader's Adviser" to "Trail Guide to the Digital Frontier," real-life librarians retain the best qualities of the librarians one meets in fiction: the humane compassion and the desire to open new realms for others that we see in Cosmo Cupples, in Peggy Cort (in spite of the way she sells herself short), in Miss Mergan, Marie Snyder, Elizabeth Cloud, Helen Raymond, and other fictional librarians doing their work at their best, from the joy of doing it, because their best work is what the world and their patrons need. With any luck, they always will.

WORKS DISCUSSED

Amis, Kingsley. *That Uncertain Feeling.* New York: Harcourt, Brace, 1956.

Anderson, Sherwood. *Beyond Desire.* New York: Liveright, 1932.

Bradbury, Ray. "Exchange." In his *Quicker Than the Eye.* New York: Avon, 1996, p. 207-219 (First publication).

Brinig, Myron. *The Sun Sets in the West.* New York: Farrar & Rinehart, 1935.

Davis, Clyde Brion. *The Anointed.* New York and Toronto: Farrar & Rinehart, 1937.

Dell, Floyd. *Moon-Calf.* New York: Knopf, 1920.

Derleth, August. *The Shield of the Valiant.* New York: Scribner, 1945.

Giovanni, Nikki. "The Library." In *Brothers and Sisters: Modern Stories by Black Americans.* Edited by Arnold Adoff. New York: Macmillan, 1970, p. 141-146 (First publication).

Hersey, John. *The Child Buyer: A Novel in the Form of Hearings Before the Standing Committee on Education, Welfare & Public Morality of a Certain State Senate, Investigating the Conspiracy of Mr. Wissey Jones, with Others, to Purchase a Male Child.* New York: Knopf, 1960.

Kristof, Agota. *The Proof.* New York: Grove Weidenfeld, 1991. Translation of *La Preuve.* Paris: Editions du Seuil, 1988.

Lane, Rose Wilder. *He Was a Man.* New York and London: Harper, 1925.

Lewis, Sinclair. *Main Street.* New York: Harcourt, Brace, 1920.

London, Jack. *The Valley of the Moon.* New York: Macmillan, 1913.

McCracken, Elizabeth. *The Giant's House.* New York: Dial, 1996.

MacDonald, George. *Alec Forbes of Howglen.* London: Hurst & Blackett, 1865, 3 vols.

Murakami, Haruki. *Hard-Boiled Wonderland and the End of the World.* New York: Kodansha, 1991. Translation of *Sekai no Owari to Hado-Boirudu Wandarando.* Tokyo: Shinchosha, 1985.

Walpole, Sir Hugh. *The Cathedral.* London: Macmillan, 1922.

Yates, Elizabeth. *Nearby.* New York: Coward-McCann, 1947.

Best Books and Readers

Bill Katz

SUMMARY. Best book lists have been a tradition among librarians since the Alexandria Library. They continue to be important in shaping reading habits, although modern technology has tended to shift the lists to a lesser place in the library. With them has gone the focus on reader guidance and services. Both should be enthusiastically supported. The primary purpose of the library is to provide readers with the best in reading. *[Article copies available for a fee from The Haworth Document Delivery Service: 1-800-342-9678. E-mail address: <getinfo@haworthpressinc.com> Website: <http://www.haworthpressinc.com>]*

KEYWORDS. Best books, readers' advisory

"What advice would you give to a creative 23-year-old looking to make a difference in the world?" Read.[1]

Attitudes change from generation to generation, but one assumption is

Bill Katz is Professor at the State University of New York, Albany School of Information Science and Policy, and Editor of *The Acquisitions Librarian*.

[Haworth co-indexing entry note]: "Best Books and Readers." Katz, Bill. Co-published simultaneously in *The Acquisitions Librarian* (The Haworth Information Press, an imprint of The Haworth Press, Inc.) No. 25, 2001, pp. 189-200; and: *Readers, Reading and Librarians* (ed: Bill Katz) The Haworth Information Press, an imprint of The Haworth Press, Inc., 2001, pp. 189-200. Single or multiple copies of this article are available for a fee from The Haworth Document Delivery Service [1-800-342-9678, 9:00 a.m. - 5:00 p.m. (EST). E-mail address: getinfo@haworthpressinc.com].

189

carried through the ages: reading is relevant and available for any individual this side of illiteracy.[2] An intricate, although not always essential part of the reading experience is an authoritative list of "best books," or a "canon." The list serves many purposes in and out of a library. Primarily it is a gentle guide for readers who want to make a difference in their lives, and, yes, in the world.

Today's best books embrace received opinions that have an important relation to everyday activities. Reading certain books is both a pleasurable and practical experience. The first is self-evident. The pragmatic argument is that intellectual skills learned through reading landmark books can be applied to solving problems in professional careers. A trained intellect, honed by reading Homer or Hawthorne, offers a measure of understanding available to solve life's difficult questions.

With conviction, dedication and select books as support, librarians from the Alexandria Library to the local public library in an American town, have shaped the intellectual capacities of readers over the centuries. By the close of the nineteenth century the public librarians had preached the gospel of "best" and "better" reading across the Western world.

A list of accepted books and the term "canon" were not synonymous even by the mid 18th century. Neither Samuel Johnson's *Dictionary of the English Language* (1755) nor the French Academy has an entry for "canon" which refers to a list of secular titles with lasting literary qualities. Diderot's *Encyclopaedia* (1751-1780) defines it in the Medieval sense as a "list of books recognized as divine" by Jews and Christians. There were uses of canon in the sense of today's definition but only as subcurrents in the stream of literature.[3]

Canon became associated with selected, best books when first employed in 1768 by David Ruhnken. He dropped earlier designations of such lists and turned to "canon" for the first time. "His coinage met with world wide and lasting success, as the term was found to be so convenient."[4] By the close of the eighteenth century, Ruhnken's definition became part of the language and was understood as a list of standard texts which represented cultural choices for individual and classroom use. Today critics apply the term to any period or time or group. There can be the "canon of German 20th century literature" or the "canon of African sculpture" and so on.

The canon surely is a list of best books. It is not elitist. It is concerned with civilized choices. It is a standard list. Too many people, from individuals to government agencies, seem to confuse standards with elitism. They are as opposite as good and bad or McDonalds and a four-star restaurant.

Most understand the best books as those great books, from Homer to the present, which traditionally constitute the core of a liberal education. One must know them to be termed truly educated. There are two assumptions. First, any select list recognizes there is such a thing as best and great books, which contain universal ideas that are worthy of study from one generation to the next. The truth of the books transcends time, race, class and nationality. Second, the choice presupposes a consensus among those who select the titles and those who read and study the books.

The argument for the "best" is as energetic as it is steeped in history: (1) Canons supply inspiration to all, from students to writers and artists, in that they offer a retrospective list of the superior thoughts of civilizations. (2) Lists are not frozen in time, but subject to foreign influences. In fact "canons not only conserve indigenous cultural achievement . . . but have also aided the assimilation of foreign cultures . . . Canons have served the cause not of essentialism but of diversity."[5] (3) The best book is important in the educational process, particularly as a lifeline between the present culture and the cultural pasts.

The primary test for inclusion is that a book should have so much value that "regardless of its origins and their relevance to immediate social problems, it would be better to have studied than not."[6]

Critic and literary columnist, May Becker followed the usual book list pattern. Her mid-1920s *A Reader's Guide Book* was directed to those who wanted a list of books which "would give me something of a background equivalent to a college education." At the same time another would-be reader wanted a list that would help him "to acquire a worldly polish–an air of savoir faire."

In her classic statement about library book selection, Helen Haines in 1935 suggested several principles that helped to categorize qualities of excellence. Her first principle, as most of the others, was ambivalent enough to satisfy almost everyone: "Select books that will tend toward the development and enrichment of life." She did not define the phrase "development and enrichment," assuming the reader understood. It is a fair assumption.[7]

The best book represents the ideal curriculum. Until the mid-twentieth century there was a consensus, at least for the few who were educated at the university level, as to what constituted the canon. The explosion of higher education, the rise of alternative approaches to everything from music to the male-female relationship, the civil rights movement and, yes, air conditioning severely jolted the complacency of those who determined the canon and its modifications. Unfortunately, in the riot of opinion, best book lists often were thrown out along with numerous standards of education. Familiar clichés filled the air. Readers are their own best guides. Every book is equal to every other book. Give 'em what they want. If it's not often read, it's not worth keeping in the library.

The barbarians no longer were at the gate. They had broken into the library.[8]

Refutation of the anti-intellectual screams is not the purpose here, although something must be said about the notion that everything is equal, all books are the same. Consider how this flies in the face of common sense and experience. For example, the typical, ubiquitous test of excellence, of merit, of quality, is measurement. Everything from a painting and a meal to an automobile and a piece of clothing can be given a quality tag that automatically places it in the hierarchy of value. Obviously a Picasso is more valuable than a Norman Rockwell, a dinner in a four-star French restaurant more memorable than in McDonalds, or a designer dress of more appeal than one off the rack at Sears. A car costing over $100,000 is usually more powerful than one under $10,000. Scales of value, which few will argue with, are a daily experience.

Quality arguments have been heard too often down through history to have any real meaning for librarians who understand human needs. It is the reader with the book that counts, no matter whether that book is on a screen, in print or listened to via a CD or tape. Individuals deserve the best quality available for their particular reading interests and, yes, skills.

The concern with people from all areas with various cultural and educational experiences, is part of library service, and has been since the first public library opened its doors. Such recognition does not mean one abandons historical standards of quality. No reader welcomes condescension. Best books must be for all readers. Tapering the discussion to a thinner point, equilibrium is needed in collection development. Lists of best books insure this balance. The argument should not be whether or not to dismiss such lists, but how to modify them to meet the needs of specific readers.

The problem associated with best book lists has been about since the beginning, and a brief study of those beginnings is necessary to fully appreciate why canon is so necessary.

In general, several assumptions are true throughout the centuries. First, the canon represents continuity in the midst of change. Second, it represents an estimate of a long-lasting public esteem of certain books. Third, though while in the early Christian period the canon of holy books was taken as literally from God, authority normally rests with laypersons who determine which titles will be included or deleted.

Aristophanes (c. 257-180 BC) as head of the Alexandrian Library (c. 194 BC), in addition to being one of the world's first great lexicographers and bibliographers, established what appears to be the earliest select list of the best classical poets. This proved to be the first recorded canon. It was a sort of sifting of the whole literature, as stored in the Alexandria Library and registered in Callimachus' *Pinakes.* Later Aristarchus (c. 217-145 BC), the supreme Homeric critic, was head of the Library (c. 153 BC). He was one of the earliest to put together an established list of the best classical writers.

Historically there has never been a fixed canon, and generation after generation has modified the canon of the past. Among the earliest rebels was Augustine who, in his *The City of God* (413-426 AD), makes the familiar case for questioning the authority of secular canon makers. Turning to the classical lists he comments that they are not to be trusted as they are put together by a "few babblers engaged in quarrelsome debates in schools and gymnasia." Conversely the Bible was a true canon in that it represented God speaking through the apostles and earlier through Moses. Augustine makes one of the best arguments for a "closed" canon based on a restricted number of unique texts. This viewpoint differs from Greek philosophers who considered the canon as flexible and changing depending on human activities. (Later critics often call for the best of both positions.)

Prior to eighteenth century England, and for much longer in the remainder of Europe, works of art and fine books existed only for the few, for members of the ruling court. These aristocrats set the rules, were arbiters of taste for the limited society beyond the courts. Laypeople, for the most part, were content to ignore these works to read, when they did, the Bible and to a lesser extent broadsides and other ephemeral.

With the division of the arts and sciences, and the consequent argument whether the modern world was better than the ancient Greeks and Romans, there came a revolution in the way people looked at culture. No longer was it all a matter of mastering Latin and Greek, but a question of whether the contemporary writers were equal to their ancient cousins. The so-called "modern" elevated current culture to the "high" culture status. The move fitted in with the advent of a truly middle class commercial society which wanted to establish its own rules, free of precedent, for "best" and "better" in the arts.

The nineteenth century "information explosion" brought about by new technologies, a more literate population and the vast increase of book production, called up a new, pervasive cry. "What shall I read?"[9] Here both amateur and professional critics responded with enthusiastic lists, expansion of the canon by hundreds and later by thousands of titles. Alongside of the list makers were the librarians who borrowed and added to the critics' opinions to produce their own, even more influential listings of "best books."

Additions and passes were determined by influential writers. Francis Jeffrey of the *Edinburgh Review,* for example, established "universal standards of truth and nature" to evaluate authors. Coleridge often asked critics and readers to support fixed canons of criticism, without actually explaining what points were in the canon.

The battle was on–and would continue to this day–as regards who selects individuals for the canon and just who was to enter the sacred halls. Repudiating with equal energy Jeffrey's theories and Coleridge's definition, *Blackwood's Magazine* attacked the *Edinburgh* as a "self-elected literary tribunal," and so it went. Rules of previous centuries were abandoned and modified in the search for a canon suitable for Victorian needs. Lists were drawn and redrawn as how to evaluate a classic. A book should show eloquence, taste, imagination, pathos, eloquence and scores of more adjectives and adverbs in order to become part of the canon. One partial solution was to reach at least a short list of entirely fixed titles. Matthew Arnold, for example, urged a short list of works and authors with whom all could agree: Homer, Virgil, Shakespeare, Dante, Milton and the Bible.

The nineteenth century canon for the average reader, for the working classes, was established by Charles Knight and his *Penny Magazine,* as well as other similar periodicals and newspapers both in England and the United States. The editors established, largely from scratch, a working class canon. And in evaluating works, they considered the importance of their readers.

The successful canon makers in the nineteenth century combined literary leaders and librarians who realized there was more than a single group of middle class readers, that all readers, no matter what their level of sophistication, should be served. Conversely, some best book compilers failed to realize that the dominant middle class was not the only audience. Their blindness resulted in lists and canon which did not last more than a generation or so.

The canon cannot be static. Values and convictions change and as they change the canon must keep up by adding titles, deleting others. At the same time the criteria of excellence for evaluation should not and rarely does change.

Lists of best books were not simply for recreation. They did, and do serve a pragmatic need. For example, knowledge of English literature became imperative by the 1870s when the English civil service, as well as the East India Company, considered acquaintance with the subject was necessary. Questions of such knowledge began to appear on the examinations. The focus was primarily on composition, with a nod to general literature and history.

"It was largely out of pressure to pass the civil service exams that some universities began to offer courses in English literature . . . The most popular study aid . . . from 1873 until 1887 was Henry Morley's *First Sketch of English Literature* . . . a monstrous tome which attempted to cover literary history from the Celts through the reign of Queen Victoria."[10]

Other study guides, both in England and America (E. R. Hooker, *Study Book in English Literature,* 1910; A. J. Wyatt, *The Tutorial History of English Literature,* 1900) established the literary canon. Titles varied, but "the most important aesthetics were conformity to the 'facts' and compatibility with imperial ideology."[11]

Technology sped the development of a wider reading audience. Printers and publishers learned to produce numerous copies of books, papers and magazines rather than a few. The book developed at an astonishing rate and in so doing sought customers and writers and artists to meet the needs of those new customers, those new readers. This enabled the new commercial middle classes to enjoy a vast number of choices.

At the same time, this same new class of reader rejected out of hand the popular ballads, folktales and broadsheets associated with the lower classes. The conviction was that these popular works lacked the refinement found in the works assigned to "high culture." The growing public library was not far behind. In the 1876 "Special Report on the Public Libraries of the United States," one F. B. Perkins observed:

> Silly reading, "trash," at least what is such to many persons, must to a considerable extent be supplied by the public library, and those who intend to organize a library for the public, for popular reading, and who intend to exclude "trash," might as well stop before they begin. But what is trash to some, is, if not nutriment, at least stimulus, to others. Readers improve; if it were not so, reading would not be a particularly useful practice. The habit of reading is the first indispensable step. That habit once established, it is a recognized fact that readers go from poor to better sorts of reading. No case has ever been cited where a reader, beginning with lofty philosophy, pure religion, profound science, and useful information, has gradually run down in his reading until his declining years were disreputably wasted on dime novels and story weeklies. The idea is ridiculous, even on the bare statement of it. But the experience of librarians is unanimous to the contrary, that those who begin with dime novels and story weeklies may be expected to grow into a liking for a better sort. . . .[12]

Carrying the sword for "silly reading" and "trash" in order to improve the reader, to eventually elevate taste, remained a common rallying cry among librarians until well after the Second World War. Note the assumption. X may be bad taste, but with Y the reader's taste improves and with the ultimate Z that same slob has broken into the magic canon, has, indeed, become a civilized reader . . . and, not incidentally, very, very old.

Librarians wanted it both ways. They encouraged people to beat a path to the library by the bait of what would now be an equivalent lowbrow program on television, or a magna movie. Once trapped the reader would be lead down the golden road to the books deemed appropriate. Working librarians knew this was just short of a lie, but it proved justification for pushing Cicero aside for the antics of criminals in Cicero.

By the late nineteenth century there were too many books about. Choice was no longer based on "What books should I read?" as "What books should I avoid?" This remains much the same today. The situation, then and now, was summed up by a bookman in 1886: "A scholar of the old days could hardly get sight of more than a few thousand books. Now he can get to London or Paris in a few hours, and see millions for the mere asking. We can now do, or see, or hear, in twelve hours, what it took our ancestors twelve months to do, or to see, or to hear. When the books of a year and of a library were counted by hundreds and thousands, learned men could really know what was best to be known, and mastered that best."[13]

The nineteenth century information explosion was highlighted by editor and librarian Frederick Perkins who pointed out that in 1872, to keep up with the production of books "would require the reading of about sixty-eight volumes a day, without allowing for reading up such arrears as the classics."[14]

In *Handbook for Readers and Students* (New York: 1843), an editor warns "be not alarmed because so many books are recommended," and adds "dare to be ignorant of many things."

There were, in fact, almost as many suggestions on how to avoid books as how to read. Ralph Waldo Emerson had three rules which checked the information explosion: "(1) Never read any book that is not a year old. (2) Never read any but famous books. (3) Never read any books but what you like."[15]

The English critic, philosopher and legal professor Harrison makes the point that "the most useful help to reading is to know what we should not read . . . in the overgrown jungle of information."[16] He concludes "the first intellectual task of our age is rightly to order and make serviceable the vast realm of printed material which . . . centuries have swept across our path."[17]

The logical response was to establish a canon, a reading program which would stress tested works of the past while allowing entry of new, equally tested titles from year to year, generation to generation. At the same time, one must check "an insatiable appetite for new novels" as this "makes it hard to read a masterpiece."[18] With that Harrison devotes some 400 pages to essays suggesting authors of interest from Homer through popular writers of the nineteenth century.

Modern library users do not think of the canon as such, or even "best books," but are inclined to want to read that which will give them useful knowledge, or self-knowledge. Few think in terms of politics or politically correct positions to take about a given book. On the other hand, a great store of useful knowledge does make the reader a better judge of the political circus. Also "the civic importance of cultural literacy lies in the fact that true enfranchisement depends upon knowledge, knowledge upon literacy, and literacy upon cultural literacy."[19]

In all fairness to critics, the "catch-22" is what is meant by "cultural literacy." For every Harrison, there were a few book list compilers throughout the centuries who reflected a less appetizing element of readers and reading. One example is Noah Porter who in the early 1900s suggested the only true test of worth, the only real method to enter the list of best books, was to offer a book which was "pervaded by those ethical faiths and emotions that are distinctly Christian." He championed only works that wed church and state.[20]

Scores of guides like Harrison's appeared toward the end of the nineteenth, and into a good part of our present century. Themes changed, as did bias against almost any type of fiction (a notion carried by the American Library Association right up until the early 1960s). In the reader aids is to be found the working canon, the true best book lists. Today's critics fail to appreciate what this means. The ever-changing guides make the point that the canon, the best book lists were modified as needed by time and audience. The lesson is as applicable for today's librarian as for those 100 or so years ago.

Rallying to the need for more objective compilations, the American Library Association launched a select list of books for libraries in 1879. After a preliminary 1893 edition, the *A.L.A. Catalog: 8,000 Volumes for a Popular Library with Notes* was published in 1904 by the United States Government Printing Office. The child of Melvil Dewey and the Library of Congress, among others, it became the primary guide in book selection, particularly for public libraries. The 8,000 volumes, selected and briefly annotated by committees of librarians, were the first official library canon. By 1926, and after three supplements, a revised edition *(The A.L.A. Catalog)* was published with 10,295 titles by the American Library Association in Chicago. "Selectively, the volume represents the cooperative work of more than 400 collaborators."[21] Haines made some interesting comparisons between the first and second edition; she points out religion, fiction, history and science were reduced while bibliography, philosophy, sociology, useful and fine arts were increased. She explains all of this with "the broadening and changing trends of public demand" as well as the "increasing catholicity and discrimination in library book selection."[22]

Shifting attitudes in the 1920s changed the direction of the lists. Compilers, concerned people who think reading 100 or 1,000 books automatically would assure character and culture, turned away from the manual/how-to/ self-improvement support for the lists. To obtain real culture, thought as well as passive reading was required. Reading demands an active mind.

Developed from courses she taught in her own Philadelphia Bookseller's School, Bessie Graham edited the *Bookman's Manual* in 1921. As a general guide to as much as what would sell as to a core bookstore collection, the *Manual* has been published ever since. (The name is changed to *The Reader's Adviser*. The 14th edition was published in 1994 by Reed/Bowker.) Today the choice is circular in that selection is based on what is most likely to be found in a library, not only in a bookstore.

Scores of different types of book lists, or to employ an oxymoron "ephemeral canons" are published in the English speaking world each year. Library periodicals such as the *Library Journal,* frequently feature annotated lists in specialized areas from writer's guide to laymen's medical books. Although less frequently than in past decades, book publishers periodically issue guides such as *Books of the Century,* a select group of books chosen by New York public librarians, or *The Harvard Guide to Influential Books,* the choices of "113 eminent Harvard profs." Bookstores, too, support efforts such as the *Reader's Catalog,* "your guide to 40,000 best books in print," and a shadow of more famous earlier efforts. Periodicals often print suggestions for the best books in various interests or areas. These may range from the standard summer and Christmas suggested lists to "International Books of the Year," a regular feature in *The Times Literary Supplement.*

There never is a shortage of specialized lists issued by individual libraries. Thanks to the Internet, many of these are now available online. They cover everything from the superior titles dealing with animals and pets to sports, hobbies and recreation. One example: The Chicago Public Library (*http://cpl*.lib.uic.edu/001hwlc/litlists/litlists.html). This site offers "selected fiction reading lists" from standard novels to "murder in Chicago."

Despite of, or perhaps because of, the arguments about canon regarding what constitutes "best" books, there are now more recommended lists of books than ever before. This is evident by a cursory check of what is available in basic bibliographies.

Under subject headings "best books" (which covers both formal canon lists and library and individual best book lists), the National Union Catalog, OCLC, and RLIN indicate relative importance through the centuries by the number of titles available. The search is only an indication, and limited to English, but it at least indicates relative interest.

From 1500 to 1700 there were five books in the "best book" category. From 1700 to 1800 the number increased to 76. From 1800 to 1850 some 77 books were published, and from 1850 to 1875 only 38. The startling increase in number of lists/canons comes in the last 25 years of Queen Victoria's reign, i.e., 1875-1901. Also this was the time of more universal education and the development of a strong public library system in the United States and less so in England. Between 1875 and 1901 more "best book" lists were published than in the previous 375 years: over 247.

Between 1901 and the outbreak of the second World War in 1939, close to 800 such titles were published. From the end of the War the number of lists has increased; e.g., from 1980 to 1990 about 991 works were issued, and from 1990 to 1998 the number stood at close to 850.

Numbers are deceptive. What once was truly "best," these days is almost any list of books devoted to a category, from Christmas to travel to multicultural. There is a particular interest in guides for children and young people. If the numbers are impressive, or at least do not seem to diminish, but grow, the truth is that these types of list are a far cry from those at the turn of the century.

Gradually the library lists changed to include not only multiple subjects but choices of current books. The emphasis shifted away from listing only time-tested works to approval marks for the "best" in every area from fiction to biography and history.

Who are these modern canon makers, these librarians who make up the "best book" lists? They seem to be just about every other reading librarian from one end of America to the other. What are the criteria? This varies. Decisions are based as much upon authoritative reviews as the reading tastes of the individual librarians. Add a considerable amount of confidence in knowing the needs of readers, and the modern canon, or to be more specific, the modern canons, represent not only best books, but the best from professional librarians, people who are no more afraid of making choices than they are of the sometimes bitter debates about those selections.

Ernest Barker, a British librarian, in the mid-1920s, reflected in his earnest words the numerous problems with libraries determining what was acceptable. "What are the dozen books, or poems, or passages of literature most likely to be chosen, by common consent, as those which have established themselves definitely as a national possession or influence," was Barker's rhetorical query. His answer: "What matters most is . . . the range and vogue of acceptance, and the degree of the effect produced on social thought and imagination."[23]

That rule is just vague enough, just idealistic enough to serve as a jumping off place for any worthwhile best book list. What matters most is that such lists continue as helpful guides for dedicated readers. Equally important is the intense interest of modern librarians in the importance of reading. No one should undermine that interest. The literature seems to have deserted the first and foremost professional duty of formal and informal reader guidance. It's almost a dead cliché, but like most clichés there is much truth in its basic approach to people and books.

No matter what it may be called, the reader advisory services of a library are the very soul of the library. They must be sustained. It is suggested here that one of the bulwarks is the "best books" list, the canon.

When the final word is in, the real truth is that "the library itself [has] superseded the canonical list. A widespread popular attitude exists that if it's in the . . . library, it must be worth reading."[24] That is a sacred, historical trust which is worth support by anyone with the title of librarian.

NOTES

1. Gore Vidal, quoted in *Wired,* July, 1998, p. 131.

2. A basic assumption about a classic is that "it is read a long time after it is written . . . by the competent" reader. Kermode points out that "the notion of competence is, I think, essential." Frank Kermode, *The Classics,* London: Faber & Faber, 1975, p. 117.

3. Jan Gorak, *The Making of the Modern Canon,* London: Athlone, 1991, pp. 45-6, 50.

4. Rudolpf Pfeiffer, *History of Classical Scholarship,* Oxford University Press, 1968, p. 207.

5. Gorak, op. cit., p. 88.

6. *The New York Times Book Review,* October 27, 1996, p. 15, quote from Frank Kermode.

7. Helen Haines, *Living With Books,* 2nd ed., New York: Columbia University Press, 1935, p. 23.

8. For a civilized, easy to understand discussion of the current canon/best book controversies see Richard Heinzkill, "The Literary Canon and Collection Building," *Collection Management,* Vol. 3 (1/2), 1990, pp. 51-64.

9. Harold Bloom, *The Western Canon,* New York: Harcourt Brace, 1994, p. 526: "What shall I read? is no longer the question, since so few now read, in the era of television and cinema. The pragmatic question has become: What shall I not bother to read?" As noted later, this has been a problem for generations, i.e., what not to read.

10. Karen Michalson, *Victorian Fantasy Literature,* Lewiston, NY: Edwin Mellen Press, 1990, p. 164-165.

11. Ibid., p. 167.

12. *Library Journal,* June 15, 1996, p. 88. This is a quote from the 1876 report.

13. Frederick Harrison, *The Choice of Books,* London: Macmillan, 1886.

14. Frederick Perkins, ed., *The Best Reading,* rev. ed., New York: G.P. Putnam's Sons, 1974, p. 281.

15. Ibid., p. 291.

16. Harrison, op. cit., p. 3.

17. Ibid., p. 18.

18. Ibid., p. 24. Harrison, confronted with "telephones, microphones . . . streampresses, and engines in general . . . leaves the poor human brain panting and throbbing." He saw the day when "the power of flying at will through space would probably extinguish civilization . . . for it would release us from the wholesome bondage of place and rest."

19. E.D. Hirsch, *Cultural Literacy: What Every American Needs to Know,* New York: Vintage Press, 1987.

20. Noah Porter, *Books and Reading,* New York: Charles Scribner's Sons, 1901, p. 114.

21. Haines, op. cit., p. 61.

22. Ibid., p. 62.

23. Gorak, op. cit., p. 64.

24. Ibid., p. 70.

A Prevalence of Lists

Marjorie Lewis

SUMMARY. Making lists is an American thing–Americans make chronological, alphabetical, best-to-worst (and sometimes, worst-to-best) lists, and then the public argues over inclusion and exclusion. It's become a national pastime of sorts. For librarians, however, making lists and using them, or using other people's lists, has become a necessity in these times in which harried skeleton staffs are expected to keep track of the enormous output of books *and evaluate them besides*! But librarians should evaluate all such lists themselves and know when and how to use them appropriately and efficiently. *[Article copies available for a fee from The Haworth Document Delivery Service: 1-800-342-9678. E-mail address: <getinfo@haworthpressinc.com> Website: <http://www.haworthpressinc.com>]*

KEYWORDS. Best books, readers' advisory, compilation of lists

Who'd have thought it–When I said I'd like to write about "lists" *months* ago, who knew that lists would have occupied the minds of the American elite and public most of the summer–even nosing out you-know-who and you-know-what.

Lists of all kinds organize our lives at home, at school, at business, and, as you know, in libraries where we call lists of books "bibliographies." Perhaps lists are an attempt to make order out of chaos. As things become more complicated and products, from information to groceries, proliferate, lists become more and more important and ubiquitous.

Americans seem to love lists. Best-dressed, worst dressed, Emmies, Os-

Marjorie Lewis is a retired Public and School Librarian, P.O. Box 186, Canaan, NY 12029.

[Haworth co-indexing entry note]: "A Prevalence of Lists." Lewis, Marjorie. Co-published simultaneously in *The Acquisitions Librarian* (The Haworth Information Press, an imprint of The Haworth Press, Inc.) No. 25, 2001, pp. 201-205; and: *Readers, Reading and Librarians* (ed: Bill Katz) The Haworth Information Press, an imprint of The Haworth Press, Inc., 2001, pp. 201-205. Single or multiple copies of this article are available for a fee from The Haworth Document Delivery Service [1-800-342-9678, 9:00 a.m. - 5:00 p.m. (EST). E-mail address: getinfo@haworthpressinc.com].

cars, Obies, Tonys, you name it and there's a list–but most of those are yearly. This summer, we've been treated to two lists which profess all-time importance. Maybe it's the approaching millennium that has raised lists to such visibility that newspapers and magazines, television specials, and web sites give them such enormous importance that there is scarcely a magazine, or pundit, or even you and I, who haven't found fault and carried on about the presumptuousness of such lists. It's as if we wish to wrap things up in neat packages before the year 2000. And as if the movies and the book industry wanted to get a head start on other lists which are sure to follow, there have been the publication of and public preoccupation with The 100 Best Movies, which were voted upon by the members of the American Film Institute and were touted on TV by the likes of Susan Lucci and Larry King, and, for Modern Library, The 100 Best Books which were voted upon by a panel of ten, of whom all but one are male with an average age of 69, and all of whom are white. Well, the hue and cry over both lists temporarily put national and world affairs on the sideline. The whining, and complaining, and anger that greeted both the choices and the rankings are still echoing through our culture, a considerable time after the release of such doings.

The ramifications of such lists are far-reaching. As far as the movie list goes, video rental libraries, off-beat movie theaters, and cinema schools have a new canon. Or, at least, a canon which they never had before. For us, as librarians, the book list has implications to which we had better attend–into our libraries come autodidacts, students, teachers, and your everyday reader who want to *need* to read what's on that list. Librarians are checking their collections to be sure they own books on the lists. Books that have not been ordered in any great quantity in decades must suddenly be ordered and accessioned immediately. Such as esoteric titles like *Zuleika Dobson* by Max Beerbohm which was newly published in an elegant edition in 1985 by Yale University Press. One wonders how many libraries bought that edition; indeed, how many *people* bought it. And Conrad's *Nostromo*. My heart goes out to young students in courses for which the list has become a new canon, to say nothing of professors and teachers who need to update their reading, critical skills, and lesson plans before they head into the classroom. Various panel members have called the list "stodgy" and even "weird." But the last word on all this: Edmund Morris (a panel member of the book list), in *The New York Times* Book Review "Bookend" feature a few months ago, "I'm sure I'm not the only member who secretly feels that all lists are dumb."

All lists, however, are not dumb. Some fulfill important niches. Librarians love and need lists. We always have. We use lists from professional magazines, a few consumer publications, from professional organizations, schools, and our own libraries. Lists help the harried librarian who, with not enough help, must do floor work, give computer help, aid patrons in finding materials, and myriad other duties. Who has time for reading and evaluation? Often, librarians depend on others to do it for them. Years ago, when I was in a public library, we were warned against "reading at our desks." The public felt, we were told, that librarians with time to read at their desks were not working as hard as they should! I soon found out that I could read *anything* at all if I had a red pencil in my hand, which has held me in good stead through twenty more years of librarianship. Unless, then, reading time is scheduled into the librarian's day, when can that librarian read, evaluate, and decide upon new materials? Lists are essential.

I am a collector of lists. As a storyteller, I like verbal lists–literary lists, lists that read aloud well. A good literary list has imagination, rhythm, snap. Among my favorites: the list of the people who came to Gatsby's party, the counselors' lists in Thurber's fairy tale *Many Moons* which remind the befuddled and worried king of all the things they have done for him, and Heide's list of the wonderful things that Treehorn (in *The Shrinking of Treehorn*) has ordered from cereal boxes. I also have folders full of decades of lists of suggested books on various themes, for a variety of grade levels. Lists are drawn up by all kinds of people and organizations. Some are published as bibliographies in glossy four-color form, others I have cut out of newspapers. I have mimeographed lists (we know how old that is!) of college prep reading grouped according to appropriate high school years which is pretentious and sober to a fault. I have William Bennett's self-selected list of books for 7th and 8th graders. I have a long list, published by the Family Research Council, of books which–to their horror–are no longer in library collections and which, they contend, MUST be republished and repurchased. I cannot bear to throw out lists from all manner of professional publications claiming to be "The Best" of a particular year, although nobody has come up with what constitutes "The Best." The supreme Best, as we are led to believe, is that 100 Best Books list from Modern Library. To mitigate that antagonism toward the term "Best" it has been suggested that "Best" be supplanted by "Important" or "Significant."

Two years ago, I edited a compilation of thirty-five years of Outstanding Books for the College Bound for the American Library Association, Young Adult Library Services Association. OBCB is a list that has appeared about forty times since 1959. Young Adult librarians, experienced with both books and their young adult patrons, meet as a committee and, in genre gatherings, decide upon retrospective titles as well as new titles that should be that year's harvest. But, the problem is: What constitutes "Outstanding?" Who are the "College Bound?" And, by what right does the committee function? After all, "Outstanding" changes with social changes and popular culture and that which is so designated as "outstanding" one year may be outdated in style or content another; the "College Bound" now is constituted of all post-secondary school ages attending all manner of community colleges, tele-courses, Ivy League universities, or simply studying on their own. As for the committee (dare I say it?), all librarians are not readers or evaluators of quality.

What is the harried librarian to do?

First of all, know who is compiling the list.

No matter where the list has originated, who are the people who have constructed it; do they have the qualifications to do it?

Is the list one of rank?

The "best" at the top? And, as I said before, who says so?

Is the list a selective subject one?

Is the list all-inclusive (every book on the American Revolution that the list-maker(s) could find)?

Are full citations given so that purchase of the book can be made? Are too many of the books out-of-print? For core collection building, pursuit of OOPS makes sense but for general collections, such books may not be worth the trouble. Know if titles not available in your library are available on inter-library loan.

Is the list for the professional? Is it a "buying" list?

Is the list for the patron? If so, are there annotations so that the patron can find out a bit about the book before searching for it? Doris Kearns Goodwin, in *Wait Till Next Year,* her book about growing up happily in Long Island, talks about a beloved and gifted teacher she had who, at the end of the school year, " . . . handed out exhaustive summer reading lists that she had carefully compiled [with the help of a librarian, one hopes] with enticing synopses under each title. We would compete with one another," says Goodwin, "to see who could finish the most books on the list."

Do lists from outside sources (county library systems, etc.) have notations on them as to whether the library indeed has the books in their collections? Too many libraries simply place beautifully colored and printed lists from outside sources where the patron can see them, but fail to check their own collections to see if the library *has* them.

When was the list compiled? Lists become outdated very quickly. If the library keeps a retrospective file of lists, note on the list the year it was compiled before filing away.

Do the compilers of the list have a vested interest in the titles included? Are there political or social emphases?

For what ages is the list compiled?

All of the above questions need to be answered by librarians using such lists.

"I've got a little list. . . . " sings Koko in *The Mikado* by Gilbert and Sullivan. Librarians, who've got myriad lists, as usual have awesome responsibilities to *know the lists they use or put out for patron use*. It's just one more thing to do, of course, but–listen–that's what we signed on for. For librarians, lists are life-blood. Who ever heard of a (forgive me!) "listless librarian."

Index